Dictionary of
QUALITATIVE
INQUIRY
SECOND EDITION

Thomas A. Schwandt

 Sage Publications
International Educational and Professional Publisher
Thousand Oaks ▪ London ▪ New Delhi

For information:

Sage Publications, Inc.
2455 Teller Road
Thousand Oaks, California 91320
E-mail: order@sagepub.com

Sage Publications Ltd.
6 Bonhill Street
London EC2A 4PU
United Kingdom

Sage Publications India Pvt. Ltd.
M-32 Market
Greater Kailash I
New Delhi 110 048 India

Printed in the United States of America

Library of Congress Cataloging-in-Publication Data

Schwandt, Thomas A.
    Dictionary of qualitative inquiry / by Thomas A. Schwandt.— 2nd ed.
        p. cm.
    Rev. ed. of: Qualitative inquiry. c1997.
    Includes bibliographical references.
        ISBN 0-7619-2165-6 (cloth: acid-free paper)
        ISBN 0-7619-2166-4 (pbk.: acid-free paper)
    1. Social sciences—Methodology—Dictionaries. 2. Social
sciences—Research—Dictionaries. I. Schwandt, Thomas A.
Qualitative inquiry. II. Title.
H61 .S4435 2001
300'.7'2—dc21   00-012062

This book is printed on acid-free paper.

        03   04   05   06   7   6   5   4   3   2

Acquiring Editor:	C. Deborah Laughton
Editorial Assistant:	Eileen Carr
Production Editor:	Sanford Robinson
Editorial Assistant:	Kathryn Journey
Typesetter:	Janelle LeMaster
Cover Designer:	Jane Quaney

Dictionary of
QUALITATIVE
INQUIRY
SECOND EDITION

Contents

Preface   xvii

Introduction   xxiii

Conventions   xxxiv

Dictionary

Action   1
Action Research   3
Agency (vs. Structure)   4
Analytic Generalization   5
Analytic Induction   5
Analyzing Qualitative Data   6
Antinaturalism   8
Applied Research   8
Auditing   8
Audit Trail   9
Authenticity   9
Authenticity Criteria   11
Authority   11
Autoethnography   13

Behaviorism   14
Bias   15
Biography   16
Body   17
Bracketing (Epoché)   19
Bricolage/Bricoleur   20

Case   22
Case Study Research   22
Causal Analysis/Causality   23
Chicago School of Sociology   25
Coding   26
Computer-Assisted Data Analysis   27
Confirmability   29
Conservative Hermeneutics   29
Constant Comparison, Method of   30
Constructivism   30
Content Analysis   34
Context   35
Context of Discovery/Context of Justification   35
Contextualism   36
Conversation Analysis   37
Covering Law Model of Explanation   38
Credibility   39
Crisis of Legitimation   39
Crisis of Representation   41
Criteria   42
Critical Ethnography   44
Critical Hermeneutics   44
Critical Social Science   45
Critical Theory   46
Cross-Case Analysis   46

Cultural Relativism   48
Cultural Studies   49
Culture   50

Data Collection   51
Data Management, Storage, Retrieval   51
Deconstructionism   51
Deduction   54
Deductive-Nomological Explanation   54
Dependability   54
Description   54
Descriptive Statistics   56
Deskwork   57
Dialogic Text   57
Différance   57
Discourse/Discourse Analysis   57
Discourse Theory   58
Discursive Practice   59
Disengagement   59
Disinterested Social Science   59
Document Analysis   60
Double Hermeneutic   60
Dramaturgy   61
Dualism   62

Embodied   63
Emergent Design   63
Emic/Etic   65
Emotion   66
Empirical Research   67
Empiricism   67
End of Philosophy   69

Epistemic Criterion   70

Epistemology   71

Erklärung   72

Essentialism   72

Ethics of Qualitative Inquiry   73

Ethnocentrism   76

Ethnographic Authority   77

Ethnographic Naturalism   77

Ethnographic Realism   78

Ethnography   80

Ethnomethodology   81

Evidence   82

Existentialism   83

Experience   84

Experimental Text   86

Explanation   87

External Validity   88

Fact   89

Fact-Value Distinction   89

Fallibilism   91

Falsification   91

Feminist Epistemologies   92

Fidelity to Method/Fidelity to Phenomenon   94

Field   94

Field Journal   96

Fieldnotes   96

Field Relations   98

Field Studies   99

Fieldwork   99

Foundationalist Epistemologies   101

Frankfurt School   102

Functionalism   102

Geisteswissenschaften   104

Genealogy   104

Generalization   105

Generating Data   108

Grand Narrative   108

Grand Theory   109

Grounded Theory Methodology   110

Hermeneutic Circle   112

Hermeneutic Method   114

Hermeneutics   115

Hermeneutics of Suspicion   116

Historicism   117

Historicity   117

Holism   118

Human Action   119

Hyperreality   119

Hypothetico-Deductive Method   120

Idealism   121

Identity   122

Ideology   123

Idiographic Interpretation   123

Indexicality   124

Inductive Analysis   125

Inductive-Statistical Explanation   125

Inference   125

Informant   126

Inscription   128

Insider/Outsider Perspective   128

Instrumentalism   129

Intentionalism   130

Intentionality   130

Interest	132
Interpretation	133
Interpretive Anthropology	133
Interpretive Turn	134
Interpretivism	134
Intersubjectivity	134
Intertextuality	135
Interviewing	135
Judgment	137
Justification of a Claim	138
Knowledge	139
Language	142
Language Games	144
Lawlike Generalization	146
Lebenswelt	146
Life-History Methodology	146
Life-World	147
Literary Turn (in Social Science)	148
Literature Review	149
Lived Experience	149
Logical Empiricism	149
Logical Positivism	150
Logocentrism	152
Marginal Native	153
Materialist Explanation	153
Meaning	153
Meaning Realism	155
Member Check	155
Memoing	156

Metaethnography   157
Metanarrative   157
Metaphysics   157
Method   158
Methodology   161
Methods of Text Analysis   163
Microethnography   164
Misunderstanding   164
Mixed Methods   164
Multiple Realities   166

Naïve Realism   168
Narrative   168
Narrative Analysis   169
Narrative Criteria   169
Narrative Ethics   169
Narrative Explanation   170
Narrative Inquiry   171
Narrative Psychology   171
Narrative Realism   172
Native's Point of View   172
Naturalism   172
Naturalistic Inquiry   173
Naturalistic Interpretation of the Social Sciences   174
Natural Setting   174
Naturwissenschaften   174
Negative Case   175
Nomothetic Knowledge   175
Nonfoundational Epistemologies   175

Objectivism   176
Objectivist Hermeneutics   177
Objectivity   177

Observation 179

Ocular Epistemology 180

Ontological Hermeneutics 180

Ontology 180

Other (the Other, Otherness) 180

Paradigm 183

Paradigmatic Knowledge Claim 184

Participant Observation 185

Participatory Action Research (PAR) 187

Peer Debriefing 188

Performance/Performative/Performativity 188

Phenomenological Sociology 190

Phenomenology 191

Philosophical Hermeneutics 193

Phronesis 194

Play 194

Pluralism 195

Poiesis 197

Politics of Research 197

Positivism 199

Postempiricism 200

Postmodern Ethnography 200

Postmodern Feminism 201

Postmodernism 201

Postpositivism 203

Poststructuralism 203

Practice 204

Pragmatism 204

Praxis 205

Prejudice 210

(The) Problem of the Criterion 210

Propositional Knowledge   211
Purposive Sampling   212

Qualitative   213
Qualitative Evaluation   214
Quantification   215
Quantitative   215

Radical Hermeneutics   216
Rationalism   216
Rationality   217
Reactivity   219
Realism   219
Realist Tale   222
Reciprocity   222
Reductionism   223
Reflexivity   223
Relativism   225
Reliability   226
Representation   227
Research Design   228
Respondent   229
Respondent Validation   229
Review of Literature   229

Sampling Logic   232
Science   234
Scientific Method   235
Scientism   235
Semiotics   236
Sensitizing Concepts   236
Skepticism   237

Social Constructionism   237
Sociology of Scientific Knowledge (SSK)   237
Spectator Theory of Knowledge   238
Standpoint Epistemologies   238
Statistical Explanation   239
Statistical Generalization   240
Structuralism   240
Subjectivism   241
Subjectivity   242
Subject-Object Relationship   243
Symbolic Interactionism   244

Tacit (Personal) Knowledge   246
Teleology   248
Text   248
Textual Analysis, Methods of   250
Textualism   251
Textualization   251
Theoretical Candor   251
Theoretical Sampling   251
Theoretical Saturation   252
Theory   252
Theory-Laden Observation   253
Theory-Observation Distinction   253
Theory of Signs   255
Theory-Practice Relationship   255
Thick Description   255
Transcription   255
Transferability   257
Triangulation   257
Trustworthiness Criteria   258
Truth   259

Underdetermination of Theory by Data 262

Understanding 262

Unity of Method 265

Use of Qualitative Inquiry 265

Validation Hermeneutics 267

Validity 267

Value-Free Social Science 270

Value-Neutrality 270

Verification 270

Verisimilitude 271

Verstehen 272

Verstehende Sociology 276

Voice 277

Weltanschauung 279

Writing Strategies 279

About the Author 281

We accept the fact that the subject presents itself historically under different aspects at different times or from a different standpoint. We accept that these aspects do not simply cancel one another out as research proceeds, but are like mutually exclusive conditions that exist each by themselves and combine only in us. Our historical consciousness is always filled with a variety of voices in which the echo of the past is to be heard. It is present in the multifariousness of such voices: This constitutes the nature of the tradition in which we want to share and have a part.

—H.-G. Gadamer, *Truth and Method,*
2nd rev. ed., J. Weinsheimer & D. G. Marshall, trans.
New York: Crossroad, 1989, p. 378.

Preface

Every linguistic experience of the world is experience of the world, not experience of language.

> —H.-G. Gadamer, *Truth and Method*,
> trans. J. Weinsheimer & D. G. Marshall, 2nd rev. ed.
> New York: Crossroads, 1989, p. 546.

When you take a word in your mouth, you have not taken up some arbitrary tool which can be thrown in a corner if it doesn't do the job, but you are committed to a line of thought that comes from afar and reaches beyond you.

> —H.-G. Gadamer, *Truth and Method*,
> trans. J. Weinsheimer & D. G. Marshall, 2nd rev. ed.
> New York: Crossroads, 1989, pp. 547-548.

This book is a commentary on the meaning of approximately 300 selected words in a specific research language. This commentary involves a combination of explication, explanation, analysis, and critique. The language in question is the set of terms and phrases that partially shape the nature, purpose, logic, meaning, and methods of the practices called qualitative inquiry. The *Dictionary* is intended as a guidebook for this vocabulary. A guide to the vocabulary of the practices of qualitative inquiry can be particularly useful because concepts acquire different interpretations both within and across the various theoretical perspectives and philosophies—for example, naturalism, interpretivism, social constructionism, feminist theory, phenomenological sociology, philosophical hermeneutics, critical theory, postmodernism, and poststructuralism—that shape the activity of qualitative inquiry.

The *Dictionary* is a catalog of ideas and concepts written from a particular point of view; thus, the book is more partisan than is characteristic of a dictionary. Entries are more like annotations (critical and explanatory remarks) than definitions. I have tried to make these annotations inviting, inclusive of multiple and often contested points of view, and occasionally provocative. My aim has been to discuss terms in such a way that further exploration is stimulated and not foreclosed. Since the publication of the first edition, many references to the *Dictionary* have appeared in publications. Although I am pleased to see the book being used, I find it a bit disconcerting when a definition of a term as found in this dictionary is cited as if it were *the* definition. I do not intend that the *Dictionary* be used in that way. (In fact, the publisher and I argued over the use of the very term *dictionary* as an appropriate title for this book—obviously, I lost that argument.) The book is intended to stimulate continued examination of the nature and purpose of qualitative inquiry practices and not to dampen discussion by offering (as does a genuine dictionary) the generally agreed-on definitions and usage of a word.

This second edition adds 110 words to the first edition. The additions reflect, in part, the appearance of new language in the practices of qualitative inquiry since the first edition was composed more than 5 years ago. New terms also came about from suggestions from readers of the first edition. As was the case in preparing the first edition, I owe a great debt to my graduate students at Indiana University, who served as a source of ideas for the terms explained here and as a sounding board for my explications. Finally, new entries resulted from my own sense of the need to revise, clarify, and expand on terms and commentary in the first edition.

This edition continues to reflect the orientation of the first edition, namely, to promote investigation of philosophical and methodological assumptions that foreground the language of qualitative inquiry. Thus, for example, the entry on interviewing does not catalog and define the many types of interviews but attempts to explain how we conceive of what it means to interview and what is at stake in generating data by means of interviews. Taken in their entirety, the entries are less a technical guide to method and more a guide to concepts and theoretical orientations in qualitative studies. This choice not only reflects my own way of thinking about social inquiry but also acknowledges the fact that there are many published resources that offer far more detailed explanations of methods than could be attempted here.

To make it easier for readers to undertake further examination of issues, in this edition I added key references for every entry. The selection of references was guided by a pedagogical interest in helping acquaint readers with the complexity of the issues that shape the various understandings of the concepts examined here. On occasion, the same reference is used for more than one entry. Of course, choice of references reflects my own predilections.

This dictionary can be used in a variety of ways. It can be a glossary for the vocabulary of qualitative inquiry in introductory courses on qualitative methods and methodologies or a supplement or complement to texts representative of different theoretical perspectives in courses on the foundations of qualitative inquiry. In courses that combine examination of theoretical perspectives and methodologies, students can use the *Dictionary* as a starting pointing to launch their own investigations into various topics that they then present to members of the class. Students could work individually or in small groups with clusters of related terms to explore interrelationships. The explication of a term found in the *Dictionary* can be a starting point from which to pursue more thorough examination. Any number of combinations of terms (both related and contrasting) are possible for this kind of exploration. Several of these clusters are suggested as follows:

Ethnographic Realism Causal	Causal Analysis/Causality
Ethnographic Naturalism	Explanation
Interpretivism	Inference
Verstehende Sociology	Analytic Generalization
Naturalistic Inquiry	Generalization
Field	Sampling Logic
Criteria	Criteria
Crisis of Legitimation	Authenticity Criteria
(The) Problem of the Criterion	Trustworthiness Criteria
Evidence	Reliability
Verification	Validity

Hermeneutic Method
Conservative Hermeneutics
Philosophical Hermeneutics
Deconstructionism
Play

Verstehen
Intentionalism
Idiographic Interpretation
Verstehende Sociology
Naturalistic Inquiry

Methodology
Naturalism
Antinaturalism
Pluralism
Critical Social Science
Paradigm
Mixed Methods

Native's Point of View
Emic/Etic
Other
Ethnocentrism
Bias

Realism
Skepticism
Constructivism
Objectivism

Coding
Computer-Assisted Data Analysis
Grounded Theory Methodology
Generating Data

Crisis of Legitimation
Authority
Postmodernism
Poststructuralism
Deconstructionism

Experience
Intentionality
Subject-Object Relationship
Body

Inscription
Description
Representation
Transcription
Observation

Epistemology
Knowledge
Paradigmatic Knowledge Claim
End of Philosophy

Meaning
Understanding
Intentionalism
Description

Authority
Crisis of Representation
Ethnographic Realism
Reflexivity
Literary Turn (in Social Science)

Reciprocity
Field Relations
Ethics of Qualitative Inquiry
Politics of Research
Reflexivity

Disinterested Social Science
Theory
Critical Social Science
Fact-Value Distinction

The *Dictionary* might also be used to explore the features of a particular approach to qualitative inquiry or to compare approaches by using clusters of terms as a starting point for the exploration. For example, one could examine critical feminist ethnography and ask, "How does this approach to qualitative inquiry address the following notions?"

Criteria	Explanation	Field
Bias	Causal analysis/ausality	Other
Reliability	Generalization	Subject-Object relationship
Validity	Evidence	Representation

One could also compare critical feminist ethnography to a symbolic interactionist approach by examining how each regards the same set of terms or a different set that suits one's purpose—for example, Field, Criteria, Description, Meaning, Observation, Representation, and Understanding.

For many reasons, it is becoming exceedingly difficult to catalog the vocabulary of qualitative inquiry. First, investigations into the meaning of social reality informed by a wide variety of often quite different (and in various ways, contradictory) epistemologies, political persuasions, and ethical frameworks all fall under the broad banner of "qualitative inquiry." Thus, for example, the significance and meaning of ideas such as the politics of research or value neutrality are quite different in studies informed by standpoint epistemologies versus those committed to naturalism. Also, the notions of meaning and truth bear little resemblance in scientific realism, deconstructionism, and philosophical hermeneutics. Second, the meaning of the very terms that we use to name a theoretical perspective or philosophy are often disputed. Consider, for example, the contested definitions of social constructionism, postmodernism, or poststructuralism. Third, pinning down the vocabulary of qualitative inquiry is also troublesome because not all inquiries bearing that label have the same social object in view. For some, the object of interest is the meaning of social action; for others, it is the accomplishment of that action; some regard their own experience as the proper object; and, for still others, society or human action as an object for analysis gives way to examining what is constructed in the process of communication. Fourth, as is readily evident in the second edition of the *Handbook of Qualitative Research* (Denzin & Lincoln, eds., 2nd ed., Sage, 2000), qualitative inquiry is both a cross-disciplinary and interdisciplinary activity. This means that vocabularies and conceptual meanings from disciplines and fields as diverse as psychology, communication studies, history, sociology, literary studies, and philosophy have become blended into new vocabularies with different currency and usage.

   None of this means that the language of the practice of qualitative inquiry is indeterminable. Rather, what it signifies is that the aim and significance of the practice is constantly being reinterpreted. This reinterpretation is inevitable given that we are language beings, an idea central to both deconstructionism and philosophical hermeneutics. We are not the ones in charge of language; language is in charge of us. How one makes sense of this characteristic of our being human, however, matters a great deal. On the one hand, one can believe that there is no final, authentic meaning; there is always and only an irreducible equivocation and undecidability of meaning in the concepts of the practice of qualitative inquiry (or in any other practice). On the other hand, one can hold that the notion of a discoverable, fixed, authentic meaning is mistaken but maintain that genuine meaning does emerge in the encounter with that which we seek to understand in the event or "happening" of understanding. In this way of making sense of ourselves, we are conversational partners with other speakers and with texts—partners engaged in a joint search for meaning.

Introduction

This dictionary is intended to be a contribution to the ongoing effort to understand the aims and methods of the activities collectively called qualitative inquiry. Although I have tried to be ecumenical in my choice of the vocabulary that in part constitutes those activities, there is no denying the fact that the text is written from my particular point of view about the meaning of the practice of human inquiry in general and of qualitative inquiry in particular. Hence, the following reflections on the preconceptions that shaped (and were in turn re-shaped in) the act of writing this dictionary are offered as a framework for understanding the composition of this particular text. These reflections may also serve as a source of ideas for the use of this text. A usual introduction might attempt to spell out the key features of qualitative inquiry. There are many other sources for the same, however; hardly a book is published about qualitative study that does not offer a list of key assumptions, defining characteristics, and so on. What is offered here are some alternative ideas for how we might think about teaching and learning the practice.

Grand Synthesis or Constellation?

Our modernist tendency in surveying the entire scene of the multiple practices of qualitative inquiry is to impose order on the unruly, largely unorganized (and often conflicting) assumptions, features, characteristics, approaches, perspectives, philosophies, and methods that comprise the subject matter of qualitative research methodology. We aim to construct a sense of the subject matter's structure by employing some means of categorizing the various practices by their methodologies, philosophical assumptions, historical lineage, and so on.[1] This tendency has two corollaries: First, it encourages efforts at achieving integration and grand synthesis. This is accomplished by discovering foundational principles, unifying themes, a vocabulary of the practice, a definitive set of propositions about the practice(s) of qualitative inquiry, or all these. Second, this approach to knowing the field of qualitative inquiry is detached, uninvolved, and spectator-like. It is a kind of knowing that requires objectification of that which we seek to understand. It is a knowing from the `outside.' This general knowledge is expressed as a set of assertions about methodology that apply to different situations, circumstances, and problems for which qualitative inquiry is thought to be most appropriate. These assertions constitute the "theory" of the practice, and they can be explained, investigated, transmitted to novices, contrasted with assertions about other methodological practices, and so forth.[2]

The study of the practices of qualitative inquiry, however, need not (and perhaps should not) be undertaken in this way. Wittgenstein, among others, has pointed out how words involve a play of different uses and definitions in a "multiplicity of language games."[3] Qualitative inquiry can be thought of using this analogy. It is a set of multiple practices in which words in methodological and philosophical vocabularies acquire different meanings in their use or in particular acts of speaking about the meaning of the practice. These different ways of speaking form something more like a constellation of contested practices than an integrated, readily surveyable order.[4] There are multiple sources and kinds of disputes, but generally they involve different ways of conceiving of the aim of qualitative inquiry stemming from different traditions of thought.

Rather than *gaze* on this site of contested practices and its apologists, defenders, critics, and practitioner-disputants from the outside, so to speak, one can *engage* it by becoming an interlocutor with other practitioners and with texts that form the various traditions of qualitative study. Adopting a posture as partner in the dialogue or conversation about the purpose and means of qualitative inquiry makes possible a different kind of knowing—a knowing from 'within' a particular situation. Here, knowing what qualitative inquiry is involves wrestling with what it means *to be* a qualitative practitioner of one sort or the other. This kind of knowledge does not take the form of a set of empirically tested propositions, assertions, principles, methods, statements, or ethical codes that define roles and responsibilities that one then adopts to become a so-called qualitative inquirer. The knowledge at issue here is not the general, propositional kind. Rather, it is concerned with understanding specific cases of qualitative inquiry in particular circumstances and dealing with all the complexity, ambiguity, emotions, and volitions entailed in these circumstances. General principles that define qualitative methodologies are not ignored, but they take on meaning only in light of particular cases. The trick is neither to become overwhelmed by the details of particular circumstances nor to be blind to general assumptions, principles, and commitments that define traditions of qualitative study. Rather, one strives to adopt a posture of "perceptive equilibrium"—a dialogue between principles and particulars.[5] In this way, one acquires and learns to exercise the judgment (practical-moral wisdom) required for the practice of qualitative inquiry. Simply although somewhat crudely stated, one does not discover the orderly reality of either something called the identity or role of the qualitative inquirer or something called the principles of practice of qualitative inquiry; rather, one continually constructs and reconstructs an understanding of the practice.

The Pedagogical Encounter
With Qualitative Texts

In the act of interpreting a text, whether a written text or conversation with another person, we bring certain fore-conceptions or prejudices that shape our efforts at interpretation. Once we recognize the hermeneutic, dialogical character of the engagement of interpreter and text, we become aware of how these fore-conceptions are challenged—how ideas about the meaning of a text are advanced and reshaped in the educative exchange that comprises the encounter. Furthermore, the understanding that results from the encounter is fundamentally a self-understanding because

> [i]nterpretation consists of a interchange that involves not only a questioning of subject matter between interpreter and the in-

terpreted, but a self-questioning. The questioning is not just unidirectional or monological; it is reflective or dialogical. All understanding is self-understanding. Interpretation is a questioning of ourselves not only with respect to the subject matter ... it is also a questioning of ourselves with respect to ourselves and our circumstance.[6]

So it was for me in the composition of this dictionary. As I encountered, once again, the vocabulary I have used for many years in talking about the practices of qualitative inquiry, I became aware of how my prior knowledge was being engaged in a critical conversation about the definition and meaning of the practices of qualitative inquiry. My self-understanding—my understanding of self in relation to and application of what I was interpreting—changed.[7] My wish is that students of the aim and methods of qualitative inquiry can experience the same as they encounter this text or others.

The hermeneutic, educative, or pedagogical encounter with qualitative inquiry practices, whether in the interaction with this text or others or in conversations with interpreters and practitioners, can be characterized in terms of several additional principles.[8] First, interpretation is both constrained and enabled by traditions and preconceptions. A tradition is not simply some conceptual place from which we come to interpret but it also is projected ahead of us in shaping our way of understanding. In the process of interpretation, this tradition undergoes rearrangement and transformation. In this sense, the act of learning qualitative inquiry is always "productive." Second, the act of interpretation is structured as questioning. Questioning opens both the self-understanding of the interpreter and the meaning of a text to be interpreted to possibilities and restructuring. Third, interpreting or understanding always involves application, but "[a]pplication is meant not in the instrumental or external sense of practicality, but in the more fundamental sense of making something relevant to oneself."[9] The kind of application at stake here is a particular kind of knowledge that was identified earlier as knowing from within or practical-moral knowledge. Gadamer explains that this is "clearly not objective knowledge—i.e., the knower is not standing over against a situation that he [sic] merely observes; he is directly affected by what he knows. It is something that he has to do." It also differs from technical know-how in that it requires not cleverness in application but understanding:

We discover that the person who is understanding does not know and judge as one who stands apart and unaffected but rather he [sic] thinks along with the other from the perspective of a specific bond of belonging, as if he too were affected.[10]

The Theory Versus Practice Divide

Shortly before completing the first edition, I heard the following anecdote from a colleague at a social research institute in Norway. He had recently attended a conference in health research at which presentations were made about the purpose, significance, and meaning of health care. Two different kinds of papers were presented at that conference. Some drew on social and political philosophy to discuss ideas such as the phenomenology of care and the place of health institutions in society. Other papers presented empirical data and the analyses of routine concerns and practices surrounding the daily care of patients (e.g., administering injections and bathing patients). He told me that near the close of the conference he was chatting with another sociologist and asked him what he thought of the presentations. The fellow remarked, "there seemed to be little between Habermas and a bedpan."

This remark is telling for describing various efforts to define and teach social research generally and qualitative research in particular. Typically, on the one hand, we are confronted with texts about the theory of social inquiry. These texts, and the pedagogical circumstances for which they are intended, describe and explain the aim of social theorizing. They draw from various perspectives in twentieth-century Continental philosophy (e.g., critical theory, phenomenology, hermeneutics, structuralism, and poststructuralism), Weberian sociology, the blend of American pragmatism and symbolic interactionism, feminist theory, and so on. These texts address the debates about the definition and purpose of social science, the nature of the social world, what constitutes knowledge of that world, the definition of human as opposed to natural sciences, the authority and legitimacy of the social inquirer, and so on. Collectively, this set of material is referred to broadly as the theory or philosophy of qualitative inquiry.

On the other hand, we have texts that carefully describe procedures for generating, analyzing, interpreting, and writing up qualitative data. These texts, and the pedagogical circumstances for which they are intended, focus on the nuts and bolts of fieldwork methods, strategies for framing and interpreting data, and issues of field relations. They serve as instructional aids in the form of fieldwork guides, handbooks, or personal accounts of fieldwork experience from which we learn about the means of dealing with logistical, procedural, ethical, and political situations. Collectively, this is the stuff referred to as the practice of qualitative work. A common assumption is that this stuff of practice is about everything that theory is not.

Not only is there often little in between these two kinds of approaches to teaching and learning qualitative inquiry but also the effort to sharply distinguish the theory from the practice of qualitative inquiry promotes a false dualism.[11] The continuity of interactions between thinking and doing, between reflection and action, or between technical expertise and the good to be served by what is produced by means of that expertise is evident when we rehabilitate the Aristotelian concept of praxis and apply it to our understanding of the practice of human inquiry.[12]

Praxis is defined not in opposition to theory but in contrast to poiesis.[13] The latter is a kind of action directed at the specific end of making or creating a product. The end or goal of poiesis can be specified in advance of undertaking the activity. It requires, in turn, a form of knowledge called *techné*—technical knowledge or expertise. When the practice of social inquiry is modeled on a trade or craft such as carpentry, then the practice is being defined as an activity of poiesis.

Praxis also has a goal or end-in-view, but that goal is not to produce some product but to realize some morally worthwhile good. As such, it requires a form of reasoning called *phronesis* (ethical know-how or practical-moral knowledge). Phronesis is characterized by judgment and deliberation. It is different from technical reasoning, in which we simply consider the relative effectiveness of different means to some particular end. When the practice of human inquiry is thought to be analogous to "doing" ethics and politics, it can be said to be defined as an activity of praxis.

The end or purpose to be realized through praxis cannot simply be produced or made by following some specific preestablished procedures or means. The purpose is not fixed and unchangeable and can be accomplished only through simultaneous contemplation of means and ends. Practice is thus "morally committed action."[14]

The end-in-view of praxis at any given time in the history of a practice is intelligible in terms of the practical-moral knowledge comprising the inherited tradition of the practice. To engage in a practice is to be initiated into the theories, concepts, beliefs, understandings, values, and indeed the very language that constitute the practice. A practice is thus laden with theoretical and pretheoretical understandings located in the tradition of the practice. A practitioner simultaneously acknowledges the authority of that tradition and subjects it to criticism. In other words, the "tradition is not mechanically or passively reproduced: It is constantly being reinterpreted and revised through dialogue and discussion about how to pursue the practical goods which constitute the tradition."[15] Acting and thinking, practice and theory are thus linked in a continuous process of self-examination and self-transformation.

Conceived in this way, the practice of social inquiry cannot be adequately defined as an atheoretical "making" that requires only technical expertise or know-how. Social inquiry is not simply poiesis, a technical activity that does not itself change its own ends through reflection on those ends. Social inquiry is also a distinctive praxis, a form of reflective action that transforms the theory that guides it. Hence, to divorce the study of the nature and aim of social theorizing; the definition of the human sciences; the study of the ways of knowing; the epistemological relationship of subject-object; the philosophies of structuralism, poststructuralism, and phenomenology; and so on from the practical activities of generating and interpreting data in social inquiry is to misunderstand the very concept of what it means to practice social inquiry.

On Framing Qualitative Studies

The practice of social inquiry in the modern Western tradition is historically modeled as a scientific practice. The activity of social inquiry is thought to be science-like, which means its aim is both to pursue and to use scientific theory and to employ theoretical reasoning. For example, many qualitative or interpretive studies stemming from symbolic interactionist, phenomenological, ethnomethodological, and *Verstehen* perspectives employ a social scientific frame: a way of collecting and interpreting qualitative data that places a premium on the validity, relevance, and importance of both topic and findings.[16] The frame is oriented to asking questions about the type, frequency, magnitude, structure, process, causes, consequences, and meanings of sociopolitical phenomena and developing answers to those questions. In this frame, the inquirer faces a problematic situation calling for a solution. Solutions take the form of substantive or middle-range theory explaining or accounting for sociopolitical phenomena. These solutions are theoretical because they have the characteristics of being atemporal or universal (i.e., held to be true across a variety of specific cases) and necessary (i.e., not accidental).[17] A researcher makes sense of the individual case in light of universal principles. In the professional fields, the social scientific enterprise serves the decision-making needs of teachers, social service workers, managers, administrators, health care providers, and so on by providing them with this general knowledge of definitions, principles, concepts, and theories that these practitioners can then, in turn, apply to solve specific problems.

Apologists for the less well-understood hermeneutic tradition that is also a part of the historical narrative of social inquiry, however, challenge this scientific framing of human inquiry. In the hermeneutic tradition, both the practice of social inquiry and the practices of teaching, administering, caring, and so forth served by social inquiry are framed as dialogical, interpretive encounters. Neither the social inquirer nor the practitioner is thought to face a problem to be solved as much as a dilemma or mystery that requires interpretation and self-understanding. The distinction between the two can be illustrated as follows:

> A problem is something that can be totally objectified and resolved in objective terms because the person confronting the problem can completely detach himself from it and view it externally. . . . A mystery is something that involves the person in such a way that the person cannot step outside of it in order to see it in an objective manner. She is caught within the situation with no possibility of escape and no possibility of clear-cut solutions. Indeed, ambiguity is the rule within a mystery.[18]

Furthermore, to understand a mystery is to deal with actual, concrete events and people, in specific places and times, in particular circumstances. Universal principles become understandable only in light of specific cases. The kind of reasoning required here involves judgment, deliberation, and the assembly of a variety of empirical, ethical, and political considerations necessary to cope with or make sense of the situation. The understanding that comes from this kind of reasoning has a unique quality:

> Understanding, like action, always remains a risk and never leaves room for the simple application of a general knowledge of rules to the statements or texts to be understood. Furthermore, where it is successful, understanding means a growth in inner awareness, which as a new experience enters into the texture of our own mental experience. Understanding is an adventure, and like any other adventure is dangerous. . . . It affords unique opportunities as well. It is capable of contributing in a special way to the broadening of our human experiences, our self-knowledge, and our horizon, for everything understanding mediates is mediated along with ourselves.[19]

One of the most difficult concepts to grasp about the philosophy of qualitative inquiry is this hermeneutic reframing that entails a radically different way of thinking about what it means to be a social inquirer, a radically different form of reasoning, and a radically different kind of knowledge. In this reframing, social inquiry (including qualitative inquiry) is less a science (as construed in the Western tradition of method, mathematics, measurement, and theoretical reasoning) and more a kind of practical philosophy.[20] Understanding the notion that qualitative inquiry is actually a contested site of multiple practices depends in large part on grasping something of this hermeneutic reframing.

Hermeneutics in social inquiry arises in the first instance as a form of opposition to the dominance of logical positivist and logical empiricist perspectives in the human sciences: It is the source of defining interpretation as a genuine alternative to explanation. In the second instance, it is on the "field of hermeneutics" that contemporary controversies unfold among apologists for philosophical, critical, and deconstructivist perspectives over adequate accounts of the right aim and meaning of interpretation.

Notes

1. John Shotter describes this as the "modernist way of theory" (Conversational Realities, Newbury Park, CA: Sage, 1993, p. 57) The distinction between knowing from the 'outside' and knowing from 'within' is based in part on Shotter's discussion of an alternative to this modernist way.

2. The contrast between this kind of conceptual, purely cognitive knowledge and practical wisdom (discussed later) is explained in Jos. P. A. M. Kessels and Fred A. J. Korthagen, "The Relationship Between Theory and Practice: Back to the Classics" *Educational Researcher*, 1996, 2, 18; see also Shirley Pendlebury, "Reason and Story in Wise Practice," in Hunter McEwan and Kieran Egan, eds., *Narrative in Teaching, Learning and Research* (New York: Teachers College Press, 1995), pp. 50-65.

3. Ludwig Wittgenstein, *Philosophical Investigations* (New York: Macmillan, 1968), p. 23.

4. Richard Bernstein borrows from T. Adorno to define a constellation as a "juxtaposed rather than integrated cluster of changing elements that resist reduction to a common denominator, essential core, or generative first principle" (*The New Constellation: The Ethical-Political Horizons of Modernity/Postmodernity*, Cambridge: MIT Press, 1991, p. 8).

5. Pendlebury, "Reason and Story in Wise Practice," p. 55.

6. Shaun Gallagher, *Hermeneutics and Education* (Albany: State University of New York Press, 1992), p. 157.

7. Both Gadamer and Ricouer emphasize that hermeneutical self-understanding is not to be equated with the modernist notion of the interpreter's (subject's) reflective discovery of self-consciousness. See Gallagher, *Hermeneutics and Education*, p. 158.

8. These characteristics are drawn from Gallagher, *Hermeneutics and Education*, pp. 188-191, 348-351.

9. Ibid., p. 190.

10. Hans-Georg Gadamer, *Truth and Method*, as quoted in Gallagher, *Hermeneutics and Education*, p. 153.

11. What is claimed here for qualitative inquiry holds true for all social science inquiry more generally.

12. For views of hermeneutics as practical philosophy, see Hans-Georg Gadamer, *Reason in the Age of Science*, trans. F. G. Lawrence (Cambridge: MIT Press, 1981), and Charles Taylor, *Philosophical Papers, Vol. 2* (Cambridge, UK: Cambridge University Press, 1985).

13. The following discussion is based on Wilfred Carr's explication of praxis. See his *For Education* (Buckingham, UK: Open University Press, 1995), pp. 68ff.

14. Ibid., p. 68.

15. Ibid., p. 69.

16. See the discussion of this frame in John Lofland and Lyn H. Lofland, *Analyzing Social Settings* (3rd ed.; Belmont, CA: Wadsworth, 1995), pp. 149ff.

17. See the discussion of theoretical versus practical reasoning in Albert R. Jonsen and Stephen Toulmin, *The Abuse of Casuistry* (Berkeley: University of California Press, 1988), pp. 23-46.

18. Gallagher, *Hermeneutics and Education*, p. 152.

19. Gadamer, *Reason in the Age of Science*, pp. 110-111.

20. For two examples of what this might look like, see (in education) Hunter McEwan, "Narrative Understanding in the Study of Teaching," in Hunter McEwan and Kieran Egan, eds., *Narrative in Teaching, Learning, and Research* (New York: Teachers College Press, 1995), pp. 166-183; and (in management) John Shotter, "The Manager as Practical Author: Conversations for Action," in *Conversational Realities* (Newbury Park, CA: Sage, 1993), pp. 148-159.

Conventions

❖ Terms are listed alphabetically without regard to hyphens and spaces between words.

❖ Cross-references are given at the end of each entry and signaled by the bold-faced designation **See also**. Cross-references may direct readers to related or, in some cases, contrasting terms.

❖ *Italics* are used for foreign words and phrases, titles of books and journals, and for emphasis.

❖ Single quotes are used to indicate a novel use of a word or phrase.

❖ Some entries contain terms or phrases discussed elsewhere in the *Dictionary*. When explanation of another term would be helpful for understanding a particular entry, the term in question appears in ***bold-faced italics***.

ACTION   Qualitative inquirers often refer to their object of study as that of human or social action as opposed to behavior. This language, in part, reflects a distinction between meaningful action and merely reactive behavior introduced by Max Weber (1864-1920) and elaborated by symbolic interactionists such as George Herbert Mead (1863-1931). Weber defined *sociology* as a science concerned with the interpretative understanding of social action and *social action* as behavior meaningfully oriented toward the behavior of others. His fourfold typology of social action included instrumentally rational (*zweckrational*), value-rational (*wertrational*), affectual, and traditional action. In addition to Weber, Parsons, Dewey, Mead, Garfinkel, Giddens, Habermas, and others have all elaborated theories of action. For example, Habermas is well-known for his sharp critique of strategic, instrumental, or purposive-rational social action as the guiding *interest* of social inquiry. Habermas builds a case for social inquiry on communicative human action grounded in an emancipatory cognitive interest (vs. *zweckrational* grounded in a technical, instrumental cognitive interest). This idea is influential in shaping some qualitative methodologies that draw on the tradition of *critical social science.*

All approaches to qualitative inquiry at least assume some theory of social action. Generally, these theories display one of two general orientations: They either stress the importance of subjective consciousness (intention) in directing action or they emphasize the significance of social *praxis* (the enactment or performance of social conduct). The former are varieties of the theory of *intentionalism*—a theory that says that the meaning of an action

1

A

derives from the intentions of the actor (agent). Hence, the inquirer must adopt some means of making sense of this intention by getting inside the head of the agent, so to speak, or engaging in some kind of psychological reenactment. The latter stress the intentionality of the act and argue that to interpret the meaning of an act, the inquirer must connect the act to the wider context of the agent's life, the social setting in which the act is performed, and so on.

The emphasis on action reflects two important ideas. First, behavior is purposive, intentional, and goal directed, not simply a physical response to a stimulus (as claimed, for example, in *behaviorism*). The human agent attaches subjective meaning to his or her behavior. Second, interpreting subjective meaning requires understanding not simply individual beliefs, attitudes, motives, intentions, values, and the like but also intersubjective or shared meanings, values, understandings, and so on that interpenetrate individual thought and action. Thus, the qualitative inquirer assumes that subjectivity is not a matter of individual psychological attributes but is constituted intersubjectively. Charles Taylor argues that a strict neo-behaviorist, empiricist account that claims human action can be explained by linking actors' physically observable behaviors to an inventory of individual actors' attitudes, beliefs, and other psychological states is mistaken because it completely overlooks the notion of intersubjective, shared meanings. **See also AGENCY, MEANING, *VERSTEHEN*.**

Key References

Cohen, J., "Theories of Action and Praxis," in B. S. Turner, ed., *The Blackwell Companion to Social Theory*. Oxford, UK: Blackwell, 1996.

Habermas, J., *The Theory of Communicative Action, Vol. 1. Reason and Rationalization of Society*, T. McCarthy, ed. & trans. Boston: Beacon, 1981.

Joas, H., *The Creativity of Action*, J. Gaines & P. Keast, trans. Chicago: University of Chicago Press, 1996.

Taylor, C., "Interpretation and the Sciences of Man." *Review of Metaphysics*, 1971, 25, 3-51.

Weber, M., "Basic Sociological Terms," in G. Roth & C. Wittich, trans., *Economy and Society*. New York: Bedminster, 1968.

ACTION RESEARCH   The term was coined by social psychologist Kurt Lewin (1890-1947) in the 1940s to describe a particular kind of research that united the experimental approach of social science with programs of social action to address social problems. Lewin argued that social problems (as opposed to a scientist's own theoretical interests) should serve as the impulse for social research. He developed a model of social inquiry that involved a spiral of interlocking cycles of planning, acting, observing, and reflecting. Although Lewin's approach was well received in organizational research in the 1960s and 1970s, action research has been subject to various criticisms within the social scientific community, including that it is not 'real' research because it does not meet criteria of a valid scientific methodology, that it is little more than refined common sense and not rigorous empirical research, and that it blurs an important distinction that should be maintained between theory and practice. Various forms of action research are alive and well today, however, in the fields of education, organizational and community development, and work life research.

Theories and methodologies of action research are found under a variety of different labels—for example, action inquiry, action science, participatory inquiry, pragmatic action research, collaborative inquiry, cooperative inquiry, and participatory action research. For example, building on the work of both Lewin and John Dewey (1859-1952), Chris Argyris and Donald Schön (1931-1977) developed a particular form of action research called action science. It seeks to advance basic (or theoretical) knowledge while it simultaneously aims to solve practical problems in organizations and communities. It provides strategies for both problem framing or setting and problem solving and links the two activities in a feedback cycle called "double loop learning." Action scientists work collaboratively with participants to solve problems of practice in particular organizational learning contexts. Reflection and experimentation are encouraged as ongoing processes. Action science employs a variety of methods for generating data, including observations, interviews, action experiments, and participant-written cases and accounts.

According to Wilfred Carr and Stephen Kemmis, all action research has the aims of improvement and involvement: Involvement refers to the participation of practitioners in all phases of

A

planning, acting, observing, and reflecting. Improvement is a matter of changing the situation in which a particular social practice takes place, enhancing the understanding that practitioners have of their practice or their capacity to control it, remaking the practice, or all these. **See also PARTICIPATORY ACTION RESEARCH.**

Key References

Argyris, C., Putnam, R., & McClain Smith, D., *Action Science.* San Francisco: Jossey-Bass, 1985.

Carr, W., & Kemmis, S., *Becoming Critical.* London: Falmer, 1986.

Greenwood, D., & Levin, M., *Introduction to Action Research.* Thousand Oaks, CA: Sage, 1998.

Schön, D., *The Reflective Practitioner: How Professionals Think in Action.* New York: Basic Books, 1983.

AGENCY (VS. STRUCTURE)   Broadly understood, the term *human agency* signals the capacity of individuals to perceive their situation, reason about it, consciously monitor their action, form motives, and so on. The agency versus structure problem is the sociological version of the philosophical problem of free will versus determinism. In developing social theory, scholars take various positions on the relative weight to be attached to human actions (agency) or external structures or forces. Consider, for example, the difference between functionalist theories that emphasize the social system or the contribution of social institutions to the constitution of society versus *symbolic interactionism* and *ethnomethodology* that place human agency at the core of society. The social theories of Anthony Giddens and Pierre Bourdieu are examples of attempts to resolve or overcome the tension between structure and agency.

Key References

Baert, P., *Social Theory in the Twentieth Century.* New York: New York University Press, 1998.

Holton, R. J., "Classical Sociological Theory," in B. S. Turner, ed., *The Blackwell Companion to Social Theory.* Oxford, UK: Blackwell, 1996.

ANALYTIC GENERALIZATION   Also called theoretical elaboration, this is a type of *generalization* in which the inquirer attempts
to link findings from a particular *case* to a *theory*. (Here, theory
means something more like a set of theoretical tools, models, or
concepts rather than a formalized set of propositions, laws, and
generalizations comprising a systematic, unified causal explanation of social phenomena.) A study of some phenomenon in a particular set of circumstances (i.e., a case) is used as evidence to support, contest, refine, or elaborate a theory, model, or concept (note
that the case is never regarded as a definitive test of the theory). It
appears that this notion is what the interpretive anthropologist
Clifford Geertz (1973) has in mind when he says it is the job of the
ethnographer to make small facts speak to large issues.

Many researchers argue that the findings from qualitative studies of cases or instances of phenomena are most appropriately
generalizable to concepts, theoretical propositions, or models and
not to universes or populations of cases or instances. Thus, analytic generalization is contrasted with statistical generalization.
(In *statistical generalization*, a case is a sample drawn from a
population of cases. An inference is then made about the population based on the study of the characteristics of the sample.) **See
also CASE STUDY RESEARCH, GENERALIZATION.**

Key References

Geertz, C., "Thick Description: Toward an Interpretive Theory of Culture," in C. Geertz, ed., *The Interpretation of Cultures*. New York: Basic
Books, 1973.

Vaughan, D., "Theory Elaboration: The Heuristics of Case Analysis," in
C. C. Ragin & H. S. Becker, eds., *What Is a Case? Exploring the Foundations of Social Inquiry*. Cambridge, UK: Cambridge University Press,
1992.

Yin, R., *Case Study Research*, 2nd ed. Thousand Oaks, CA: Sage, 1994.

ANALYTIC INDUCTION   This is a strategy for analyzing qualitative data based on the assumption that the inquirer should formu-
late propositions that apply to all instances (or cases) of the problem under analysis. After initial examination of the data, the
inquirer develops working hypotheses to explain the data. One
example, instance, episode, or case in the data corpus is examined

to determine whether the hypothesis fits the facts of that instance. If the hypothesis fits, the inquirer moves to the next instance and again tests for fit. If the hypothesis does not fit the facts, the hypothesis is revised or the phenomenon to be explained is redefined to exclude that instance. An instance that does not fit the hypothesis is called a *negative case*. The intent here is to use negative instances for continuous refinement of the hypothesis until all instances can be satisfactorily explained. See also ANALYZING QUALITATIVE DATA.

Key References

Fielding, N. G., ed., *Actions and Structure*. London: Sage, 1988.

Manning, P. K., "Analytic Induction," in K. Plummer, ed., *Symbolic Interactionism, Vol. 2. Contemporary Issues*. Brookfield, VT: Elgar, 1991. (Original work published in R. Smith & P. K. Manning, eds., *Qualitative Methods*. Cambridge, MA: Ballinger, 1982)

Silverman, D., *Interpreting Qualitative Data: Methods of Analyzing Talk, Text, and Interaction*. London: Sage, 1993.

ANALYZING QUALITATIVE DATA   Broadly conceived, this is the activity of making sense of, interpreting, or theorizing data. It is both art and science, and it is undertaken by means of a variety of procedures that facilitate working back and forth between data and ideas. Analysis begins with the processes of organizing, reducing, and describing the data and continues through the activity of drawing conclusions or interpretations from the data and warranting those interpretations. If data could speak for themselves, analysis would not be necessary.

Some qualitative inquirers place a premium on analysis as a science and stress the fact that analysis should be rigorous, disciplined, systematic, carefully documented, and methodical. To analyze means to break down a whole into its component or constituent parts. Through reassembly of the parts, one comes to understand the integrity of the whole. Thus, the qualitative analyst breaks down the whole corpus of data (fieldnotes, transcriptions, etc.) by categorizing and coding its segments and then tries to establish a pattern for the whole by relating the codes or categories to one another. Having knowledge of the correct application of the right analytic procedures (e.g., *constant comparison method, analytic induction, grounded theory* analysis, and typological analysis) figures prominently in this way of thinking about analysis. Other inquirers, although generally no less empirical in their approach to making sense of data, draw a distinction between analysis and interpretation. They emphasize that interpretation is an art of understanding (including re-presenting one's understanding in writing) that is not fully definable in terms of procedure.

Whether viewed as science or art, analysis in qualitative inquiry is recursive and begins almost at the outset of generating data. The inquirer employs a variety of analytic strategies that involve sorting, organizing, and reducing the data to something manageable and then exploring ways to reassemble the data to interpret them. Sorting and organizing requires comparing, contrasting, and labeling the data. This initial step is necessary to bring some order to the largely undifferentiated mass of data that the inquirer has generated from observations, interviews, and so on. Sorting can involve making frequency counts of the data, developing categories or typologies to account for all the data, selecting concepts that define relationships among categories, formulating working hypotheses or assertions that explain the data, or all these. Choosing concepts, developing typologies, and so on are, in effect, ways of developing an analytic vocabulary by means of which the inquirer fosters the aim of his or her research (i.e., to answer questions such as What is happening? What are people doing? What does it mean to them? How are the realities of everyday life accomplished? How is the social world constituted by its members? and Why is it constituted this way rather than that?). The results of data analysis can be presented in tables, graphs, charts, concept maps, and narrative accounts. **See also CODING, COMPUTER-ASSISTED DATA ANALYSIS, EMERGENT DESIGN, HERMENEUTIC METHOD, TEXTUAL ANALYSIS.**

Key References

Bernard, H. R., *Research Methods in Anthropology: Qualitative and Quantitative Approaches,* 2nd ed. Thousand Oaks, CA: Sage, 1994.

Gubrium, J. F., & Holstein, J. A., *The New Language of Qualitative Method.* Oxford, UK: Oxford University Press, 1997.

Miles, M., & Huberman, A. M., *Qualitative Data Analysis: An Expanded Sourcebook*, 2nd ed. Thousand Oaks, CA: Sage, 1994.

Wolcott, H. F., *Transforming Qualitative Data: Description, Analysis, and Interpretation*. Thousand Oaks, CA: Sage, 1994.

ANTINATURALISM   This is one of four basic approaches to the study of social phenomena (the others are *naturalism, pluralism,* and *critical social science*). Antinaturalists claim that the study of social phenomena cannot or should not be undertaken using the same methods of inquiry and with the same goal and modes of explanation that the natural sciences employ to study natural phenomena. For the antinaturalist, there are particular and distinctive features of the social world: (a) The social or human sciences deal with phenomena that are intentional—the meaningful action of individuals—whereas the subject matter of the natural sciences is the behavior of physical phenomena; consequently, (b) social phenomena, unlike natural phenomena, do not admit to causal explanation—the inquirer must attempt to understand (vs. explain) social action by reference to the ways in which humans experience their activities and give meaning to them. Antinaturalists can be found among scholars who embrace *Verstehen* approaches, *phenomenological sociology,* and *philosophical hermeneutics* as well as some feminist inquirers. **See also ACTION, AUTHENTICITY, EXPLANATION, INTENTIONALISM.**

Key References

Outhwaite, W., *Understanding Social Life: The Method Called* Verstehen. London: Allen & Unwin, 1975.

Taylor, C., *Philosophy and the Human Sciences, Philosophical Papers* 2. Cambridge, UK: Cambridge University Press, 1985.

APPLIED RESEARCH   See USE OF QUALITATIVE INQUIRY.

AUDITING   A procedure whereby an independent, third-party examiner systematically reviews an audit trail maintained by the inquirer. The purpose of the audit is to render a judgment about the dependability of procedures employed by the inquirer and the extent to which the conclusions or findings of the study are confirmable. An audit trail is a systematically maintained documentation system. It is an organized collection of materials that includes the data generated in a study; a statement of the theoretical framework that shaped the study at the outset; explanations of concepts, models, and the like that were developed as part of the effort to make sense of the data (often the product of *memoing*); a description of the procedures used to generate data and analyze them; a statement of the findings or conclusions of the investigation; notes about the process of conducting the study; personal notes; and copies of instruments used to guide the generation and analysis of data. The audit trail can serve dual purposes: It can be used by the inquirer as a means of managing record keeping and encouraging reflexivity about procedures, and, as noted previously, it can be used by a third-party examiner to attest to the use of dependable procedures and the generation of confirmable findings on the part of the inquirer. **See also TRUSTWORTHINESS CRITERIA.**

Key References

Lincoln, Y. S., & Guba, E. G., *Naturalistic Inquiry*. Beverly Hills, CA: Sage, 1985.

Schwandt, T. A., & Halpern, E. S., *Linking Auditing and Metaevaluation*. Newbury Park, CA: Sage, 1989.

AUDIT TRAIL   See AUDITING.

AUTHENTICITY   Two senses of this term are part of the lexicon of qualitative inquiry. First, authenticity is regarded as a feature unique to *naturalistic inquiry* (and *ethnographic naturalism*), an approach to inquiry that aims to generate a genuine or true (i.e., 'authentic') understanding of people's experiences. This genuine understanding, also spoken of as viewing the world from the actors' point of view, is achieved through the methods of unstructured interviewing and participant observation. Second, authenticity is a key notion in the German idealist tradition, in the German tradition of phenomenology, and in the philosophical and literary tradition of existentialism. Broadly speaking, key figures in these traditions—for example, Husserl (1859-1938), Heidegger (1889-1976), Nietzsche (1844-1900), Sartre (1905-1980), and Merleau-Ponty (1907-1961)—shared a strong hostility to technological modernity and to the ideology of scientism. Moreover, they argued, although in different ways, that our fundamental way of experiencing and engaging the world as human beings is through structures of meaning or significance. For these scholars, human existence is fundamentally different in kind than the being of natural objects studied in the natural sciences. They saw in modernity and scientism a danger to treat human existence or human being as simply another kind of natural 'object' to be studied via the methods of the natural sciences. They feared that this way of thinking led to viewing human existence in objectifying and alienating ways—being was becoming stripped of its unique significance. For example, Sartre argued that regarding the 'self' as a subject for science required adopting the third-person point of view that is disengaged from the experience of self during everyday engaged existence. It is in this context that authenticity refers to a notion of being or existence that is not objectified. An authentic life is a condition of significance; it is emotionally appropriate living, clearly facing up to one's responsibility for what one's life has been and is becoming. The opposites of authenticity are inauthenticity, estrangement, objectification, and alienation, all of which point, in different ways, to a life dehumanized and stripped of responsibility and purpose, to a flight from the fundamental situatedness and embodiedness of self. Living authentically—resisting unthinking conformism, the objectification of existence, and possessive individualism—is often regarded as the central problem of modern social and political life. **See also EXPERIENCE.**

Key References

Cooper, D. E., "Modern European Philosophy," in N. Bunnin & E. P. Tsui-James, eds., *The Blackwell Companion to Philosophy*. Oxford, UK: Blackwell, 1996.

Guignon, C., "Heidegger's 'Authenticity' Revisited." *Review of Metaphysics*, 1984, 38, 321-339.

Taylor, C., *The Ethics of Authenticity*. Cambridge, MA: Harvard University Press, 1991.

AUTHENTICITY CRITERIA   This is a set of *criteria* (and associated procedures) developed by Egon Guba and Yvonna Lincoln for judging the kind of qualitative inquiry that has its origins in a constructivist epistemology. The criteria are as follows: (a) fairness—refers to the extent to which respondents' different constructions of concerns and issues and their underlying values are solicited and represented in a balanced, even-handed way by the inquirer (constructions are defined by Guba and Lincoln as the outcomes of various ways that individuals have of making sense of some situation, event, and so on); (b) ontological authenticity—concerned with the extent to which respondents' own constructions are enhanced or made more informed and sophisticated as a result of their having participated in the inquiry; (c) educative authenticity—concerned with the extent to which participants in an inquiry develop greater understanding and appreciation of the constructions of others; (d) catalytic authenticity—refers to the extent to which action is stimulated and facilitated by the inquiry process; and (e) tactical authenticity—refers to the extent to which participants in the inquiry are empowered to act. **See also CONSTRUCTIVISM, PROBLEM OF CRITERIA, TRUSTWORTHINESS CRITERIA.**

Key Reference

Guba, E. G., & Lincoln, Y. S., *Fourth Generation Evaluation*. Newbury Park, CA: Sage, 1989.

AUTHORITY   This notion figures prominently in postmodern and poststructuralist criticisms of *ethnography* wherein it is commonplace to criticize a text's 'call to authority.' This concern about the authority of any ethnographic account is intimately connected to the current *crisis of legitimation* in the human sciences. Critics claim that traditional ethnographers establish their authority through two textual (rhetorical) strategies. First, there is an experiential appeal—the ethnographer claims that he or she was 'there,' in the *'field,'* and thereby acquired firsthand the experience of the other's world, way of life, and so on. Second, the ethnographer as author then suppresses in the act of writing the "I" of the observer. He or she is absent from the text as a genuine author with personal subjectivities, interests, and dispositions and simply impersonally narrates what he or she saw and heard. Taken collectively, these two strategies serve to establish the ethnographer's account as authoritative. In other words, the reader is led to believe that whatever the ethnographer experienced by being in the field, and accordingly reported in the text, would be more or less what any equally well-trained observer would experience and report.

According to postmodern and poststructuralist critics, this bid to establish the authority of the text is closely wedded to the realist assumption that there is a genuine, valid account of the way life 'really is' for those being studied and that this 'real' life can be (relatively) unproblematically captured and represented in the ethnographer's account. Hence, criticism of a text's call to authority is at once a criticism of an ideology of the immediacy of experience and the transparency of representation. For the postmodern ethnographer, there is no such thing as a `real' account of the way of life of others—all accounts are contested, partial, incomplete, written from some particular standpoint, advance some particular interest, and so on. Any claim that a particular textual account is a valid *representation* (a faithful, accurate rendering) of others' life-worlds is nothing more than an effort on the part of the author to persuade the reader that the author's account is authoritative. Thus, traditional concerns with *validity* are replaced by concerns with how a text seeks to legitimate itself—how the authority of the text is established. The postmodern ethnographer seeks to decenter his or her own authority, to render more visible the ways in which the text produces a particular *inscription* of reality, and to disperse or share the authoritativeness of a textual account by featuring more dialogic and polyvocal textual forms. **See also CRISIS OF REPRESENTATION, ETHNOGRAPHIC REALISM, LITERARY TURN (IN SOCIAL SCIENCE).**

Key References

Clifford, J., "On Ethnographic Authority." *Representations,* 1983, 1(2), 118-146.

Clifford, J., & Marcus, G. E., eds., *Writing Culture: The Poetics and Politics of Ethnography.* Berkeley: University of California Press, 1986.

Van Maanen, J., *Tales of the Field: On Writing Ethnography.* Chicago: University of Chicago Press, 1988.

AUTOETHNOGRAPHY   Originally defined as the cultural study of one's own people, this term now commonly refers to a particular form of writing that seeks to unite ethnographic (looking outward at a world beyond one's own) and autobiographical (gazing inward for a story of one's self) intentions. The aim in composing an autoethnographic account is to keep both the subject (knower) and object (that which is being examined) in simultaneous view. It is commonly claimed that the striking stories that frequently comprise autoethnography are intended to illustrate and evoke rather than to state or make a claim, and that the author of such a text aims to invite readers into the text to relive the experience rather than to interpret or analyze what the author is saying. **See also EXPERIENCE, NARRATIVE, WRITING STRATEGIES.**

Key References

Ellis, C., "Evocative Autoethnography: Writing Emotionally About Our Lives," in W. G. Tierney & Y. S. Lincoln, eds., *Representation and the Text: Re-Framing the Narrative Voice.* Albany: State University of New York Press, 1997.

Ellis, C., & Bochner, A. P., "Autoethnography, Personal Narrative, Reflexivity: Researcher as Subject," in N. K. Denzin & Y. S. Lincoln, eds., *Handbook of Qualitative Research,* 2nd ed. Thousand Oaks, CA: Sage, 2000.

Hayano, D. M., "Autoethnography." *Human Organization,* 1979, 38, 99-104.

Reed-Danahay, D., *Auto/Ethnography: Rewriting the Self and the Social.* Oxford, UK: Berg, 1997.

BEHAVIORISM As a sociopsychological theory, scientific or methodological behaviorism is the view that the only truly scientific investigation is that which limits itself to behavioral data—that is, that which can be measured and observed, especially patterns of physical responses to environmental stimuli. The theory emphasizes determinable and invariant principles of human conduct and social behavior. It is strongly deterministic: Behaviors are associated in *lawlike* ways with environmental stimuli and reinforcements. It is also reductionistic in that it holds that there is no need to invent complex mental constructs to explain why behavior happens. Although the theory is most often associated with behavioral and educational psychology, it is also evident in research traditions in other fields, particularly in political science. As a philosophical doctrine, behaviorism figured prominently in the thinking of *logical positivism.* Also spoken of as the doctrine of physicalism, philosophical behaviorism meant that the mental states of individuals (their intentions, beliefs, etc.) and indeed all that is considered social are ultimately explainable in terms of physical (i.e., behavioral) expressions. **See also AC-TION, REDUCTIONISM.**

Key References

Ayer, A. J., ed., *Logical Positivism.* Glencoe, IL: Free Press, 1959.

Taylor, C., *The Explanation of Behaviour.* London: Routledge Kegan Paul, 1964.

BIAS   Two senses of this term figure prominently in criticisms of qualitative inquiry. In the first sense, readily found in dictionaries, bias denotes a tendency in inquirers that prevents unprejudiced consideration or judgment. For example, the tendency to rely on a particular *informant* or to cross the line between rapport and friendship in dealing with informants, respondents, or participants can lead to the prejudicial drawing of inferences or generalizing from nontypical or nonrepresentative persons or events. Also, the tendency to be unaware of how one's interactions in a field site threaten, disrupt, create, or sustain patterns of social interaction might result in a prejudicial account of social behavior in the site. In the second sense, bias means individual preferences, predispositions, or predilections that prevent neutrality and objectivity. This sense of the term bias is evident when an inquirer is criticized for taking the side of or advocating for a particular group of informants (and the inquirer is thus thought to be incapable of rendering a neutral account of the social action), for imposing a priori a theoretical framework or interpretation on the data, or when it appears as though the researcher uses data to confirm a hypothesis or belief held before the study was undertaken.

Although biases of these kinds are a problem for all methodologies for social investigation, they are thought to be particularly acute in forms of qualitative inquiry that rely on fieldwork because the latter is admittedly an intensely personal experience. *Fieldwork* requires the active, sustained, and long-term involvement of the inquirer with respondents and the cultivation of empathy with and attachment to the people one studies to gain access to their own understandings of their life ways. Hence, bias resulting from overreliance on accessible or key informants, selective attention to dramatic events or statements, or both; the biasing effects of the presence of the inquirer in the site of investigation; and biases stemming from the effects of the respondents and the site on the inquirer can be particularly difficult problems in fieldwork.

It is beyond dispute that sound inquiry practice requires critical reflection on one's actions and predispositions and awareness of the potential both of being deceived and of deceiving one's self. The extent to which bias is believed to be a problem in qualitative studies, however, is related to assumptions about objective *method.* A significant subset of qualitative inquiry is wedded to a conception of method as a device for setting aside or controlling bias. The devotion to method as holding the key to sound inquiry is predicated on the assumption that we need some means of removing our tendencies as everyday human beings to be biased or prejudiced in our investigations of social life so that we may come to have genuine, legitimate, objective knowledge. Since Descartes, at least, social science (and philosophy) has been obsessed with this understanding and pursuit of a strong sense of method.

In light of this understanding of method, bias or prejudice is always defined negatively as something that interferes with, prevents, or inhibits having true, genuine knowledge. It is precisely this understanding of method and prejudice, however, that is severely criticized by advocates of *philosophical hermeneutics*. For example, Gadamer's critique of the Cartesian notion of method as providing a sure path to knowledge is based in large part on a rehabilitation of the word "prejudice." Building on the work of Martin Heidegger (1889-1976), Gadamer argued that prejudice ('prejudgment') can neither be eliminated nor set aside because it is an inescapable condition of being and knowing. In fact, our understanding of ourselves and our world depends on having prejudgment. What we must do to achieve understanding is to reflect on prejudice (prejudgment) and distinguish enabling from disabling prejudice. **See also** OBJECTIVITY, REFLEXIVITY, SUBJECTIVITY.

Key References

Gadamer, H.-G., *Truth and Method*, 2nd rev. ed., J. Weinsheimer & D. G. Marshall, trans. New York: Crossroad, 1989.

LeCompte, M. D., & Preissle, J., *Ethnography and Qualitative Design in Educational Research*, 2nd ed. New York: Academic Press, 1993.

BIOGRAPHY   Like the term *ethnography*, biography refers to both a product and a process. It is an account (in writing, film, etc.) of an individual's life and the activity of composing that account. The biographical method is an assembly of procedures for generating and interpreting the stories or narratives of individuals' lives. Biographies, life histories, and the biographical method are often used in qualitative research, especially given the increasing interest in *narrative* methodologies.

The biographical method, also spoken of as life-history methodology, is a generic term for a variety of approaches to qualitative study that focus on the generation, analysis, and presentation of the data of a life history (the unfolding of an individual's experiences over time), life story, personal experience narrative, autobiography, and biography. Data can be generated from interviews and from personal documents (letters, journals, diaries, etc.). The methodology assumes that social *action* can best be understood from the accounts and perspectives of the people involved, and thus the focus is on an individual subjective definition and experience of life. Because most qualitative inquirers assume that the subjective world of experience is at once intersubjectively constituted, however, life-history approaches seek to interrelate the private and the public, the personal and the social. Private, personal, biographic, and subjective perspectives are linked to meanings, definitions, concepts, and practices that are historical, structural, public, and social.

Biographical methods take up many interrelated methodological, philosophical, and epistemological concerns regarding what constitutes a biography (e.g., is it a retelling or an active production of a consistent understanding of a life), subjectivity, life course, *experience*, and how to best describe, interpret, and write a life-history text. Diverse methodologies are influenced by assumptions from critical theory of society and phenomenological, hermeneutic, semiotic, and poststructural perspectives. **See also INTERVIEWING, NARRATIVE ANALYSIS.**

Key References

Berteaux, D., ed., *Biography and Society: The Life-History Approach in the Social Sciences.* London: Sage, 1981.

Denzin, N. K., *Interpretive Biography.* Newbury Park, CA: Sage, 1989.

Weymann, A., & Heinz, W. R., eds., *Biography and Society.* Weinheim, Germany: Beltz, 1995.

BODY   In the history of *epistemology* at least since Descartes, the ideal epistemic agent (the one who engages in knowing, i.e., the knower or subject) is an individual, disengaged, disembodied mind. This conception is captured in the familiar binary oppositions: mind-body, reason-desire, and mental-manual. The mind or the purely mental is associated with reason, rationality, and knowledge. The body or the purely physical is associated with emotions, desires, passions, personal involvement, and commitments.

Two twentieth-century strands of thought are largely responsible for restoring a concern with the body (and all its associations) to our thinking about epistemology. One strand emanates from the work of the French phenomenologist Maurice Merleau-Ponty (1908-1961) along with the feminist scholarship of Luce Irigaray, Gayatri Spivak, Judith Butler, Naomi Schor, Hèlene Cixous, and many others. Here, the central idea is that the lived body is not an object in the world distinct from the knowing subject. Rather, we experience the world as embodied subjects; the body is the original knowing 'subject.' Merleau-Ponty explained that our agency is essentially embodied, and that the lived body is the center of our actions and desires that we never fully grasp or control by personal decision. This idea of embodied agency also occupies a central place in Charles Taylor's *philosophical hermeneutics*. Feminist scholars have argued that the lived body is not an ahistorical, biologically given, acultural object but is represented and used in specific ways in particular cultures. Hence, the lived body is crucial to understanding woman's social and psychical existence. A second strand of thought is associated with the work of Nietzsche (1844-1900), Deleuze, and Foucault (1926-1984). Here, the body is regarded as a social site or surface on which law, morality, and values are inscribed. Foucault's work has been particularly influential in shaping the sociology of the body. See also INTENTIONALITY.

Key References

Butler, J., *Gender Trouble: Feminism and the Subversion of Identity*. New York: Routledge, 1990.

Grosz, E., *Volatile Bodies: Toward a Corporeal Feminism*. Bloomington: Indiana University Press, 1994.

Merleau-Ponty, M., *Phenomenology of Perception*. C. Morris, trans. London: Routledge Kegan Paul, 1962. (Original work published 1945)

Schatzki, T., & Natter, W., eds., *The Social and Political Body*. New York: Guilford, 1996.

Taylor, C., *Philosophical Arguments*. Cambridge, MA: Harvard University Press, 1995.

Turner, B., *Regulating Bodies: Essays in Medical Sociology*. London: Routledge, 1992.

B

BRACKETING (EPOCHÉ)   The term originates in Husserl's (1859-1938) phenomenology (*The Idea of Phenomenology*, posthumously published in 1950, English trans. W. P. Alston & G. Nakhnikian, 1964), which was strongly opposed to philosophical *realism*—the doctrine claiming that an external world exists independent of one's knowledge of it. Husserl argued that the everyday assumption of the independent existence of what is perceived and thought about (what he called "the natural attitude") should be suspended so that one could investigate what is perceived and thought about without that assumption. In other words, one should suspend judgment about the existence of the world and 'bracket' or set aside existential assumptions made in everyday life and in the sciences. By performing such a reduction or bracketing, it becomes possible to focus on the intrinsic nature or *phenomenology* of conscious acts such as perceiving or remembering. The *phenomenological* sociology of Alfred Schutz (1899-1956) developed this idea of setting aside or bracketing everyday assumptions to concentrate on the phenomenology of the experience of the everyday world (i.e., on *how* that experience is constituted). Schutz's work, in turn, influenced the development of *ethnomethodology*. Ethnomethodologists bracket, set aside, or suspend commonsense assumptions about social reality to understand *how* it is that actors experience their world as real, concrete, factual, and objective—in short, to understand how the taken-for-granted features of social life are accomplished. **See also LIFE-WORLD.**

Key References

Garfinkel, H., *Studies in Ethnomethodology*. Englewood Cliffs, NJ: Prentice Hall, 1967.

Gubrium, J. F., & Holstein, J. A., *The New Language of Qualitative Method*. Oxford, UK: Oxford University Press, 1997.

B

BRICOLAGE/BRICOLEUR   Even a cursory glance at the massive tome, *The Handbook of Qualitative Research* (2nd ed., Sage, 2000), will reveal that qualitative inquiry comprises a variety of method- ological and philosophical ideas drawn from traditions of interpretivism, phenomenology, hermeneutics, ethnomethod- ology, ethnography, semiotics, cultural studies, feminism, critical theory, and so on. Given this diversity in intellectual origins, strat- egies, methods, and practices, it becomes difficult to define in any precise way who the qualitative inquirer is and what it is that he or she does. Of late, some scholars in qualitative inquiry have found the terms *qualitative researcher* and *qualitative research* to be inade- quate descriptors of what they believe to be the manifold *identity* and *practice* of the qualitative inquirer and have substituted the terms *bricolage* and *bricoleur* as alternatives. For example, Norman Denzin and Yvonna Lincoln (*The Handbook of Qualitative Research*, Sage, 1994) describe the multiple methodologies used in qualita- tive inquiry as *bricolage* and the qualitative inquirer as *bricoleur*, one who is "adept at performing a large number of diverse tasks, ranging from interviewing to observing, to interpreting personal and historical documents, to intensive self-reflection and intro- spection . . . [and one who] reads widely and is knowledgeable about the many interpretive paradigms (feminism, Marxism, cul- tural studies, constructivism) that can be brought to any particu- lar problem." (p. 2)

As a *bricoleur*, the qualitative inquirer is capable of donning multiple identities—researcher, scientist, artist, critic, and per- former—and engaging in different kinds of *bricolage* that consist of particular configurations of (or ways of relating) various frag- ments of inherited methodologies, methods, empirical materials, perspectives, understandings, ways of presentation, situated re- sponsiveness, and so on into a coherent, reasoned approach to a research situation and problem. The *bricolage* appears to vary de- pending on one's allegiance to different notions of interpretation, understanding, representation, and so on drawn from various in- tellectual and practice traditions.

The terms are traceable to Lévi-Strauss, who, in seeking to de- fine the savage mind, defined a *bricoleur* as "someone who works with his hands and uses devious means." He sharply contrasted the *bricoleur* and the engineer. The *bricoleur* draws on a heterogeneous collection of inherited odds and ends kept at hand on the chance they might someday prove useful for some project. What the *bricoleur* produces is *bricolage*—a kind of pieced-togethered (in contrast to algorithmically guided) but structured solution to a problem. (Jacques Derrida [1978, p. 285] criticized this binary distinction, arguing that "if one calls *bricolage* the necessity of borrowing one's concepts from the text of a heritage which is more or less coherent or ruined, it must be said that every discourse is *bricoleur.*")

The mixing of methodologies, discourses, substantive theories, and the like that *bricolage* signifies can be read in a variety of ways. Some might view it as a sign of methodological and theoretical impurity in the field of qualitative inquiry—a symptom of a pathology that must be diagnosed, explained, and somehow remedied. Others might read *bricolage* as a kind of necessary and productive insecurity about confining qualitative inquiry to disciplinary boundaries. Still others may view *bricolage* as a way of signaling that the object of qualitative inquiry and the practice itself are relational and processual (a network of interlocking discourses) rather than fixed and formal.

Key References

Denzin, N. K., & Lincoln, Y. S., "Introduction: The Discipline and Practice of Qualitative Research," in *The Handbook of Qualitative Research,* 2nd ed. Thousand Oaks, CA: Sage, 2000.

Derrida, J., *Writing and Differences.* A. Bass, trans. Chicago: University of Chicago Press, 1978.

Freadman, A., "The Vagabond Arts," in A. Freadman, ed., *In the Place of French: Essays in and Around French Studies in Honour of Michael Spencer.* Mt. Nebo, Australia: University of Queensland, 1992.

Lévi-Strauss, C., *The Savage Mind.* Chicago: University of Chicago Press, 1966.

Weinstein, D., & Weinstein, M. A., "Georg Simmel: Sociological Flaneur Bricoleur." *Theory, Culture and Society,* 1991, 8, 151-168.

CASE   The terms *case* and *unit of analysis* are often used interchangeably in social research, but to a qualitative inquirer the term case means something more than just "*n* of 1." In the sociological and anthropological literature, a case is typically regarded as a specific and bounded (in time and place) instance of a phenomenon selected for study. The phenomenon of interest may be a person, process, event, group, organization, and so on. Empirical cases are routinely used in the study of law, business, and medicine. Cases are generally characterized, on the one hand, by their concreteness and circumstantial specificity and, on the other hand, by their theoretical interest or generalizability. There is disagreement as to whether the case is an empirical unit ('out there' to be discovered and observed) or a theoretical construct that serves the interest of the investigator. Hence, the sociologist Howard Becker advises that instead of asking "What is a case?" inquirers should continually ask themselves "What is this a case *of?*" **See also CASE STUDY RESEARCH.**

Key Reference

Ragin, C. C., & Becker, H. S., *What Is a Case? Exploring the Foundations of Social Inquiry.* Cambridge, UK: Cambridge University Press, 1992.

CASE STUDY RESEARCH   This is a strategy for doing social inquiry, although what constitutes the strategy is a matter of debate.

One useful way of thinking of this approach to inquiry is in terms of the distinction between case study and variable study: In case study, the *case* is at center stage, not variables. Robert Yin argues that a case study strategy is preferred when the inquirer seeks answers to how or why questions, when the inquirer has little control over events being studied, when the object of study is a contemporary phenomenon in a real-life context, when boundaries between the phenomenon and the context are not clear, and when it is desirable to use multiple sources of evidence. Robert Stake emphasizes that the foremost concern of case study research is to generate knowledge of the particular. He explains that case study seeks to discern and pursue understanding of issues intrinsic to the case. He acknowledges, however, that cases can be chosen and studied because they are thought to be instrumentally useful in furthering understanding of a particular problem, issue, concept, and so on. Both Stake and Yin argue that case studies can be used for theoretical elaboration or *analytic generalization*. **See also CROSS-CASE ANALYSIS.**

Key References

Hamel, J. (with S. Dufour & D. Fortin), *Case Study Methods*. Newbury Park, CA: Sage, 1993.

Stake, R., *The Art of Case Study Research*. Thousand Oaks, CA: Sage, 1995.

Yin, R., *Case Study Research: Design and Methods*, rev. ed. Newbury Park, CA: Sage, 1989.

CAUSAL ANALYSIS/CAUSALITY   Causation is intimately related to *explanation;* asking for an explanation of an event is often to ask *why* it happened. Hence, for many social scientists, deterministic (universal) and statistical (probabilistic) causal laws are thought to play a pivotal role in defining what constitutes a legitimate explanation of social phenomena. Although causal relations are important in social inquiry, exactly how to define a causal relationship is one of the most difficult topics in epistemology and the philosophy of science. There is little general agreement on how to establish causation. Some philosophers and social scientists argue that cause means an underlying *lawlike* mechanism that accounts for the regular observed association of events. Others support an inductive model of causation: A statement of a cause summarizes the regular association of events of type C with events of type E. Still others claim that a cause is best defined as a necessary and sufficient condition for the occurrence of an event.

Experimental designs are generally regarded as the most appropriate means for testing causal inferences. Qualitative inquirers usually do not use such designs, but from that fact we cannot conclude that the study of cause is unimportant in all qualitative work. For example, the strategy of *analytic induction* was developed as a nonexperimental method suitable for establishing causal accounts using qualitative data. Moreover, there are many varieties of qualitative inquiry that aim to develop causal accounts of social phenomena using structural, functional, and materialist explanations. Thus, it is irresponsible and untrue to say that qualitative inquiry as a whole eschews causal analysis. Some defenders of qualitative work have argued that qualitative inquiry is somehow more attuned to the idea of multiple, probabilistic causes of events than so-called quantitative approaches to the social sciences. This is not necessarily true either, however, because quantitative studies in the social sciences rely a great deal on statistical (i.e., probabilistic) explanations involving multiple causes and do not always assume a deterministic view of causality. Some scholars claim that a concern with causality in qualitative inquiry was characteristic of its 'modernist phase' that has now ended. That will no doubt come as news to many qualitative inquirers still concerned with causal questions.

To understand the importance (or lack thereof) that causal analysis assumes in qualitative inquiry, we must consider the doctrine of *naturalism*. Defenders of naturalism in social science argue that the goal of social inquiry is to create causal explanations of human behavior (however it may be that cause is defined). Phenomenological and hermeneutic approaches to qualitative inquiry reject causal explanation as the proper goal of the human sciences. They argue that we can only understand or interpret human **action**; we cannot give a causal explanation of it. Some feminist researchers share in this rejection of naturalism. Also, postmodern approaches to social inquiry aim to deconstruct all language of cause and effect. **See also EXPLANATION.**

Key References

Denzin, N. K., & Lincoln, Y. S., "Introduction: The Discipline and Practice of Qualitative Research," in *The Handbook of Qualitative Research*, 2nd ed. Thousand Oaks, CA: Sage, 2000.

Little, D., *Varieties of Social Explanation*. Boulder, CO: Westview, 1991.

Ragin, C. C., *The Comparative Method: Moving Beyond Qualitative and Quantitative Strategies*. Berkeley: University of California Press, 1987.

CHICAGO SCHOOL OF SOCIOLOGY   The Chicago school or tradition of sociology developed in the period from about 1920 to 1940 in the Department of Social Science and Anthropology at the University of Chicago and is associated with the work of Robert Park (1864-1944), W. I. Thomas (1863-1947), Ernest Burgess (1886-1966), Everett C. Hughes, and their students. It is generally recognized as the primary source of sociological fieldwork. Park introduced the sociology of Georg Simmel (1858-1918) to the sociologists of the Chicago school; other important influences on their work included the pragmatism of G. H. Mead (1863-1931) and John Dewey (1859-1952), the *symbolic interactionism* of Herbert Blumer (1900-1987), and interactions with socioanthropologist colleagues at Chicago. Chicago sociologists practiced a rich variety of ethnographic fieldwork, including life histories; community studies; urban ethnographies of 'deviant subcultures,' including taxi dancers, hobos, and gang members (reflecting Park's advice to students to explore and document the subcultures of the city of Chicago); and studies combining a focus on the nature of work, professional identity, role, and status that developed from the intellectual direction provided by Hughes. The tradition figures prominently not simply in the history of fieldwork but also in the professional identity of contemporary sociologists, as noted by Van Maanen (1988, p. 20): "Although now well dispersed, the Chicago School still represents a sort of mythical Eden to many contemporary sociologists who locate their personal pedigree and purpose in the profession by tracing back their lineage on the family tree planted in Chicago."

Key References

Bulmer, M., *The Chicago School of Sociology*. Chicago: University of Chicago Press, 1984.

Hammersley, M., *The Dilemma of Qualitative Method: Herbert Blumer and the Chicago Tradition.* London: Routledge, 1989.

Van Maanen, J., *Tales of the Field.* Chicago: University of Chicago Press, 1988.

CODING   To begin the process of analyzing the large volume of data generated in the form of transcripts, fieldnotes, photographs, and the like, the qualitative inquirer often engages in the activity of coding. Coding is a procedure that disaggregates the data, breaks it down into manageable segments, and identifies or names those segments. Although it is impossible to identify and name without at least an implicit conceptual structure, coding is often classified as relatively descriptive or analytical and explanatory depending on the degree of interpretation involved. Coding requires constantly comparing and contrasting various successive segments of the data and subsequently categorizing them. Coding can be accomplished in at least three different ways that can be combined:

1. An a priori, content-specific scheme is first developed from careful study of the problem or topic under investigation and the theoretical interests that drive the inquiry. The codes are derived directly by the social inquirer from the language of the problem area or theoretical field. Data are then examined and sorted into this scheme.

2. An a priori, noncontent-specific scheme is developed, and data are sorted into the scheme. Noncontent-specific schemes are ways of accounting for the data by sorting it into a typology. The typology may be based on commonsense reasoning (e.g., type of event, time of occurrence, participants involved, reactions of participants, and physical setting) or derived from the assumptions of a particular methodological framework such as symbolic interactionism (e.g., practices, episodes, encounters, roles, and relationships).

3. A grounded, a posteriori, inductive, context-sensitive scheme is developed. This scheme may also begin with a simple typology, but here analysts (a) work with the actual language of respondents to generate the codes or categories and (b) work

back and forth between the data segments and the codes or categories to refine the meaning of categories as they proceed through the data.

Depending on the approach taken, the process of coding can yield either a fully labeled (coded) set of data that can be retrieved and manipulated for further analysis or new data documents (e.g., analytical memos and graphic displays) used in further analysis. Qualitative data can be coded for the purpose of generating theories and concepts as well as for testing hypotheses.

Perhaps the three most troublesome tendencies to be aware of in coding are (a) the tendency to code largely at the descriptive level rather than to code for the purposes of explaining or developing an understanding of 'what's going on here'; (b) the tendency to think of coding as a mechanical, straightforward, algorithmic process, thereby ignoring the prior conceptualization and theoretical understandings that are involved; and (c) the tendency to regard codes or categories as 'fixed' or unchanging labels, thereby ignoring their organic, dynamic character. **See also ANALYZING QUALITATIVE DATA, COMPUTER-ASSISTED DATA ANALYSIS, CONTENT ANALYSIS, GROUNDED THEORY METHODOLOGY, MEMOING, TEXTUAL ANALYSIS.**

Key References

Lofland, J., & Lofland, L. H., *Analyzing Social Settings,* 3rd ed. Belmont, CA: Wadsworth, 1995.

Miles, M. B., & Huberman, A. M., *Qualitative Data Analysis,* 2nd ed. Thousand Oaks, CA: Sage, 1994.

Strauss, A., *Qualitative Analysis for Social Scientists.* Cambridge, UK: Cambridge University Press, 1987.

COMPUTER-ASSISTED DATA ANALYSIS   This is a growing subfield of a larger movement concerned with technological innovation in qualitative inquiry. New audio-recording devices, laptop computers, portable high-quality video cameras, and software for data analysis and visual imaging are making possible new procedures for generating and analyzing qualitative data. The introduction of computer software for facilitating qualitative data analysis coincides with and is partially responsible for the concern about developing rigorous, systematic methods of processing data. Software tools are used for recording, storing, indexing, cross-indexing, coding, sorting, and so on. They facilitate the management of large volumes of data and enable the analyst to locate, label (categorize or code), cross-reference, and compile various combinations of segments of textual data.

In some discussions of software tools for data analysis, the implicit assumption often seems to be that because computer-managed analysis is by definition more algorithmic, systematic, and rigorous, it is therefore better. Although computer-assisted tools make qualitative inquiry a different practice, "different" is not synonymous with "better." One need not be a neo-Luddite to be concerned about how the introduction of these tools contributes to the definition of the discursive practice called qualitative inquiry. As Neil Postman (*Technopoly*, Vintage, 1993) reminds us, embedded in every tool is an ideological bias, a predisposition to construct the world to which the tool will be applied as one thing rather than another. Although developers and frequent users of qualitative analysis tools may customarily reflect on these embedded predispositions, it is not entirely clear that the causal user does so. The operations made possible by software are not neutral tools; rather, they structure the undertaking of qualitative inquiry. John Seidel, the developer of ETHNOGRAPH, notes that the following dangers accompany the benefits of software tools: (a) an infatuation with the volume of data one can deal with leading to sacrificing resolution for scope; (b) a reification of the relationship between researcher and data wherein the researcher assumes that data are 'things out there' that can in a relatively simple and straightforward manner be discovered, identified, collected, counted, and sorted, thereby ignoring the fact that data are artifacts of complex processes of identifying, naming, indexing, and coding that, in turn, are shaped by theoretical and methodological assumptions; and (c) a distancing of the researcher from the data. **See also FIELDNOTES.**

Key References

Fielding, N. G., & Lee, R. M., *Computer Analysis and Qualitative Research.* London: Sage, 1998.

Seidel, J., "Method and Madness in the Application of Computer Technology to Qualitative Data Analysis," in N. G. Fielding & R. M. Lee, eds., *Using Computers in Qualitative Research*. Newbury Park, CA: Sage, 1991.

Weitzman, E., & Miles, M. B., *Computer Programs for Qualitative Data Analysis: A Software Sourcebook*. Thousand Oaks, CA: Sage, 1995.

CONFIRMABILITY   See TRUSTWORTHINESS CRITERIA.

C

CONSERVATIVE HERMENEUTICS   Also called validation or objectivist *hermeneutics,* this theory of interpretation defines hermeneutics as a method for the validation of the meaning embedded in a text. Its principal advocates are the Italian legal historian Emilio Betti and the American professor of literature E. D. Hirsch. Both Betti and Hirsch argue that an author's intended meaning of a text is a fixed, determinate entity or object that can be depicted or portrayed accurately. This meaning is the external reference point against which competing interpretations of a text are judged to be valid or invalid. In this version of hermeneutics, *method* plays a key role in helping prevent the misinterpretation of a text—that is, the danger of reading something into the text because of the interpreter's own bias or standpoint. Method is regarded as a means of stepping outside the *hermeneutic circle* to achieve historical objectivity and validity in interpretation. This kind of hermeneutics contrasts sharply with *critical hermeneutics, philosophical hermeneutics,* and *deconstructionism.*

Key References

Betti, E., "Hermeneutics as the General Methodology of the *Geisteswissenschaften*," in J. Bleicher, ed., *Contemporary Hermeneutics*. London: Routledge Kegan Paul, 1980.

Gallagher, S., *Hermeneutics and Education*. Albany: State University of New York Press, 1992.

Hirsch, E. D., *Validity in Interpretation*. New Haven, CT: Yale University Press, 1967.

Hirsch, E. D., *The Aims of Interpretation*. Chicago: University of Chicago Press, 1976.

CONSTANT COMPARISON, METHOD OF   In this method for *analyzing qualitative data,* devised by Barney Glaser and Anselm Strauss, data in the form of fieldnotes, observations, interviews, and the like are coded inductively, and then each segment of the data is taken in turn and (a) compared to one or more categories to determine its relevance and (b) compared with other segments of data similarly categorized. As segments are compared, new analytic categories and new relationships between categories may be discovered. **See also CODING, GROUNDED THEORY METHODOLOGY.**

Key References

Glaser, B., & Strauss, A., *Awareness of Dying.* Chicago: Aldine, 1965.

Glaser, B., & Strauss, A., *The Discovery of Grounded Theory.* Chicago: Aldine, 1967.

CONSTRUCTIVISM   This is a particularly elusive term with different meanings depending on the discourse in which it is used. For example, constructivism in mathematics and logic, or the ideas of construct and construct validity that play a central role in the methodologies of experimental psychology and psychometrics, bear little resemblance to the notions of constructivism readily found in the contemporary literature in the social sciences. Also, the latter generally have very little to do with everyday garden-variety constructivism, which is the belief that the mind is active in the construction of knowledge. Most of us would agree that knowing is not passive—a simple imprinting of sense data on the mind—but active; that is, the mind does something with these impressions—at the very least it forms abstractions or concepts. In this sense, constructivism means that human beings do not find or discover knowledge so much as construct or make it. We invent concepts, models, and schemes to make sense of experience, and we continually test and modify these constructions in the light of new experience. Furthermore, there is an inevitable historical and sociocultural dimension to this construction. We do not construct our interpretations in isolation but against a backdrop of shared understandings, practices, language, and so forth. This ordinary sense of constructivism holds that all knowledge claims and their evaluation take place within a conceptual framework through which the world is described and explained. Everyday constructivism thus opposes *naïve realism* and strict *empiricism,* which assume that there can be some kind of unmediated, direct grasp of the empirical world and that knowledge (i.e., the mind) simply reflects or mirrors what is 'out there.'

Notions of constructivism encountered in the social sciences generally go far beyond this ordinary sense of constructing. There are two broad strands of constructivist thought. One strand, known as radical constructivism or psychological constructivism, focuses more on the individual knower and acts of cognition, and its most well-know advocate is Ernst von Glasersfeld. The central idea in radical constructivism is that human knowledge cannot consist in accurate representation or faithful copying of an external reality—that is, of a reality that is nonphenomenal (existing apart from the knower's experiences). Knowledge is redefined procedurally—as an unending series of processes of inner construction. The reliability of constructions is determined instrumentally in terms of their evolutionary viability. Radical constructivism claims a debt to the genetic *epistemology* of Jean Piaget (1896-1980). Although Piaget is perhaps better known for his work in developmental psychology, he did considerable work in theory of knowledge. He rejected both *empiricism* and *rationalism* and, like Kant (1724-1804), held that knowledge of the world is mediated by cognitive structures. Unlike Kant, however, Piaget did not consider these structures to be given a priori but rather viewed them as the products of a process of construction resulting from the interaction of mind and environment (see his *Introduction à l'epistemologie génétique,* 3 vols., 1950; *The Origins of Intelligence in Children,* Norton, 1952).

A second strand of constructivism focuses more on social process and interaction and is generally known as social constructionism. Social constructionism has some affinity to theories of *symbolic interactionism* and *ethnomethodology* that emphasize the actor's definition of the situation—that seek to understand how social actors recognize, produce, and reproduce social actions and how they come to share an intersubjective understanding of specific life circumstances. The classic work in this area is Peter Berger and Thomas Luckmann's *The Social Construction of Reality* (Doubleday, 1966).

Ian Hacking argues that social constructionist arguments generally arise as follows: Scholars claim that some particular X (childhood, gender, poverty, frailty, disability, etc.) is taken for granted or appears to be inevitable. They argue that X need not be at all as it is at present; it is not determined by the nature of things, nor is it inevitable. They aim to undermine the idea that X has an 'essence.' Diana Fuss (1989), for example, claims that

> what is at stake for the constructionist are systems of representations, social and material practices, laws of discourses, and ideological effects. In short, constructionists are concerned above all with the production and organization of differences, and they therefore reject the idea that any essential or natural givens precede the process of social determination. (p. 3)

The constructionist seeks to explain how human beings interpret or construct some X in specific linguistic, social, and historical contexts. In addition, many constructionists hold that X is something that should be severely criticized, changed, or overthrown.

In making sense of constructionism, it is important to distinguish just what is being constructed. Again, Hacking is helpful here in explaining that three broad types of things are said to be socially constructed (imagine substituting one of the following for X in the previous paragraph): (a) items or objects that are in the world in a commonsensical meaning of the phrase—for example, states (childhood), practices (domestic abuse), conditions (health), actions (labeling something criminal or deviant), behavior (attention deficit disorder), experiences (of being disabled), and relations (gender); (b) ideas, including conceptions, beliefs, theories, and attitudes toward; and (c) facts, truth, reality, and knowledge —in sum, everything.

There are both weak and strong versions of social constructionism, depending on their respective views regarding the social construction of everything. Both versions share the view that our concepts, theories, ideas, and so forth do not chart, map, or straightforwardly represent or mirror reality. The weak variety, however, would not hold that *every* object, idea, and so forth in the world, and indeed *every* aspect of the world (i.e., every thing in itself), is a social construct. Instead of this kind of universal constructivism, weak constructionism might focus on how our experience of some particular object or idea, our classifications of same, and our interest in same are socially constructed. This is a roundabout way of saying that weak social constructionism does not deny reality in the ordinary commonplace sense of that term. For example, one might write a social history of the notion of disability, schizophrenia, altruism, mental illness, family, domestic violence, gender, childhood, and so forth revealing how each is culturally produced or unmasking each as an ideology and still maintain that it is real. Strong social constructionists do appear to deny any *ontology* of the real whatsoever. Gergen (1994), for example, argues that "one must be suspicious of all attempts to establish *fundamental* ontologies—incorrigible inventories of *the real*" (p. 75). Taken literally, that may well mean that everything in the world and about the world is nothing but a sociolinguistic product of historically situated interactions—a kind of linguistic or semantic *idealism*. Moreover, many strong social constructionists endorse radical perspectivalism, a doctrine that claims that our experience, thought, and speech about reality or reality itself or all these are a function of the particular conceptual scheme or framework (e.g., culture, form of life, language game, on paradigm) in which we live, and that different conceptual schemes yield incommensurable understandings of experience and reality. **See also ESSENTIALISM, FACT, FALLIBILISM.**

Key References

Collin, F., *Social Reality*. London: Routledge, 1997.

Fuss, D., *Essentially Speaking: Feminism, Nature, and Difference*. New York: Routledge, 1989.

Gergen, K. J., *Realities and Relationships: Soundings in Social Construction*. Cambridge, MA: Harvard University Press, 1994.

Hacking, I., *The Social Construction of What?* Cambridge, MA: Harvard University Press, 1999.

Phillips, D. C., ed., *Constructivism in Education: Opinions and Second Opinions on Controversial Issues,* National Society for the Study of Education 99th Yearbook, Vol. 1. Chicago: University of Chicago Press, 2000.

Potter, J., *Representing Reality: Discourse, Rhetoric, and Social Construction.* London: Sage, 1996.

Sarbin, T. R., & Kitsue, J. I., eds., *Constructing the Social.* Thousand Oaks, CA: Sage, 1994.

von Glasersfeld, E., *Radical Constructivism: A Way of Knowing and Learning.* London: Falmer, 1995.

CONTENT ANALYSIS   This is a generic name for a variety of means of *textual analysis* that involve comparing, contrasting, and categorizing a corpus of data to test hypotheses. The analysis usually, but not always, relies on some statistical procedures for drawing samples and establishing intercoder reliability. The central steps to this procedure include (a) creating a set of codes; (b) systematically applying those codes to some set of textual data; (c) establishing the interrater reliability of coders when more than one coder is employed; (d) creating a matrix of variables from the texts and codes; and (e) analyzing the matrix by means of some univariate, bivariate, or multivariate statistical procedure. The data to be coded may be cultural artifacts (texts of various kinds, documents, records, billboards, television shows, films, advertisements, etc.) or events. Although classic context analysis emphasizes systematic, objective, quantitative description of content derived from researcher-developed categories, contemporary forms of content analysis include both numeric and interpretive means of analyzing data. **See also ANALYZING QUALITATIVE DATA, CODING.**

Key References

Krippendorf, K., *Content Analysis: An Introduction to Its Methodology.* Beverly Hills, CA: Sage, 1980.

Reinharz, S., *Feminist Methods in Social Research.* Oxford, UK: Oxford University Press, 1992. (See the chapter on content analysis)

Weber, R. P., *Basic Content Analysis,* 2nd ed. Newbury Park, CA: Sage, 1990.

CONTEXT   See CONTEXTUALISM.

CONTEXT OF DISCOVERY/CONTEXT OF JUSTIFICATION   The philosophy of *logical positivism* was based on a strict *empiricism* that relied only on perception and induction in the formation of scientific claims. *Theory* and theoretical terms were nothing more than a language that functioned as a filing system for organizing data and hypotheses. Moreover, the starting points for scientific discovery—that is, the theoretical interests and dispositions of inquirers—were largely regarded as irrelevant to the task of developing justifiable scientific claims. The philosophy of *logical empiricism* reintroduced the ideas of discovery and theoretical dispositions as relevant features of the picture of scientific claim making. It did so, however, in a way so as not to subvert the primary importance of empirical testing. Logical empiricists argued that there is indeed a process of intellectual discovery and theoretical speculation that produces new ideas and hypotheses. Here, in the context of discovery, the imagination, intellectual interests, values, dispositions, and theoretical inclinations of individual scientists, as well as the role of institutional commitments and values influencing the scientist's choices, are all relevant matters. These extrascientific ('external') concerns, however, are completely irrelevant (and must be eliminated) once the scientist embarks on the process of the epistemological validation of an hypothesis—that is, the context of justification. It is in this ('internal') context, governed as it is by epistemic concerns and procedures, that a scientific claim is checked, tested, and critically evaluated.

This sharp distinction was first introduced in 1938 by Hans Reichenbach (1891-1953) and was featured in the philosophies of science of both Karl Popper (1902-1994) and Ernest Nagel (1901-1985). The distinction met with sharp criticism from philosophers, who argued that a complete understanding of the epistemology of science could only be had by recognizing science as a social enterprise and by considering the interrelationships between the dynamics of theory development, the acceptance and rejection of theories, the choice of which experiments to perform to test a theory, and so on.

Despite the rather thoroughgoing criticism of this doctrine, it continues to serve as a key methodological principle in the philosophy of *naturalism*. Defenders of naturalism generally argue that epistemological concerns are primary, and that it is important to distinguish between ideology (or history or sociology) and epistemology when discussing the testing and growth of scientific knowledge. According to this view, emotions, interests, ideologies, and values have a bearing on or influence the problems one addresses and the hypotheses one develops but are irrelevant to cognitive assessment of those problems and hypotheses. Moreover, the spirit of the doctrine is evident in other contemporary efforts to come to terms with the relationship between a normative philosophy of science (the traditional concerns of epistemology) and an empirical sociology of knowledge. For example, some feminists argue that a distinction between the two contexts cannot be maintained, and defenders of the Strong Programme in the *Sociology of Scientific Knowledge* appear to collapse the distinction and argue that knowledge is whatever we take it to be. **See also FACT-VALUE DISTINCTION, TACIT (PERSONAL) KNOWLEDGE.**

Key References

Hollis, M., *The Philosophy of Social Science: An Introduction.* Cambridge, UK: Cambridge University Press, 1994.

Reichenbach, H., *Experience and Prediction.* Chicago: University of Chicago Press, 1938.

CONTEXTUALISM   Several senses of this term play an important role in current thinking about qualitative inquiry. In one sense, contextualism refers to a humanistic theory that explains the kinds of beings that we are. This theory holds that human nature is only specified and made intelligible by the particular context in which it is found. Clifford Geertz's views of human nature in *The Interpretation of Cultures* (Basic Books, 1971) reflect this theory. In a second sense, contextualism refers to the nature of interpretations. Hermeneutic contextualism is the view that interpretations are always context bound—that is, they always take place within some background of beliefs and practices (culture, form of life, language game, or tradition) that is never at once and completely capable of articulation. Moreover, interpretations are context bound in the sense that a specific situation determines the form and direction of an interpretation. A third sense of context as formative is related to the second. In *cultural studies,* context or contextualism indicates not simply an empirical environment given beforehand against which some *action* is to be understood. Context is not simply a background of influences and determinants of meaning, identity, speech, and so forth that is detachable from those human actions. Nor is context simply the set of interrelated conditions in which something occurs or exists. Rather, context is *produced* in the social practice of asking questions about meaning, identity, speech, and so on.

Key References

Grossberg, L., *Bringing it all Back Home: Essays on Cultural Studies.* Durham, NC: Duke University Press, 1997.

Hoy, D. R., Bohman, J. F., & Shusterman, R., eds., *The Interpretive Turn: Philosophy, Science, Culture.* Ithaca, NY: Cornell University Press, 1991.

CONVERSATION ANALYSIS   This methodology for *textual analysis* arose out of *ethnomethodology.* It is concerned specifically with examining the structure of talk to reveal how speakers produce orderly social interaction. The methodology requires the detailed analysis of precise transcripts. Like ethnomethodology, conversation analysis rejects referential theories of language use that assume that words acquire meaning by standing for things and that an utterance (or sentence) means what it does because its parts refer to or correspond to elements of an actual or possible state of affairs. Because utterances 'stand for' in this way, in this theory of language use one is primarily concerned with the quality of that 'standing for'—that is, the extent to which the utterance is accurate, truthful, distorted, and so on. In contrast, conversation analysis assumes a pragmatic theory of language use in which the meaning of an utterance is the role it plays in a particular social practice. In this view, words and sentences 'do things'—they perform actions such as inviting, rebuking, complaining, and complimenting; they do not simply (or even) refer (see J. L. Austin, *How to Do Things With Words,* Oxford University Press, 1962). The conversation analyst is interested in understanding the many things that utterances can do and how they do what they do in particular social practices. **See also LANGUAGE.**

Key References

Have, P. T., *Doing Conversational Analysis: A Practical Guide.* London: Sage, 1999.

Heritage, J., "Explanations as Accounts: A Conversation Analytic Perspective," in C. Antaki, ed., *Analyzing Everyday Explanation: A Casebook of Methods.* London: Sage, 1988.

Sacks, H., *Lectures on Conversation,* Vols. 1 & 2, G. Jefferson, ed. Oxford, UK: Blackwell, 1992.

Silverman, D., "Analyzing Conversation," in C. Seale, ed., *Researching Society and Culture.* London: Sage, 1998.

Silverman, D., *Harvey Sacks: Social Science and Conversation Analysis.* Cambridge, MA: Polity, 1998.

COVERING LAW MODEL OF EXPLANATION   The most influential, although not universally accepted, view of what constitutes the logic of *explanation* in the social sciences or an adequate social *scientific* explanation is the covering law model. This model explains an event or action by subsuming (covering) it under one or more general causal laws. This model has two forms: In the case in which laws are deterministic (universal), a deductive-nomological (i.e., *lawlike*) explanation is possible. This takes the following form:

$L_1, L_2, L_3, \ldots L_n$(Testable causal laws)
$C_1, C_2, C_3, \ldots C_n$(Testable statements of background conditions)

E(Statement of the event or action to be explained)

In circumstances in which laws are statistical (probabilistic), explanation takes an inductive-statistical form:

$L_1, L_2, L_3, \ldots L_n$(Testable statistical laws)
$C_1, C_2, C_3, \ldots C_n$(Testable statements of background conditions)

===

E(Statement of the event or action to be explained)

In the former, the laws and conditions deductively entail the event or action to be explained by showing why it was necessary in the circumstances. In the latter, laws and conditions help show only why the event or action was probable (not necessary).

Much controversy surrounds the issue of whether the covering law model in general is the most appropriate definition of social scientific explanation and what constitutes a legitimate form of an inductive-statistical explanation. Nonetheless, for defenders of *logical empiricism,* this is a generally accepted account of what constitutes theoretical explanation. In this view, the goal of social science is to develop social *theory*—a unified causal explanation that ties together laws, generalizations, hypotheses, and so on. Other models or accounts of explanation (functional, structural, and materialist) are also popular in social science, but there is significant debate about whether these models are more or less variations on the kind of causal explanation defended in the covering law model or simply poor substitutes.

Key Reference

Little, D., *Varieties of Social Explanation.* Boulder, CO: Westview, 1991.

CREDIBILITY   See **TRUSTWORTHINESS CRITERIA.**

CRISIS OF LEGITIMATION   This phrase is shorthand for a set of issues that arise from questioning the *authority* of the interpretive *text* characteristic of *postmodernism* and *poststructuralism.* Authority here refers to the claim a text makes to be an accurate, true, complete account of experience, meaning, a way of life, and so forth. Traditionally, these kinds of concerns about the authority of an account are considered to be epistemological matters. In other words, an account is judged in terms of the validity, accuracy, and truthfulness of its claims. Hence, the ability of a text to persuade, sway, influence, or command an audience's attention depends, for the most part, on the extent to which the claims made in a text are accurate, warranted, and so forth. In other words, in this perspective, the quality of evidence and argument presented to warrant a claim are more important than the rhetoric and style of presentation.

Postmodernist thought regards these traditional concerns with validity as vacuous. It does so because it argues as follows: (a) The notion of validity rests on the assumption that a textual account is capable of faithfully representing some set of experiences in 'the world-out-there'; (b) various rules and procedures are employed to judge the validity of this act of representation—for example, respondent validation, triangulation, internal coherence, and careful fit to theory; (c) there is no such thing as a 'real' world of experience out there, however, only various textual constructions that create experience and in the process transform it; (d) hence, the rules and procedures employed to establish the validity of a text or to provide a warrant for claims made in a text are in actuality only devices employed by the author of a particular text to assert some kind of power over the reader by persuading the reader that the particular text in question is authoritative or legitimate; (e) because there can be no such thing as a valid and authoritative account, there can only be various kinds of accounts that, via a variety of different means (e.g., appeals to evidence, standpoint, involvement, subjectivity, emotionality, feeling, and participation) seek to persuade readers of their legitimacy; (f) hence, validity is replaced by notions of authority and legitimation, and rhetorical and political issues trump traditional epistemological concerns.

To the extent that this argument accurately captures the state of affairs in interpretive work, there would be no real crisis. There would simply be debate about the merits of various ways of persuading readers of the legitimacy of an account. A genuine crisis, however, does in fact arise because despite this turn away from epistemology and toward rhetoric and politics, the core problem of criteria remains, namely, on what basis are we to discriminate between better and worse accounts? When legitimation becomes a matter of exercising authority and power, the following question naturally arises: What are legitimate and illegitimate means of exercising power? **See also CRISIS OF REPRESENTATION, EXPERIENCE, (THE) PROBLEM OF THE CRITERION.**

Key Reference

Denzin, N. K., *Interpretive Ethnography: Ethnographic Practices for the 21st Century.* Thousand Oaks, CA: Sage, 1997.

CRISIS OF REPRESENTATION   This phrase was coined by George Marcus and Michael Fischer to refer specifically to the uncertainty within the human sciences about adequate means of describing social reality. This crisis arises from the (noncontroversial) claim that no interpretive account can ever directly or completely capture lived *experience.* Broadly conceived, the crisis is part of a more general set of ideas across the human sciences that challenge long-standing beliefs about the role of encompassing, generalizing (theoretical, methodological, and political) frameworks that guide empirical research within a discipline. Symptoms of the crisis include the borrowing of ideas and methods across disciplines (e.g., social sciences to literature, literature to philosophy, and philosophy to social science), questioning the dominance of post-World War II frameworks and theories that guided inquiry (e.g., Parsonian sociology, Marxism, and French structuralism), and the general turn away from developing theoretical models of social and natural order to debates about epistemology, method, forms of representation, and the like. Although foreshadowed and shaped in the antipositivist writing of German scholars in the late nineteenth and early twentieth century, these are the sets of ideas that, during the past three or four decades, have come to characterize the postmodern condition of the social sciences (and related conditions in literature, philosophy, arts, architecture, etc.).

Within the crisis, both radically skeptical and optimistic voices are discernible. Radical skeptics insist that what we are faced with are only texts—that is, particular *inscriptions* that create different accounts of lived experience. There is no direct, unmediated link between the inscriptions of any particular *text* and the 'real' world of experience. There are no real-world referents (no such thing as 'experience' as an object) to which the language of descriptive and explanatory accounts of human *action* can be mapped and against which it can be judged. Moreover, all attempts to describe and explain are always, at best, incomplete, reductive, and insufficient and, at worst, misleading, perverse, fraudulent, and deceptive. Texts (accounts, representations, and interpretations) only refer to other texts; the language of representation is only rhetoric. More optimistic responses acknowledge the importance of examining the rhetoric of representation but are not willing to concede that the dilemma of representation dissolves the responsibility of the social scientist to describe and explain the social world. **See also CRISIS OF LEGITIMATION, GRAND THEORY, POSTMODERNISM, REPRESENTATION.**

Key References

Atkinson, P., *The Ethnographic Imagination.* London: Routledge, 1990.

Gubrium, J., & Holstein, J., *The New Language of Qualitative Method.* Oxford, UK: Blackwell, 1997.

Marcus, G., & Fischer, M., *Anthropology as Cultural Critique.* Chicago: University of Chicago Press, 1986.

CRITERIA   Criteria are standards, benchmarks, norms, and in some cases regulative ideals that guide judgments about the goodness, quality, validity, truthfulness, and so forth of competing claims (or methodologies, theories, interpretations, etc.). A criterion is distinguishable from various procedures employed to achieve the criterion (e.g., validity of a claim is a criterion, and to demonstrate that that criterion is met might involve using procedures such as analytic induction, member checking, and triangulation).

Criteria that have been proposed for judging the processes and products of social inquiry include truth, relevance, validity, credibility, plausibility, generalizability, social action, and social transformation. Some of these criteria are epistemic (i.e., concerned with justifying knowledge claims as true, accurate, and correct), others are political (i.e., concerned with warranting the power, use, and effects of knowledge claims or the inquiry process more generally), and still others are moral or ethical standards (i.e., concerned with the right conduct of the inquirer and the inquiry process in general).

Traditionally, criteria are an essential feature of *epistemology*— they are standards by means of which one distinguishes genuine, objective knowledge from mere belief. Charles Taylor explains that the quest for a set of externally defined standards against which competing methodologies, values, theories, claims, conjectures, and so forth are independently weighed is based on the assumption that rational arbitration of differences *requires* such standards. In other words, it is absolutely necessary to have criteria because without them it would be impossible to determine whether one is behaving rationally. Criteria are considered to be decisive considerations that both parties to a dispute about competing claims must accept. Taylor is highly critical of this conception of criteria central to foundationalist epistemologies. He defends an alternative view of practical rationality and a form of argument that evaluates transitions from one interpretation to another.

Poststructuralist and postmodernist approaches to qualitative inquiry are also shaping the way we conceive of criteria. Given the growing influence of narrative approaches and experimental texts in qualitative inquiry, it is becoming more common to find discussions of rhetorical and aesthetic criteria replacing discussions of epistemic criteria. Other scholars argue that epistemological criteria cannot be neatly decoupled from political and critical agendas and ethical concerns. Some scholars in qualitative inquiry have little patience for discussing criteria within different epistemological frameworks and theoretical perspectives and prefer to focus on the craft of using various methodological procedures for producing "quality" work. **See also FACT-VALUE DISTINCTION, KNOWLEDGE, (THE) PROBLEM OF THE CRITERION, VALIDITY.**

Key References

Hammersley, M., *Reading Ethnographic Research: A Critical Guide.* London: Longman, 1990.

Richardson, L., ed., "Special Focus: Introduction—Assessing Alternative Modes of Qualitative and Ethnographic Research: How Do We Judge? Who Judges?" *Qualitative Inquiry*, 2000, 6(2), 251-291.

Seale, C. F., *The Quality of Qualitative Research.* London: Sage, 1999.

Smith, J. K., *After the Demise of Empiricism: The Problem of Judging Social and Educational Inquiry.* Norwood, NJ: Ablex, 1993.

Taylor, C., *Philosophical Arguments.* Cambridge, MA: Harvard University Press, 1995.

CRITICAL ETHNOGRAPHY   This phrase refers to ethnographic studies that engage in cultural critique by examining larger political, social, and economic issues and that focus on oppression, conflict, struggle, and power. These studies are critical of the parochial, romantic, politically conservative, and limited vision of traditional ethnographies. Critical ethnographies of this kind are often, although not necessarily, informed by Marxist and post-Marxist theory (J. Nash, *We Eat the Mines and the Mines Eat Us*, Columbia University Press, 1979; P. Willis, *Learning to Labour*, Columbia University Press, 1981; G. Nelson & L. Grossman, eds., *Marxism and the Interpretation of Culture*, University of Illinois Press, 1988). **See also CRITICAL SOCIAL SCIENCE.**

Key References

Carspecken, P., *Critical Ethnography in Educational Research: A Theoretical and Practical Guide.* New York: Routledge, 1995.

Carspecken, P., *Four Scenes for Posing the Question of Meaning and Other Essays in Critical Philosophy and Critical Methodology.* New York: Lang, 1999.

Marcus, G. E., & Fischer, M. M. J., *Anthropology as Cultural Critique.* Chicago: University of Chicago Press, 1986.

CRITICAL HERMENEUTICS   Also known as depth hermeneutics, this version of *hermeneutics* is explained by Karl Otto-Apel and Jürgen Habermas as well as other critical theorists. It is characterized by several general ideas. First, it is highly skeptical about given meanings and interpretations. It is suspicious of claims to truth and knowledge and seeks to demystify those claims by engaging in a critique of ideologies that distort understanding and communication. Second, it is emphatically normative; that is, its critiques of meanings and practices are undertaken for the purposes of transforming society and emancipating individuals from false consciousness such that undistorted communication and nonideological understandings can be realized. Finally, it is materialist—it is concerned not simply with the relationship between language, meaning, and understanding but also with concrete, empirical economic, social, organizational, and political conditions and practices that shape human beings as knowers and as social agents. Critical hermeneutics often draws on psychoanalysis as a model for the hermeneutic task integrating both causal explanation and interpretive self-understanding. **See also** CRITICAL SOCIAL SCIENCE, CRITICAL THEORY.

Key References

Habermas, J., *Knowledge and Human Interests*. J. J. Shapiro, trans. Boston: Beacon, 1971.

Kögler, H. H., *The Power of Dialogue: Critical Hermeneutics After Gadamer and Foucault*. P. Henrickson, trans. Cambridge: MIT Press, 1996.

C

CRITICAL SOCIAL SCIENCE   Generally, this is the research program undertaken by a variety of social theorists that are strongly influenced by *critical theory.* Critical theory of society, in turn, can be characterized as a blend of practical philosophy and explanatory social science, sharing and radically reforming the intentions of both. Practical philosophy is concerned with the specifics of ethical and political life (*praxis*) and the actions that must be undertaken to achieve the good life; explanatory social science produces scientific knowledge of the general causes of social *action.* Critical social science is characterized by several general themes. First, its aim, broadly conceived, is to integrate theory and practice in such a way that individuals and groups become aware of the contradictions and distortions in their belief systems and social practices and are then inspired to change those beliefs and practices. Its method here is immanent critique, which challenges belief systems and social relations not by comparing them to some set of external standards but by showing that these practices do not measure up to their own standards and are internally inconsistent, hypocritical, incoherent, and hence comprise a false consciousness. Second, critical social science is thus practical and normative and not merely descriptive and explanatory. Third, it is foregrounded in a critique of instrumental, technical reason. Critical theorists (among other social theorists) argue that this kind of means-end reasoning is pervasive; it informs the traditional empirical-analytic sciences and dominates not only societal processes and cultural meaning but also the dynamics of personality formation. Critical social scientists argue that instrumental reason aims to eliminate crises, conflict, and critique. Although founded in the Enlightenment bid to liberate people from myth, ignorance, and oppression, the rationalization of social and individual life by means of instrumental reason actually works to suppress the very self-transformative, self-reflexive, critical, liberating impulses on which it was founded. Critical inquiry supports a kind of reasoning that is practical, moral, and ethically and politically informed. Fourth, to retain or recapture the Enlightenment belief in the power of human reason to affect individual and social transformation, critical social science argues that a form of inquiry is needed that fosters enlightened self-knowledge and effective social-political action. The logic of critical social inquiry requires linking hermeneutic and explanatory social scientific interests to normative concerns. This feature of critical social science marks it as distinctly different from social science characterized by *naturalism* and *antinaturalism*. Finally, critical social science is self-reflexive. To prevent a critical theory of society from becoming another self-serving ideology, the theory must account for its own conditions of possibility and its transformative effects. It rejects the idea of *disinterested social science* and emphasizes attending to the cultural and historical conditions on which the theorist's own intellectual activity depends. **See also FRANKFURT SCHOOL, INTEREST.**

Key References

Calhoun, C., "Social Theory and the Public Sphere," in B. S. Turner, ed., *The Blackwell Companion to Social Theory.* Oxford, UK: Blackwell, 1996.

Comstock, D. E., "A Method for Critical Research," in M. Martin & L. C. McIntyre, eds., *Readings in the Philosophy of Social Science.* Cambridge: MIT Press, 1994.

Fay, B., *Critical Social Science.* Ithaca, NY: Cornell University Press, 1987.

Fay, B., & Moon, J. D., "What Would an Adequate Philosophy of Social Science Look Like?" in M. Martin & L. C. McIntyre, eds., *Readings in the Philosophy of Social Science.* Cambridge: MIT Press, 1994.

CRITICAL THEORY   See **FRANKFURT SCHOOL, THEORY.**

CROSS-CASE ANALYSIS   (also called comparative case method or comparative analysis) A study can include the examination of one case or a collection of cases to learn something about a concept, theory, social process, and so on. Cross-case or comparative approaches include functional analysis as first developed by Durkheim (1858-1917); Marx's (1818-1883) theory of modes of production in societies; Weber's (1864-1920) methods of historical comparison using ideal types; contemporary methods of quasi-experimentation using multivariate statistical analysis (T. D. Cook & D. Campbell, *Quasi-Experimentation: Design and Analysis Issues for Field Settings,* Rand McNally, 1979); and *meta-ethnography.* In cross-case analysis, two central issues are the rationale for the selection of multiple cases in a single study and the procedures for analyzing data across the cases.

Robert Yin advises that the choice of single or multiple cases is a design decision. Cases are rarely if ever chosen as a sample of some universe of cases. Rather, a single-case design is chosen because the case is thought to be critical to the elaboration or test of a theory, extreme or unique, or unusually revelatory. The choice of multiple-case designs (permitting cross-case analysis) follows what Yin calls a replication rather than a sampling logic: Additional cases are chosen for study because such cases are expected to yield similar information or findings or contrary but predictable findings. Robert Stake agrees that cases are not chosen for representativeness. He defines instrumental case study as strategy whereby a case is studied because it can shed light on a particular pregiven issue, concept, or problem. When several cases are chosen within a single study to achieve this aim, each is thought to be useful in that regard. The result is what he calls a collective case study. **See also CASE STUDY RESEARCH, CODING, SAMPLING.**

Key References

Miles, M., & Huberman, A. M., *Qualitative Data Analysis,* 2nd ed. Thousand Oaks, CA: Sage, 1994.

Ragin, C. C., *The Comparative Method: Moving Beyond Qualitative and Quantitative Strategies.* Berkeley: University of California Press, 1987.

Stake, R. E., *The Art of Case Study Research.* Thousand Oaks, CA: Sage, 1995.

Yin, R., *Case Study Research,* rev. ed. Newbury Park, CA: Sage, 1989.

CULTURAL RELATIVISM   In the 1920s and 1930s in the United States, cultural relativism was a set of methodological principles that both enabled and justified the study of cultural diversity by anthropologists. The principles encompassed respect for different conceptions of what it meant to behave rationally in different societies, endorsed the view that cultures are composed of different systems of values, and supported the notion that firsthand observation rather than simply conjecture undertaken from the comfort of one's own library was necessary to understand the ways in which cultures organized their respective ways of life. (See also **NATIVE'S POINT OF VIEW**.) In the 1950s, this set of methodological principles often came to be interpreted as a normative doctrine. As such, it led to widespread concern that anthropology was at least implicitly claiming that all cultural value systems were equal, thus making comparative moral judgments impossible. Moreover, the focus on documenting widespread cultural diversity seemed to argue against the possibility of any meaningful generalization about human societies and values, thereby casting doubt on anthropology as a genuine science. With the appearance of interpretive anthropology in the late 1960s and early 1970s, the idea of cultural relativism as method was resurrected as a rationale for engaging in *ethnography*. Marcus and Fischer (1986) claim that contemporary *interpretive anthropology* once again embodies a reinvigorated methodological principle (but not the doctrine) of cultural relativism. In their view, it is precisely because it has resurrected and strengthened this notion that the practice of ethnography is capable of "challenging all those views of reality in social thought which prematurely overlook or reduce cultural diversity for the sake of the capacity to generalize or to affirm universal values, usually from the still-privileged vantage point of global homogenization, emanating from the West" (p. 33). **See also CULTURAL STUDIES, OTHER (THE OTHER, OTHERNESS), RELATIVISM.**

Key References

Geertz, C., "Anti Anti-Relativism." *American Anthropologist*, 1984, 86(2), 263-277.

Marcus, G., & Fischer, M., *Anthropology as Cultural Critique*. Chicago: University of Chicago Press, 1986.

CULTURAL STUDIES   This is a diverse field devoted to the study of *culture,* but the particular practices of cultural study differ not only in terms of contexts in which these studies unfold (e.g., British cultural studies, Australian cultural studies, U.S. cultural studies, African cultural studies, and Pacific cultural studies) but also in methods employed (e.g., participant observation, various means of textual analysis, and statistical survey techniques), the frameworks that give rise to particular foci for a study (e.g., postcolonial relations, semiotics, gender studies, and media studies), and social theories that provide it with substantive concerns (e.g., critical race theory, neo-Marxism, feminist social theory, communications theory, and poststructuralism). All cultural studies appear to share a view that culture is both language- and practice-in-use. Culture is that shifting, contested, conflictual site of the meanings, values, norms, beliefs, actions, and so on that make up the stuff of everyday life for some social group. Cultural studies aim to examine the internal organization of those meanings, values, norms, and so on; how they relate to one another; and, hence, how certain objects and events in a culture acquire particular meaning(s). Cultural studies are also characterized by the simultaneous affirmation of culture and the attempt to deconstruct and criticize culture. In other words, these studies seek to understand how notions such as identity, social group, community, and place become constituted as same through shared language and practice; at the same time, however, these studies seriously question these very ideas as kinds of imaginary social unities that provide an explanatory basis.

Key References

Grossberg, L., Nelson, C., & Treichler, P. A., eds., *Cultural Studies.* New York: Routledge, 1992.

Morley, D., & Chen, K. H., eds., *Stuart Hall: Critical Dialogues in Cultural Studies.* New York: Routledge, 1996.

Rodman, G., "Subject to Debate: (Mis)reading Cultural Studies." *Journal of Communication Inquiry,* 1997, 21(2), 58-69.

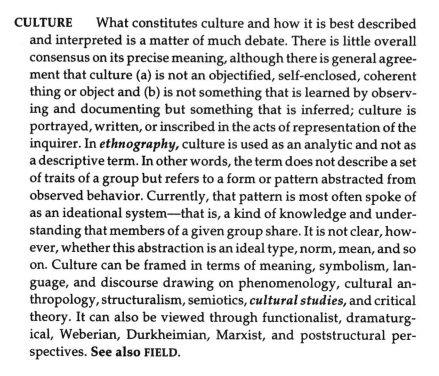

CULTURE   What constitutes culture and how it is best described and interpreted is a matter of much debate. There is little overall consensus on its precise meaning, although there is general agreement that culture (a) is not an objectified, self-enclosed, coherent thing or object and (b) is not something that is learned by observing and documenting but something that is inferred; culture is portrayed, written, or inscribed in the acts of representation of the inquirer. In *ethnography,* culture is used as an analytic and not as a descriptive term. In other words, the term does not describe a set of traits of a group but refers to a form or pattern abstracted from observed behavior. Currently, that pattern is most often spoke of as an ideational system—that is, a kind of knowledge and understanding that members of a given group share. It is not clear, however, whether this abstraction is an ideal type, norm, mean, and so on. Culture can be framed in terms of meaning, symbolism, language, and discourse drawing on phenomenology, cultural anthropology, structuralism, semiotics, *cultural studies,* and critical theory. It can also be viewed through functionalist, dramaturgical, Weberian, Durkheimian, Marxist, and poststructural perspectives. **See also** FIELD.

Key References

Alexander, J. C., & Seidman, S., eds., *Culture and Society: Contemporary Debates.* Cambridge, UK: Cambridge University Press, 1990.

Geertz, C., *The Interpretation of Cultures.* New York: Basic Books, 1973.

Rosaldo, R., "Whose Cultural Studies? Cultural Studies and the Disciplines," in P. Gibian, ed., *Mass Culture and Everyday Life.* New York: Routledge, 1997.

Wuthnow, R., et al., eds., *Cultural Analysis.* London: Routledge Kegan Paul, 1984.

DATA COLLECTION   See **DESCRIPTION, GENERATING DATA.**

DATA MANAGEMENT, STORAGE, RETRIEVAL   Simply stated, fieldwork generates lots of 'stuff' (more technically, the data corpus or the data log), and the longer one is engaged in field study, the more stuff one accumulates—tapes of interviews, audiotape transcripts, fieldnotes, personal notes, notes on readings, photographs, and copies of documents. An absolutely essential task for any field-worker is designing a system for organizing, cataloging, and indexing these materials in the data log that makes it possible to retrieve them efficiently, duplicate them, and use them for different tasks. The system one designs will, in turn, affect the way one conceptualizes the process of analyzing the data.

Key Reference

Miles, M., & Huberman, A. M., *Qualitative Data Analysis,* 2nd ed. Thousand Oaks, CA: Sage, 1994.

DECONSTRUCTIONISM   This is the kind of *hermeneutics* practiced in *poststructuralism,* also called radical hermeneutics and the *hermeneutics of suspicion.* The term *Destrucktion* was originally explained by Martin Heidegger (1889-1976), although Jacques Derrida's term *deconstruction* is the most often cited source. Derrida strongly objects to what he calls *logocentrism* or the logocentric bias of Western thought. Terms conceived as naturally referring to something are called *logi* (from the Greek *logos,* which can mean word, speech, or reason). Any account (explanation) of the world that presupposes such terms is logocentric. Derrida claims that all of Western thought assumes that there can be an authoritative, universal language that can disclose what is real, true, right, and beautiful. Western thought seeks to establish through language an order of truth and reality that will stand as an authoritative basis for judging truth-falsity, reality-illusion, right-wrong, and so on. Moreover, Western thought makes use of a set of binary oppositions or dualisms—for example, speech-writing, meaning-form, presence-absence, mind-body, masculine- feminine, and nature-culture—in its efforts to establish an order of truth and reality.

D

Derrida developed his critique of the logocentric bias of Western thought by drawing on the work of the French structural linguist, Ferdinand de Saussure (1857-1913). Saussure argued that the sense or meaning of a word (sign) is determined only by its relations to and differences from other words in a network of language. Derrida concluded that there is no interior language of thought and intention such that the sense and referent of a term (sign) is determined by its nature. In other words, there is no such thing as an object, idea, or concept present to the mind of the speaker that gives a particular word its sense or meaning. Thus, the meaning or sense of a word can never be fully present to the mind. Rather, the meaning of a word is intelligible only in terms of its relations in an infinite network of other words in a language. Words (signs) only signify other words (signs). Derrida argued that once we recognize the logocentricity of all accounts of the natural and social world, then language is only an endless play of signifiers with indeterminate meaning, and thought and intention are merely wordlike and have no intrinsic connection to some referent.

Deconstructionism is a kind of internal critique that reveals that the meaning of words occurs only in relations of sameness and difference. The act of deconstruction takes place within the terms that have shaped the text; it does not stand outside of the text but unfolds within the position being discussed in the text. The deconstruction of a text reveals that language is only a network of signs and their *différance* (an amalgam of the French terms for difference and deferral). According to Derrida, for everything affirmed in a text (e.g., authorship, meaning, man, and truth) there is an 'other' that contrasts with it. This other is thought to be absent, but in fact it is contained in that which is affirmed as a deferred or different meaning. Deconstruction is the process whereby these deferred and different meanings are revealed to be operating as invisible dimensions of ever-unfolding schemes of meanings. This *play* of meaning within a web or network of language means that meaning can never be fixed, single, and unambiguous. The aim of deconstruction is not to decode a *text* to somehow reveal its meaning or truth but to displace or unsettle taken-for-granted concepts, such as the unity of the text, the meaning or message of the text, and the authorship of the text. As Pauline Rosenau (1992) explains, deconstructionism

> involves demystifying a text, tearing it apart to reveal its internal hierarchies and its presuppositions [e.g., author-text and object-subject]. It lays out the flaws and the latent metaphysical structures of a text [e.g., unity, identity, meaning, and authorship]. A deconstructive reading of a text seeks to discover its ambivalence, blindness, logocentricity . . . [it] examines what is left out of a text, what is unnamed, what is excluded, and what is concealed. (p. 120)

Deconstruction is not undertaken for the purposes of revealing errors or showing various different interpretations because that would assume that there is *a* truth, meaning, or sense to be revealed. In this respect, deconstructionism departs from *philosophical hermeneutics* that holds there is a meaning to be constructed in the engagement of the interpreter with the text (see the dispute between Derrida and Gadamer in D. P. Michelfelder and R. E. Palmer, eds., *Dialogue and Deconstruction: The Gadamer-Derrida Exchange*, State University of New York Press, 1989). Deconstructionism shares with *critical hermeneutics* a suspicion of what purports to be the truth and thus seeks to unmask this erroneous assumption. Unlike critical hermeneutics, however, radical hermeneutics or deconstructionism holds out little hope for achieving emancipation from ideologically distorted meanings. For the deconstructionist, there is nothing more to interpretations than the endless plays of different signifiers (words) with ambiguous, conflicting meanings. **See also DUALISM, HERMENEUTICS OF SUSPICION, PLAY, SEMIOTICS.**

Key References

Caputo, J. D., *Radical Hermeneutics: Repetition, Deconstruction and the Hermeneutic Project*. Bloomington: Indiana University Press, 1987.

Cooper, D. E., "Modern European Philosophy," in N. Bunnin & E. P. Tsui-James, eds., *The Blackwell Companion to Philosophy*. Oxford, UK: Blackwell, 1996.

Culler, J., *On Deconstruction: Theory and Criticism After Structuralism*. Ithaca, NY: Cornell University Press, 1982.

Denzin, N. K., "Postmodernism and Deconstructionism," in D. R. Dickens & A. Fontana, eds., *Postmodernism and Social Theory*. New York: Guilford, 1994.

Derrida, J., *Positions*. Chicago: University of Chicago Press, 1981.

Derrida, J., *Writing and Difference*. London: Routledge Kegan Paul, 1987.

Rosenau, P., *Post-Modernism and the Social Sciences*. Princeton, NJ: Princeton University Press, 1992.

Siedman, S., *Contested Knowledge: Social Theory in the Postmodern Era*, 2nd ed. Oxford, UK: Blackwell, 1998.

DEDUCTION   See **INFERENCE.**

DEDUCTIVE-NOMOLOGICAL EXPLANATION   See **COVERING LAW MODEL OF EXPLANATION.**

DEPENDABILITY   See **TRUSTWORTHINESS CRITERIA.**

DESCRIPTION   This is the act of giving an account of that which we perceive. We can perceive objects and events, and we can perceive facts about those objects and events. For example, I can see an object, for example, airplane lights in the night sky, without in fact knowing *that* they are airplane lights. I might be mistaken: What I believe to be airplane lights may in fact be stars. In other words, one can give a descriptive account of an object or event without knowing in fact that that is what one is seeing. When we speak of description as the empirical basis for interpretive work, what we are usually concerned about is not the perception of objects or events per se but the perception of facts about them. Descriptions in interpretive work are factual claims about what we perceive—for example, *that* this person that I am observing is teaching. In other words, description is not simply an account of what I see (or hear) but also a claim *that* this is in fact the case.

What complicates the description of factual perception is that seeing facts is relative to the conceptual resources, background knowledge, language, and so on of the observer. For example, I cannot give a description of the factual perception of the event of teaching unless I have a concept of teaching and a way of classifying it among the various kinds of acts in which humans engage. That description of factual perception is relative to some conceptual scheme does not necessarily mean that believing is seeing because there still are objects and events that we perceive. Rather, it signifies that factual descriptions are not just states of affairs in the world that present themselves to us in some unmediated way. (That is why it is more appropriate to say that we generate or construct factual descriptions and do not simply collect data.) That factual descriptions depend on conceptual schemes means that such descriptions are 'theory-laden' and that there is no such a thing as pure description or 'raw' data. The knowledge that all description is theory-laden is generally accepted. Simply carving up the field of social action by deciding what to observe and what not to observe requires some foreknowledge of what is and is not important to attend to.

Careful, detailed factual description of people, objects, and *action* is said to be the empirical basis or foundation of ethnography and qualitative inquiry more generally. At least two different kinds of conceptual schemes figure prominently in the factual descriptions employed in qualitative studies. One is description of events and actions (*what* people are doing) achieved through participant observation and typically reported in the actors' own words. This kind of description is the foundation of *ethnographic naturalism* and *interpretivism.* The other kind of descriptive scheme, characteristic of *ethnomethodology,* is more concerned with *how* (not what) people do what they do. Instead of a kind of description that takes the reader to the setting and reveals who the actors are, what they are doing, and so forth, this second kind of description treats what is 'there' in interaction of actors as not simply evident to observation but constructed through social interaction. Description thus focuses on social processes—on how social life is constituted in interaction.

Both of these conceptual schemes for describing the perception of facts are challenged in postmodern and poststructuralist critiques of qualitative work. This challenge unfolds approximately as follows: (a) Description is typically regarded as distinct from interpretation. Description is thought to be a matter of the correct representation of the 'real' lived experience of actors. This real experience is thought to be something that exists 'out there' in the world, outside of any effort to re-create it and represent it in a textual account. (b) There is no such thing as 'real' experience conceived outside of its textual re-creation, however. (c) Hence, the distinction between description as primary and interpretation as secondary collapses. All description is a form of interpretation—representations exist only in textual creation. The worlds (actions and events) that we study are created through the texts that we write. (d) Thus, the notion that description of factual perception (through whatever conceptual scheme) constitutes an empirical grounding or foundation for the representations that characterize interpretive work is chimerical. **See also REPRESENTATION, THICK DESCRIPTION.**

Key References

Fay, B., *Contemporary Philosophy of Social Science*. Oxford, UK: Blackwell, 1996.

Gubrium, J., & Holstein, J., *The New Language of Qualitative Method*. Oxford, UK: Blackwell, 1997.

Wolcott, W., *Transforming Qualitative Data: Description, Analysis, and Interpretation*. Thousand Oaks, CA: Sage, 1994.

DESCRIPTIVE STATISTICS   These are mathematical techniques used for the purposes of organizing, displaying, and summarizing a set of numerical data. They include measures of central tendency (mean, median, and mode) and measures of variability (standard deviation). It is not uncommon for field studies to report the results of community or group surveys using descriptive statistics.

Key Reference

Bernard, H. R., *Social Research Methods: Qualitative and Quantitative Approaches*. Thousand Oaks, CA: Sage, 2000.

DESKWORK   This phrase indicates the task and activities of a phase of qualitative work that takes place after one has completed *fieldwork*. It refers to the activities of organizing, sense making, analyzing, and interpreting of fieldnotes and the writing up of the study.

Key Reference

Van Maanen, J., *Tales of the Field: On Writing Ethnography*. Chicago: University of Chicago Press, 1988.

DIALOGIC TEXT   See **PERFORMANCE/PERFORMATIVE/ PERFORMATIVITY.**

DIFFÉRANCE   See **DECONSTRUCTIONISM.**

DISCOURSE/DISCOURSE ANALYSIS   The study of *discourse*— understood broadly as an examination of language-in-use or the study of actually occurring language ('texts') in specific communicative contexts—is central to the kinds of analyses undertaken in *ethnomethodology, conversation analysis,* and *poststructuralism.* Discourse analysis is one of the many procedures employed in *textual analysis.* It is a general term covering a variety of approaches to the analysis of recorded talk; it is sometimes used interchangeably with conversation analysis, but it is distinguishable by its more strict focus on the content of talk than on its linguistic organization. Discourse analysis is an interdisciplinary approach drawing on insights from ethnomethodology, sociolinguistics, cognitive psychology, communication studies, and ordinary language philosophy. It is principally concerned with the analysis of the process of communication.

Discourse, however, has a somewhat different meaning when used in conversational analysis and ethnomethodology than in Foucauldian discourse analysis. In the former, discourse takes up the structure of talk in specific kinds of practices and refers to the processes whereby speakers methodically construct their worlds of meaning. It is concerned with *how*, for example, speakers accomplish ('do') intimacy, lying, trust, description of the real, and so forth. In Foucault's (1926-1984) work, the term discourse refers more broadly to systems of thought that construct subjects and their worlds. For Foucault, discourses are practices (composed of ideas, ideologies, attitudes, courses of action, and terms of reference) that systematically constitute the subjects and objects of which they speak. **See also GENEALOGY.**

Key References

Foucault, M., *The Archaeology of Knowledge.* New York: Pantheon, 1972.

Potter, J., *Representing Reality: Discourse, Rhetoric and Social Construction.* London: Sage, 1996.

Potter, J., "Discourse Analysis as a Way of Analyzing Naturally Occurring Talk," in D. Silverman, ed., *Qualitative Research: Theory, Method, and Practice.* London: Sage, 1997.

Potter, J., & Wetherell, M., "Discourse Analysis," in J. A. Smith, R. Harré, & L. Langenhove, eds., *Rethinking Methods in Psychology.* London: Sage, 1995.

Schiffrin, D., *Approaches to Discourse.* Oxford, UK: Blackwell, 1994.

DISCOURSE THEORY   Postmodern discourse theory defines all social phenomena as structured semiotically by codes and rules and therefore amenable to linguistic analysis using semiotic concepts (e.g., sign, expression, content, interpretant, and codes). This is another way of saying that meaning is not given but socially constructed. Discourse theory addresses the means (ideological, material, institutional, and relational) whereby discourses are constituted, operate, conflict, and so on. This theory challenges and often encompasses previous semiotic theories. **See also POSTSTRUCTURALISM, SEMIOTICS.**

Key Reference

Best, S., & Kellner, D., *Postmodern Theory*. New York: Guilford, 1991.

DISCURSIVE PRACTICE   See DISCOURSE, DISCOURSE THEORY.

DISENGAGEMENT   See BODY, DISINTERESTED SOCIAL SCIENCE, SUBJECT-OBJECT RELATIONSHIP.

D

DISINTERESTED SOCIAL SCIENCE   Western social science generally endorses the idea that social scientists as scientists should adopt the 'theoretical attitude'—that is, scientific contemplation at a distance. As the creator of theory, the social scientist should be a disinterested observer of the social-political world and, in that sense, disengaged from society. Social scientists should study the workings of society dispassionately and aim only at developing and testing theoretical *explanations* of the way the world is. In this way of thinking, the activity of theorizing social and political life as traditionally conceived lies outside the rest of the activity of social life. Judgments about the way the social-political world ought to be should be left to others to decide. The enterprise of social science and the individual social scientist should be value free—that is, neutral with respect to decisions about how we should live or act as humans in society. Social science can be relevant to decisions about values but only by empirically demonstrating consequences of different means to various ends or by describing and explaining the values and norms held by members of a society. This attitude or posture does not mean that science has no values whatsoever: The scientific enterprise upholds the values of dispassionate, objective, and critical investigation of scientific claims and the idea of scientifically informed (but neutral with respect to social norms) policy making.

This separation of empirical explanatory theory from normative concerns (as well as a sharp distinction between the 'is' and the 'ought,' between scientific claims about social phenomena and practical-moral discourse, or the heterogeneity of facts and values) in the work of the social inquirer is challenged by a variety of different philosophies of social inquiry, including *participatory action research*, some feminist methodologies, *critical social science*, and some versions of *philosophical hermeneutics*. **See also** FACT-VALUE DISTINCTION, THEORY.

Key References

Bernstein, R. J., *The Restructuring of Social and Political Theory*. Philadelphia: University of Pennsylvania Press, 1976.

Root, M., *Philosophy of Social Science*. Oxford, UK: Blackwell, 1993.

DOCUMENT ANALYSIS   This term refers broadly to various procedures involved in analyzing and interpreting data generated from the examination of documents and records relevant to a particular study. These sources of data include public records (e.g., political and judicial reports, government documents, media accounts, television scripts, yearbooks, and minutes of meetings), private documents (e.g., medical histories, letters, diaries, school records, personal journals, and memoirs), interview transcripts and transcripts prepared from video records, and photographs. The literature on document analysis also addresses a variety of issues concerning obtaining access to records and documents and examining their authenticity. **See also TEXTUAL ANALYSIS.**

Key References

Mason, J., *Qualitative Researching*. London: Sage, 1996.

Plummer, K., *Documents of Life: An Introduction to the Problems and Literature of a Humanistic Method*. London: Allen & Unwin, 1983.

Scott, J., *A Matter of Record: Documentary Sources in Social Research*. Cambridge, UK: Polity, 1990.

DOUBLE HERMENEUTIC   This term was coined by the social theorist Anthony Giddens, who argues that the double hermeneutic characterizes the social sciences and serves to distinguish them from the natural sciences. The social scientist studies social phenomena (i.e., human actions of various kinds), which (unlike the objects studied in natural science) are already constituted as meaningful. Humans are concept-using beings whose concepts of their action help constitute what those actions are and what they mean. Hence, the first task of the social inquirer is to understand the concepts of the social actors that are the object of study. That is, the inquirer must first get to know the world of the actors, what they already know and have to know to 'go on' with their daily social activity. From this first-level understanding, social inquirers construct second-order concepts and theories to explain what social actors are doing. These second-order concepts of the social scientist, however, can, in turn, actually become first-order concepts as they are appropriated and interpreted by social actors. In other words, the concepts and theories of the social inquirer can circulate in and out of the very social world that those concepts were first invented to analyze and explain. Social scientific theory and concepts, unlike those in natural science, can actually alter the way society behaves. There is thus a double process of interpretation.

Key Reference

Giddens, A., *The Constitution of Society: Outline of a Theory of Structuration*. Berkeley: University of California Press, 1984.

DRAMATURGY   The sociologist Erving Goffman (1922-1982) pioneered the analysis of the interactional order of social life (what people do when they are in the presence of others) via the metaphor of theater. He employed a variety of dramaturgical terms (e.g., performance, impression management, facework, and front-stage and back-stage behavior) that have become part of the vocabulary of social analysis. In postmodern social theory, this metaphor of life as theater becomes reality—society *is* theater. **See also PERFORMANCE/PERFORMATIVE/PERFORMATIVITY, PLAY.**

Key References

Branaman, A., "Goffman's Social Theory," in C. Lemert & A. Branaman, eds., *The Goffman Reader*. Oxford, UK: Blackwell, 1997.

Denzin, N. K., *Images of Postmodern Society*. Thousand Oaks, CA: Sage, 1991.

Goffman, E., *The Presentation of Self in Everyday Life*. Garden City, NJ: Doubleday, 1957.

DUALISM   This is the doctrine that reality consists of two separable parts (e.g., the distinction between appearance and reality), and it is accompanied by binary thinking commonly expressed in the distinctions valid versus invalid, good or bad, right or wrong, and true or false. It is generally acknowledged that dualism and binary thinking characterize all aspects of Western thought. The list of dualisms that figure prominently in the history of Western thought is virtually endless—fact-value, mind-body, experience-reason, sacred-profane, being-nothingness, means-end, objective-subjective, reason-emotion, objectivism-relativism, analytic-synthetic, and explanation-understanding. The poststructuralist philosophy of *deconstructionism* championed by Derrida is intimately concerned with unmasking the operation of this binary thinking in Western metaphysics. Derrida's work, however, is not the first to call our attention to the problems associated with such thinking. Much of the scholarship in the tradition of American pragmatism, including John Dewey's (1859-1952) philosophy of instrumentalism (which drew on the work of Charles Sanders Peirce, 1839-1914), the criticisms of logical positivism delivered by W. V. O. Quine, and the contemporary pragmatic stance taken in the work of Richard Bernstein, all aim to overcome the problems of modern philosophy brought on by binary thinking.

Key References

Bernstein, R. J., *Beyond Objectivism and Relativism: Science, Hermeneutics, and Praxis.* Philadelphia: University of Pennsylvania Press, 1983.

Derrida, J., *Writing and Difference.* London: Routledge, 1978.

Dewey, J., *The Quest for Certainty.* New York: Minton, Balch, 1929.

EMBODIED   See BODY.

EMERGENT DESIGN   Field-workers routinely adjust their inquiry plans and strategies in response to what they are learning as their study unfolds. For example, a field-worker may discover documents of particular importance that he or she was not aware existed, come across particular respondents who need to be interviewed when this was not anticipated, identify and cultivate a relationship with a key informant where that may have been thought impossible, decide after a study is already under way to conduct a community survey to gather a broader picture of an issue, and realize that a particular aspect of a social setting is more relevant to understanding some phenomenon than was initially imagined. By both allowing for and anticipating changes in strategies, procedures, questions to be asked, ways of generating data, and so on, the field-worker seeks to make his or her plans (i.e., design) attuned and responsive to the circumstances of the particular study.

This characteristic of planning and conducting a field study is often referred to as *emergent design*. If we use the strict sense of the word *emergent* (i.e., arising unexpectedly), it would be reasonable to say that the field-worker does encounter emergent issues or emergent circumstances or both that call for a response and, hence, the plan for fieldwork should be flexible and adaptive. As a

63

modifier for the term *design*, however, the term *emergent* can suggest that the design arises unexpectedly or that the field-worker has no design or plan at all at the outset of the study. This kind of complete laissez-faire attitude of seeing 'what happens' is ill advised. The field-worker seeks to understand and portray some problem, event, or issue and should have given careful thought in advance of undertaking the fieldwork regarding how that understanding can best be developed and how claims made about the meaning, cause, or accomplishment of human action can be warranted.

It may be more appropriate to talk of emergent *analysis* in qualitative studies. This signals the fact that the design and process of fieldwork is less linear and more circular in nature. The relevant contrast is between those studies that have clearly specified hypotheses, measures, and means of analysis spelled out in advance and studies in which hypotheses and analysis emerge from the interaction of the kinds of questions asked and the kinds of data generated. For example, the plans for a quasi-experimental study would be worked out in detail in advance of actually conducting the study (from precise specification of hypotheses, through selection of groups, to specification of variables, choice and pretesting of measures, specification of procedures for the statistical analysis of data, etc.). The means of analysis are specified in advance so that a priori hypotheses can be correctly tested. Preparation for a field study is somewhat different. A field study would be theoretically structured at the outset: The researcher would have decided how to specify (name and identify) the social action (e.g., teaching, negotiating, giving care, and bargaining) or entities (e.g., group and community) to be investigated, developed questions about the phenomenon (e.g., What happens? How does it happen? and Why does it happen?) that focus the research and give it purpose, and thought about the kinds of data sources and procedures that would generate relevant evidence. The actual analysis, however, would be less like a prespecified process of testing and verification and more like discovery. Analysis unfolds in an iterative fashion through the interaction of the processes of generating data, examining preliminary focusing questions, and considering theoretical assumptions. Analysis thus becomes a process of elaborating a version of or perspective on the phenomenon in question, revising that version or perspective as additional data are generated and new questions asked, elaborating another version, revising that version or perspective, and so on. *Memoing* and analytic *coding* are means of undertaking this iterative and emergent analysis. **See also** FIDELITY TO METHOD/FIDELITY TO PHENOMENON, GROUNDED THEORY METHODOLOGY, RESEARCH DESIGN, SENSITIZING CONCEPTS.

Key References

Flick, U., *An Introduction to Qualitative Research*. London: Sage, 1998.

Lincoln, Y. S., & Guba, E. G., *Naturalistic Inquiry*. Beverly Hills, CA: Sage, 1985.

Lofland, J., & Lofland, L. H., *Analyzing Social Settings: A Guide to Qualitative Observation and Analysis*, 3rd ed. Belmont, CA: Wadsworth, 1995.

Mason, J., *Qualitative Researching*. London: Sage, 1996.

EMIC/ETIC   Originating in linguistics (phonemic vs. phonetic), a distinction between emic and etic cultural categories was once popular in cognitive anthropology. Emic terms were indigenous —specific to a language or culture—whereas etic terms were developed by the social inquirer and used to describe and compare sociocultural systems. Etic terms were used by cognitive anthropology and other formalist approaches to ethnography as something like a codebook of concepts facilitating cross-cultural comparisons. This absolute distinction has been severely criticized on the grounds that there are no purely etic categories unbound to some specific context. Interest in distinguishing inside from outside perspectives remains, although it is now recognized that these distinctions are relative. The terms emic and etic are still occasionally used more broadly: Emic is used to refer to first-order concepts—the local language, concepts, or ways of expression used by members in a particular group or setting to name their experience. Etic is used to refer to second-order concepts—the social scientific language used by the scientist to refer to the same phenomena. Emic may also be used to refer to the processes of cataloging, description, and categorization and etic to indicate the process of explanation.

Clifford Geertz (1983, p. 57) introduced the concepts 'experience-near' and 'experience-distant' as a refinement of the emic-etic distinction. An experience-near concept is one that a respondent or informant "might naturally and effortlessly use to define what he [sic] or his fellows see, feel, think, imagine, and . . . which he would readily understand when similarly applied by others"; an experience-distant concept is one "that specialists of one sort or another . . . employ to forward their scientific, philosophical, or practical aims." Geertz explained that both kinds of concepts are necessary in ethnographic analysis because "confinement to experience-near concepts leaves the ethnographer awash in immediacies, as well as entangled in vernacular. Confinement to experience-distant ones leaves him [sic] stranded in abstractions and smothered in jargon" (p. 57). Geertz uses these concepts to defend the methodology of participant observation as a dialectic of experience and interpretation. He stresses the importance of grasping insider's perspectives through experience-near concepts while simultaneously illuminating their connection to experience-distant concepts. **See also NATIVE'S POINT OF VIEW.**

Key References

Geertz, C., *Local Knowledge*. New York: Basic Books, 1983.

Harris, M., "History and Significance of the Emic/Etic Distinction." *Annual Review of Anthropology*, 1976, 5, 329-350.

EMOTION   At least three aspects of this notion figure prominently in the broad field of qualitative inquiry. First, some feminist scholars argue that Western epistemology has tended to emphasize reason at the expense of emotion, regarding reason as the indispensable faculty for acquiring knowledge. Instead of viewing emotion as something that should be controlled and excluded by strict application of method, these scholars argue for restoring emotion (and other ways of knowing with the body) to our epistemological models. Second, in addition to the notion of emotion figuring prominently in arguments for reuniting reasoning and feeling, the sociological investigation of emotionality as a process and intersubjective accomplishment is one particular kind of qualitative study. Third, the interest in *autoethnography* and *performance* texts and related efforts to create a poetics of experience (vs. traditional modes of representation) reflects a specific concern with portraying the subjective, emotional experiences of the inquirer and evoking readers' emotional responses to the text. See also BODY, EXISTENTIALISM, SUBJECTIVITY.

Key References

Denzin, N. K., *On Understanding Emotion*. San Francisco: Jossey-Bass, 1984.

Ellis, C., "Emotional Sociology," in *Studies in Symbolic Interaction*, Vol. 12. Greenwich, CT: JAI, 1991.

Ellis, C., "Sociological Introspection and Emotional Experience." *Symbolic Interaction*, 1991, 14, 23-50.

Ellis, C., & Flaherty, M. G., eds., *Investigating Subjectivity*. Newbury Park, CA: Sage, 1992.

Jaggar, A. M., "Love and Knowledge: Emotion in Feminist Epistemology," in A. Garry & M. Pearsall, eds., *Women, Knowledge, and Reality: Explorations in Feminist Philosophy*. Boston: Unwin & Hyman, 1989.

E

EMPIRICAL RESEARCH   See EMPIRICISM.

EMPIRICISM   This is the name for a family of epistemological theories that generally accept the premise that knowledge begins with sense experience. Empiricism is often contrasted with *rationalism,* which holds that reason is the primary way of acquiring knowledge, and with *pragmatism,* which holds that action, not just any kind of experience, is both the source and test of all knowledge. The two main schools of empiricist epistemology are naïve (also called classic, radical, strict, or vulgar) empiricism and *logical empiricism.* The former is the empiricism of Bacon (1561-1626), Hume (1711-1776), and the logical positivists of the Vienna Circle. It holds that all knowledge is experiential, and that knowledge claims can be justified only by appeal to the evidence of the senses (experience, observation, and experiment). Strict empiricism relies exclusively on perception and induction in building knowledge claims and eschews any important role whatsoever for concepts and theories. (The latter are simply a convenient way—a filing system—of organizing observations.) The relationship between theory and data in strict empiricism is shown in Figure E.1a. The strict empiricist believes that data in the form of sense perceptions and observations (or observation statements) comprise the bedrock or foundation of all knowledge claims. Observations are often referred to as brute data, indicating that they are accessible to all competent observers and elemental in nature (i.e., require no further interpretation). (Note: Strict empiricists do not argue that knowledge is somehow 'given' in the brute data of experience, such that the inquirer is merely a spectator or passive recording device. On the contrary, these empiricists engage in lively debate concerning how concepts and theories [i.e., explanations and predictions] that we construct are to be related to the data of observation.)

Theory	Theory
↑	↕
Data	Data
(a)	(b)

Figure E.1. Relationship Between Theory and Data in (a) Logical Positivism and (b) Logical Empiricism

The strict empiricism of logical positivist philosophy was strongly challenged by historians and philosophers of science called the *Weltanschauung* analysts (e.g., Thomas Kuhn, Stephen Toulmin, Norwood Hanson, and Michael Polanyi), who argued that the worldviews (*Weltanschauungen*) of scientists—their prior knowledge, historical circumstances, beliefs, concepts, and so on—played a critical role in the testing and justification of scientific claims. Logical empiricism is, in part, a response to these criticisms. It is a more moderate variety of empiricism that continues to accord an important place to empirical observation but also allows for an active role played by concepts and theories in what constitutes valid knowledge. The relationship between theory and data in logical empiricism is shown in Figure E.1b.

Criticism of both varieties of empiricism is central to what is often called the *interpretive turn* in the human sciences. This turn is marked by the belief that all knowledge claims are interpretations, and that there is nothing to appeal to in judging an interpretation but other interpretations. In other words, empirical data (the data of observation and experience) cannot provide any special basis or foundation for knowledge claims that is somehow free of interpretation.

All forms of qualitative inquiry are empirical research to the extent that they deal in the data of experience. Many kinds of claims and assertions made in case study, ethnography, life history, oral history, and the like are often based on the *evidence* of observations—both those of the inquirer and the reports of people studied. When a qualitative inquirer makes a claim (assertion, statement, working hypothesis, etc.) about an event, object, process, person, or so on and offers as evidence or warrant for that claim its relationship to experience (something the inquirer or respondents saw or heard), then that inquirer is engaging in empirical inquiry. To say that qualitative inquiry is empirical research, however, is not to say that it rests on the philosophy of empiricism. Qualitative inquiry deals in empirical matters but is informed by a variety of different epistemologies, including logical empiricism, pragmatism, phenomenology, social constructionism, poststructuralism, and feminism. **See also EPISTEMOLOGY, POSTEMPIRICISM, THEORY-OBSERVATION DISTINCTION.**

Key References

Hollis, M., *The Philosophy of Social Science: An Introduction*. Cambridge, UK: Cambridge University Press, 1994.

Taylor, C., "Interpretation and the Sciences of Man." *Review of Metaphysics*, 1971, 24, 3-51. (Reprinted in Taylor, C., *Philosophical Papers 2. Philosophy and the Human Sciences*. Cambridge, UK: Cambridge University Press, 1985)

END OF PHILOSOPHY   The work of Friedrich Nietzsche (1844-1900) is looked to particularly by poststructuralists as having heralded the death of traditional philosophical concerns with clarifying the meaning of truth, reality, morality, virtue, and the like. The existentialist and phenomenological philosophy of fellow German philosopher Martin Heidegger (1889-1976) is also sometimes appealed to in the same way. Following in the wake of and building on the insights of these and other pronouncements of the death of philosophy are a variety of postphilosophical positions (e.g., *feminist theories, poststructuralism, critical theory, philosophical hermeneutics,* postanalytic philosophy, and neo-pragmatism) taken up by Sandra Harding, Nancy Fraser, Nancy Harstock, Allison Jaggar, Jacques Derrida, Michel Foucault, Hans-Georg Gadamer, Jürgen Habermas, Jean-François Lyotard, Alasdair MacIntyre, Hilary Putnam, Richard Rorty, Charles Taylor, and others.

Whether we use the phrase after philosophy, end of philosophy, postanalytic philosophy, or postphilosophy matters less than understanding the nature of the turmoil. This period is characterized by various criticisms of notions that form the core of the Enlightenment tradition: the necessity and universality of reason; the autonomous, disengaged, atomistic, sovereign, rational subject; knowledge as representation; the separation of philosophy from rhetoric and poetics; and so on. The period is marked by mergers of philosophy with other disciplines, including anthropology, literary theory, history of science, and political theory. The debates comprising this period have influenced the way social science philosophers and social scientists define the nature and aim of social inquiry; the authority, role, identity, and expertise of the inquirer; the epistemological status of claims to represent social reality; and so on. Of course, claims that traditional philosophy has come to an end have met with resistance. Thus, the contemporary scene in the broad field of qualitative inquiry is philosophically complex and has moved well beyond the tired debate of quantitative versus qualitative methods into far more interesting (and complicated) matters of the epistemology, ethics, and politics of inquiry. **See also EPISTEMOLOGY, KNOWLEDGE.**

Key References

Baynes, K., Bohman, J., & McCarthy, T., eds., *After Philosophy: End or Transformation?* Cambridge: MIT Press, 1987.

Rajchman, J., & West, C., eds., *Post-Analytic Philosophy.* New York: Columbia University Press, 1985.

EPISTEMIC CRITERION   See **CRITERIA, VALIDITY.**

EPISTEMOLOGY   This is the study of the nature of knowledge and justification. There are many theories of epistemology. For example, empiricist epistemology argues that knowledge is derived from sense experience. Genuine, legitimate knowledge consists of beliefs that can be justified by observation. Rationalist epistemology argues that reason is the sure path to knowledge. Rationalists may claim that sense experiences are an effect of external causes, that a priori ideas (concepts, theories, etc.) provide a structure for making sense of experience, that reason provides a kind of certainty that the senses cannot provide, or all these.

Rather than conceiving of the differences between so-called qualitative and quantitative inquiry in terms of tools and methods, students of qualitative inquiry might be better served by examining the differences (and similarities) among epistemologies for qualitative inquiry—for example, the epistemologies of empiricism and hermeneutics or empiricist and feminist epistemologies. Epistemologies provide much of the justification for particular methodologies (i.e., the aim, function, and assumptions of method).

Currently, many criticisms are directed at what is sometimes called the epistemological project or philosophy-as-epistemology. There are two significantly different strands of criticism here that share the same diagnosis but issue in different remedies, so to speak. The diagnosis is that both rationalist and empiricist epistemologies are foundationalist; that is, they seek permanent, indisputable criteria for knowledge—one finds it in reason, the other in sense experience. These epistemologies are also characterized by their interest in an autonomous, detached subject (knower) and a preoccupation with establishing correspondence between idea and object, concept and observation. The quest for certainty characteristic of these epistemologies has not only been found wanting but also is thought to be a futile and dysfunctional search.

Postempiricist, hermeneutic, feminist, poststructuralist, pragmatist, and critical social science approaches to social inquiry all generally accept (and have in various ways made) this diagnosis. Two different responses result, however. One response is pragmatic and fallibilistic. It holds that knowledge is by definition uncertain, and that the best we can do is make a stand on the basis of (admittedly fallible) human judgment that requires the use of both reason and evidence. This response abandons epistemology with a capital "E"—the search for the foundations or essences of knowledge—but retains the idea of epistemology with a lower-case "e"—reflection of various kinds about what it means to know. The other response is one of radical *skepticism* or episte-mological nihilism. It holds that diverse realities, plural construc-tions, the absence of certainty, intertextuality, shifting identities of subjects, and the like all add up to the undecidability of all inter-pretation. No interpretation and no judgment are decidedly better than any other. This response abandons the entire idea of episte-mology or assumes what might be called *epistemological impos-sibilism* (M. Calinescu, *Five Faces of Modernity*, Duke University Press, 1987). **See also END OF PHILOSOPHY, FALLIBILISM, KNOWL-EDGE, OBJECTIVISM, PLURALISM, PRAGMATISM.**

Key References

Bohman, J., *New Philosophy of Social Science: Problems of Indeterminacy.* Cambridge: MIT Press, 1991.

Grayling, A. C., "Epistemology," in N. Bunnin & E. P. Tsui-James, eds., *The Blackwell Companion to Social Theory.* Oxford, UK: Blackwell, 1996.

Hollis, M., "Philosophy of Social Science," in N. Bunnin & E. P. Tsui-James, eds., *The Blackwell Companion to Philosophy.* Oxford, UK: Blackwell, 1996.

ERKLÄRUNG   This is the German term for "explanation." See **EXPLANATION,** *VERSTEHEN.*

ESSENTIALISM   This is a metaphysical doctrine that holds that objects have essences—that is, intrinsic identifying or characteriz-ing properties that constitute their real, true nature. Some femi-nists, for example, argue that there are essential features of men's and women's biology, identity, and gender. For other feminists, essentialism is their foil. They claim that plurality, otherness, dif-ference, and heterogeneity characterize our understanding of no-tions such as subject, man, woman, gender, self, family, intelli-gence, and anxiety. **See also CONSTRUCTIVISM.**

Key References

Fuss, D., *Essentially Speaking: Feminism, Nature, and Difference.* New York: Routledge, 1989.

Stein, E., "Conclusion: The Essentials of Constructionism and the Construction of Essentialism," in E. Stein, ed., *Forms of Desire: Sexual Orientation and the Social Constructionist Controversy.* New York: Garland, 1992.

ETHICS OF QUALITATIVE INQUIRY   In the widest sense, the subject matter of ethics is the justification of human actions, especially as those actions affect others. The subject matter of ethics includes various ethical systems or theories and means of ethical reasoning. Ethical theories include deontological ethics (based on concepts of duty or what is right to do), consequentialist ethics (based on the idea of achieving some good state of affairs), and virtue ethics (based on the qualities of character necessary to live well). Approaches to ethical reasoning include applied ethics, which is often modeled on a deductive model of practical reasoning; *narrative ethics,* which emphasizes the importance of personal identity, the virtues of character, and the individual and collective stories in which those virtues are made intelligible; and casuistry, an approach to ethical reasoning that attempts to steer a course between these two approaches.

Addressing ethical issues in social research typically requires taking into account considerations beyond those of ethical theories and models of ethical reasoning. When social researchers consider the reasons for their own and others' actions during the conduct of research, assess the validity of those reasons, and reform their actions against the backdrop of some systematic and thoughtful account of human responsibility, they must, of necessity, recognize that ethics, epistemology, and politics are intertwined. In other words, inquirers cannot rightly understand their ethics—habits, obligations, and modes of thought that shape and define their interactions as social scientists with others—without simultaneously thinking through what constitutes legitimate, warranted knowledge of social life as well as what comprises their political commitments and responsibilities as inquirers into the nature and meaning of human affairs.

This does not necessarily mean that, given different understandings of the ethics-epistemology-politics nexus, different ethical principles (e.g., informed consent, avoidance of deception, avoidance of harm or risk, treating others always as ends and never as means, and no breaches of promise or confidence) are involved. Rather, it suggests that special attention must be paid to the means of addressing ethical and political issues (and styles of reasoning) that are associated with various ways in which we envision and enact the relationship between researcher and researched. The following are ways of thinking about that relationship in qualitative studies (Elliott, 1988):

E

1. Researcher as detached, objective, outside expert; researched as subjects, data sources, and respondents

2. Researcher as marginal participant (participant-observer); researched as informants

3. Researcher as facilitator (helping the researched activate their own capacities for self-observation, critique, and advocacy), critic, advocate, change agent, and adversary to the established and powerful; researched as coresearchers, coparticipants, and collaborators

In the relationship identified in Number 1 (and all that it entails epistemologically and politically), it is commonplace to conceive of the ethical obligations of researcher to researched in terms of a contract—a written agreement between the two parties. The contract explains the purpose of the research, the anticipated duration and extent of subjects' involvement, the procedures to be employed by the researcher, assurances of confidentiality, the potential risks and benefits to subjects, and a means whereby subjects can gain further information from the investigator. The terms of the contract include that it is voluntary on the part of the subjects, specifies the form (if any) of compensation for participation, and entails no penalty for a subject's withdrawal from a study. This contractual model of ethics is the one most often assumed in the workings of institutional review boards in universities.

In general, all features of a contractual conceptualization of ethics are entailed in the ethical and political relations between researcher and researched as characterized in Numbers 2 and 3. In these latter two ways of framing human relations in research, however, several special obligations arise due to the fact that these relationships are characterized by considerably extended personal exchanges, substantial dealings between the researcher and those whom he or she studies, and different research agendas. Moreover, because these substantial exchanges, relations, and agendas are dynamic and subject to change over time, they require of the researcher a heightened capacity to anticipate potential ethical dilemmas and demand a special kind of normative attention in the course of fieldwork. In the view of the ethicist William May, these special ethical obligations might better be understood in terms of a covenantal (as opposed to a contractual) ethic—an exchange of promises, an agreement that shapes the future between two parties, and an ethic that is responsive and reciprocal in character. May (1980) explains,

> The duties of field-workers to their host populations—duties to respect confidences, to communicate to them the aims of the research, to protect anonymity, to safeguard rights, interests, and sensitivities, to give fair return for services rendered, to anticipate the consequences of publication, to share the results of research with affected parties, and to be sensitive to the diversity of values and interests of those studied—all these duties rest on a deeper footing than a contract, on a lower pedestal than philanthropy [that pretends to a wholly gratuitous altruism], and on a more concrete foundation than Kant's universal principle of respect. (pp. 367-368)

The notion of a covenantal ethic signals the particularly weighty moral responsibility entailed in qualitative studies, the need for moral and ethical awareness—special vigilance or alertness to circumstances that demand attention—and the ever-present need to be prepared, through adequate ethical training, to address such circumstances in morally responsible ways. **See also FIELD RELATIONS, FIELDWORK, OTHER (THE OTHER, OTHERNESS), POLITICS OF RESEARCH.**

Key References

Bulmer, M., ed., *Social Research Ethics*. New York: Macmillan, 1982.

Elliott, J., "Educational Research and Outsider-Insider Relations." *Qualitative Studies in Education*, 1988, 1(2), 155-166.

Gubrium, J. F., & Silverman, D., eds., *The Politics of Field Research*. Newbury Park, CA: Sage, 1989.

May, W. F., "Doing Ethics: The Bearing of Ethical Theories on Fieldwork." *Social Problems*, 1980, 27(3), 358-370.

Walker, M. U., "Moral Understandings: Alternative 'Epistemology' for a Feminist Ethics," in E. B. Cole & S. Coultrap-McQuin, eds., *Explorations in Feminist Ethics*. Bloomington: Indiana University Press, 1992.

ETHNOCENTRISM   This is a form of *prejudice*—a predisposition or preconception—that has both a weak and a strong interpretation. A weak interpretation of ethnocentrism means that we always view the world through our own self-understandings (i.e., the understandings of 'our' group, community, culture, etc.). A strong version adds the condition that our own self-understandings are superior, and that we expect the self-understandings of others to converge with ours. *Postmodern ethnography* is highly critical of *interpretive ethnography* for being ethnocentric in the strong sense noted previously. The former also claims that the entire practice of cultural anthropology is located in a long history of Western colonialism and the globalization of Western culture.

Viewed more broadly, across the entire spectrum of qualitative studies, worries about ethnocentrism figure prominently in the *interpretive turn* in the human sciences as follows: If all efforts to understand others are always interpretations made only against the backdrop of the interpreter's way of life, culture, and so forth, are not all such interpretations inevitably ethnocentric? There are several different responses to this question. Richard Rorty, for example, claims that indeed all efforts to understand others are always made by "our own lights," and that we should be frank about that. Clifford Geertz acknowledges that interpretations cannot be anything but an attempt to portray one way of life in the categories of another, but he is highly critical of Rorty's "easy comforts of merely being ourselves." Geertz argues that the inescapable ethnocentricity (in a weak sense) of interpretations need not lead to radical *skepticism* or *relativism;* in fact, it considerably increases the moral responsibilities of the interpreter to give an accurate and responsible portrayal of others' ways of life. David Couzens Hoy, Charles Taylor, and James Bohman also accept the weak sense of ethnocentrism noted previously and, like Geertz, argue that it does not necessarily entail radical skepticism. All three argue (although in very different ways) that it is possible to engage in normative criticism of different ways of life or social practices, despite the fact that we always view the world through our own self-understandings. Both Hoy and Taylor adopt the view that "we understand *ourselves* differently as a result of encountering others who have a different self-understanding themselves." **See also OTHER (THE OTHER, OTHERNESS).**

Key References

Bohman, J., *New Philosophy of Social Science.* Cambridge: MIT Press, 1991.

Geertz, C., "The Uses of Diversity." *Michigan Quarterly Review,* 1986, 23, 105-123.

Hoy, D. C., "Is Hermeneutics Ethnocentric?," in D. R. Hiley, J. F. Bohman, & R. Shusterman, eds., *The Interpretive Turn.* Ithaca, NY: Cornell University Press, 1991.

Rorty, R., "Solidarity or Objectivity" and "On Ethnocentrism: A Reply to Clifford Geertz," in R. Rorty, ed., *Objectivity, Relativism, and Truth Philosophical Papers,* Vol. 1. Cambridge, UK: Cambridge University Press, 1991.

Taylor, C. "Understanding and Ethnocentricity," in *Philosophy and the Human Sciences, Philosophical Papers,* Vol. 2. Cambridge, UK: Cambridge University Press, 1985.

ETHNOGRAPHIC AUTHORITY   See **AUTHORITY.**

ETHNOGRAPHIC NATURALISM   Various interpretations of this doctrine, also called social realism, foreground some of the practices of qualitative inquiry. A strong interpretation of the doctrine means the inquirer must capture the 'authentic,' 'true,' or real nature of social phenomena and that this is best accomplished by 'being there' in the 'natural' setting in which such phenomena occur. A weak interpretation means respect for or attention to the nature of phenomenon under study. Furthermore, both weak and strong versions share the idea of fidelity to phenomenon and reject the idea of fidelity to methodological principles. In other words, the primary commitment of the social inquirer should be to remain true to the nature of the phenomenon under study rather than to honor a particular conception of scientific method. Ethnographic naturalism typically finds its expression in *ethnographic realism*. Defenders of postmodern approaches to ethnographic work (e.g., in sociology, Norman Denzin and Patricia Clough; in anthropology, Stephen Tyler) take strong exception to this doctrine. **See also** ETHNOGRAPHIC REALISM, EXPERIENCE, FIDELITY TO METHOD/FIDELITY TO PHENOMENON, FIELD, NATURALISTIC INQUIRY, REPRESENTATION.

Key References

Denzin, N. K., *The Research Act*, 3rd ed. Englewood Cliffs, NJ: Prentice Hall, 1989.

Gubrium, J., & Holstein, J., *The New Language of Qualitative Method*. Oxford, UK: Blackwell, 1997.

Hammersley, M., *What's Wrong With Ethnography?* London: Routledge, 1992.

Lofland, J., & Lofland, L. H., *Analyzing Social Settings*, 3rd ed. Belmont, CA: Wadsworth, 1995.

Matza, D., *Becoming Deviant*. Englewood Cliffs, NJ: Prentice Hall, 1969.

ETHNOGRAPHIC REALISM   This is the genre of ethnographic writing that reflects the assumptions of ethnographic naturalism. If *ethnography* is both process and product, then traditionally its process of *participant observation* is built on the doctrine of *ethnographic naturalism* and its product reflects the practice of ethnographic realism. The genre is composed of many literary conventions that contribute to the construction of a representational text—that is, a text that claims to represent literally the ways of life, attitudes, practices, beliefs, and so on of those studied. John Van Mannen (1988, pp. 46ff) identifies the following four conventions as characteristic of these texts or what he calls "realist tales": First, the experience of the researcher serves as a source of authority, but the author is virtually completely absent from most segments of the text. Van Maanen notes that "Ironically, by taking the 'I' (observer) out of the ethnographic report, the narrator's authority is apparently enhanced, and audience worries over personal subjectivity become moot." Second, a documentary style is employed to focus on the mundane details of everyday life revealing the powers of observation of the inquirer. This catalog of observations is often presented via standard anthropological or sociological categories that typically are used to divide the complex field of others' ways of life into something manageable (e.g., family life, work life, social networks, customs, beliefs, rituals, and kinship patterns). Details within these categories are not randomly arranged but accumulate systematically and redundantly to demonstrate something important about respondents' lived *experience* from the field-worker's point of view. Third, the native's (respondent's) point of view is painstakingly produced through extensive, closely edited quotations to convey that what is presented is not the field-worker's view but authentic and representative remarks of respondents. Finally, there is a marked absence of reflection on whether the field-worker got it right, a tendency toward a no-nonsense approach to presenting representations and accounts. Van Maanen calls this the attitude of "interpretive omnipotence" on the part of the author.

Postmodern ethnography (in both sociology and anthropology) has arisen largely as a challenge to the doctrine of ethnographic realism and the production of realist texts. In a variety of ways, it questions the notion that fieldwork texts can be direct, matter-of-fact accounts of other's experience unclouded by how the field-worker produced the product. It experiments with other textual forms that reflect the social dynamics of field-worker/respondent relations as interlocutory, dialogical, collaborative, and co-creative of understanding the lives of others. **See also AUTHORITY, EXPERIENTIAL TEXT, LITERARY TURN (IN SOCIAL SCIENCE), REPRESENTATION.**

Key References

Denzin, N. K., *Interpretive Ethnography: Ethnographic Practices for the 21st Century.* Thousand Oaks, CA: Sage, 1997.

Van Maanen, J., *Tales of the Field.* Chicago: University of Chicago Press, 1988.

ETHNOGRAPHY The methodology born in cultural anthropology, ethnography is a particular kind of qualitative inquiry distinguishable from case study research, descriptive studies, naturalistic inquiry, and so forth by the fact that it is the process and product of describing and interpreting cultural behavior. Cultural anthropology, broadly conceived as a practice, includes both ethnography, which is regarded as the activity of describing a culture, and ethnology, which is the historical-geographical study of peoples or cultures that involves classifications, comparisons, and explanations of cultural differences. Although there is considerable disagreement on the meaning of the term *culture,* both anthropological and sociological definitions of ethnography stress the centrality of culture as the analytic concept that informs the doing of ethnography.

Ethnography has in common with several other kinds of qualitative inquiries an emphasis on firsthand *field study.* Thus, ethnography is often (perhaps wrongly) used as a synonym for fieldwork and its characteristics of prolonged time in the field, generation of descriptive data, development of rapport and empathy with respondents, the use of multiple data sources, making of *fieldnotes,* and so forth. Although many kinds of qualitative inquirers may engage in fieldwork (i.e., use ethnographic methods), not all do ethnographic fieldwork (i.e., do ethnography).

Ethnography unites both process and product, *fieldwork* and written text. Fieldwork, undertaken as *participant observation,* is the process by which the ethnographer comes to know a culture; the ethnographic text is how culture is portrayed. There is general agreement that culture is not visible or tangible but is constructed by the act of ethnographic writing. Hence, understanding what it means to 'write' culture (i.e., literal *representation, inscription, transcription, textualization,* and cultural translation) is a critical concern in ethnography. **See also INTERPRETIVE ANTHROPOLOGY.**

Key References

Van Maanen, J., *Tales of the Field.* Chicago: University of Chicago Press, 1988.

Wolcott, H., "On Ethnographic Intent," in G. Spindler & L. Spindler, eds., *Interpretive Ethnography of Education: At Home and Abroad.* Hillsdale, NJ: Lawrence Erlbaum, 1987.

ETHNOMETHODOLOGY   The term was coined by Harold Garfinkel, who formed a new school of sociology around this approach. Garfinkel drew, in part, on the resources of the *phenomenological sociology* of Alfred Schutz (1899-1956) to fashion an approach to the study of social life that opposed mainstream sociology, including the functionalist sociology of Garfinkel's teacher, Talcott Parsons (1902-1979). Garfinkel objected to the idea that the normal course for human intentions and actions is set by social rules and norms that exist prior to intention and action. He claimed that mainstream sociology treated human actors as "judgmental dopes" who passively carried out prescribed actions on the basis of internalized social norms. Social action, in his view, was not to be explained by appeal to such rules or norms nor by examination of actors' subjective beliefs or intentions. Rather, the sociologist was to look at *how* actors do things and *what* they do, examining the methods, procedures, and organization of social action.

Ethnomethodology is thus interested in how people accomplish the interactions we take for granted in everyday life—for example, promising, trusting, agreeing, and negotiating. It is the study of social action as the product and achievement of knowledgeable and reflective social actors. It focuses on the ways that various aspects of the *life-world* are produced, experienced, or accomplished interactionally and discursively. As a methodology for studying social life, ethnomethodology is committed to *bracketing* the researcher's own sense of the way encounters are socially structured or accomplished to describe how members in specific setting or parties to an interaction themselves accomplish a sense of structure.

Broadly conceived, ethnomethodology covers the cognitive sociology of Aaron Cicourel, constitutive ethnography, and recent forms of the approach known as *conversation analysis.* **See also DISCOURSE ANALYSIS, LANGUAGE.**

Key References

Atkinson, J. M., & Heritage, J., eds., *Structures of Social Action*. Cambridge, UK: Cambridge University Press, 1984.

Baert, P., *Social Theory in the Twentieth Century*. New York: New York University Press, 1998.

Garfinkel, H., *Studies in Ethnomethodology*. Englewood Cliffs, NJ: Prentice Hall, 1967.

Heritage, J., "Ethnomethodology," in A. Giddens & J. Turner, eds., *Social Theory Today*. Stanford, CA: Stanford University Press, 1987.

Mehan, H., & Wood, H., *The Reality of Ethnomethodology*. New York: John Wiley, 1975.

EVIDENCE   This is information that bears on determining the validity (truth, falsity, accuracy, etc.) of a claim or what an inquirer, in part, provides to warrant a claim. Sources of evidence include the senses, reason, and testimony of others. Types of evidence appealed to in qualitative inquiry include various kinds of written texts (e.g., transcripts), verbal records, visual records, cultural artifacts, and observer accounts. Different qualitative methodologies rely on different types of evidence to support their claims.

Evidence is essential to justification, and justification takes the form of an argument about the merit(s) of a given claim. It is generally accepted that no evidence is conclusive or unassailable (and hence, no argument is foolproof). Thus, evidence must often be judged for its credibility, and that typically means examining its source and the procedures by which it was produced. When we speak of rules of evidence in different practices (e.g., social inquiry, legal proceedings, medical diagnosis, and psychiatric treatment), we are generally concerned with different means or procedures whereby evidence is judged to be credible in that particular practice.

There are many strategies for linking evidence (facts and data) to claims (provisional conclusions), but each way of making that *inference* has serious flaws. *Induction* is the strategy of piling up evidence of specific instances or cases and then inferring a general conclusion. *Confirmation* entails showing that evidence supports the claim. *Testability/falsifiability* is a strategy used to demonstrate that evidence does not necessarily contradict the claim (and thereby enhances the likelihood that the claim is true).

Some forms of postmodern qualitative inquiry argue that the account prepared by the inquirer is not to be judged as an argument based on evidence but more like a poem or novel. In other words, the inquirer's account of lived *experience* is not intended to represent that experience but to evoke some particular feelings, attitudes, or dispositions in the reader of the account. Of course, arguments based on evidence come in to play here as well. First, we would judge the claim that "accounts should evoke not represent" based on the arguments and evidence for such a claim. Also, we would judge whether any particular evocative account does the job of 'evoking' well by arguing whether or not it does so by appeal to evidence for good poetry or quality novels. **See also EM-PIRICISM, VALIDITY.**

Key References

Hammersley, M., *Reading Ethnographic Research*. London: Longman, 1990.

Weston, A., *A Rulebook for Arguments*, 2nd ed. Indianapolis, IN: Hackett, 1992.

EXISTENTIALISM   This post-World War II philosophical and literary movement that unfolded primarily in France in the work of Sartre (1905-1980), Simone de Beauvoir (1905-1986), Merleau-Ponty (1907-1961), and others combined the focus of *phenomenology* on the 'intentional' character of human existence with a radical insistence on individual *authenticity*. Its particular relevance for qualitative inquiry lies in the work of the existential sociologists of the 1970s and their successors. Existential sociology strongly objected to traditional cognitive sociology claiming that the latter was overly rational both in its approach to understanding social life and in its portrayal of the conduct of social life. It argued that traditional sociology was strongly wedded to a sharp divide between the experiencing subject (the inquirer) and the object (social life) to be understood. Existential sociology claimed that inquirers were part of the phenomenon they seek to understand and, therefore, it promoted a return to the direct, lived experience of the individual field-worker as the source of knowledge about the social world. Contemporary versions of this kind of sociology, evident in *autoethnography* and related practices, are critical of earlier forms for not incorporating a concern for emotionality, subjectivity, and the lived experience of the fieldworker into the field of representation. Postmodern 'existentialist' inquirers seek to collapse completely the distinction between the inquirer's experience and the 'field' of social action that he or she witnesses. They argue that no neat distinction can be drawn between the 'inquirer's' experience and the 'other's' world; there is only the inquirer's *inscription* or representation. **See also EXPERIENCE, INTENTIONALITY.**

Key References

Douglas, J. D., & Johnson, J. M., eds., *Existential Sociology*. Cambridge, UK: Cambridge University Press, 1977.

Ellis, C., & Flaherty, M. G., eds., *Investigating Subjectivity: Research on Lived Experience*. Newbury Park, CA: Sage, 1992.

Kotarba, J. A., & Fontana, A., eds., *The Existential Self in Society*. Chicago: University of Chicago Press, 1987.

EXPERIENCE   Qualitative inquiry deals with human lived experience. It is the *life-world* as it is lived, felt, undergone, made sense of, and accomplished by human beings that is the object of study. From the perspective of *ethnographic naturalism,* authentic experience is what inquirers aim to capture in their accounts. By using the right methods to observe and probe, the inquirer can reveal, describe, and map the lived experience of others (their interactions, intentions, the meanings they attach to their actions, etc.) and, subsequently, present it as it was actually lived or undergone by particular actors in particular circumstances. In this way of thinking, experience is distinguishable from its representation. Inquirers are capable of accomplishing this feat because they learn to operate on the border between lived experience and its representation (hence the notions of inquirer as marginal native and participant observer). The inquirer's own lived experience (as an eyewitness, participant observer) functions as a means of access to the experience of others. Often, the inquirer's own experience becomes part of the recounting or representation of the experience of others in, for example, what Van Maanen has called confessional and impressionist tales.

Many postmodern and poststructuralist approaches to qualitative inquiry object strongly to the assumption that the inquirer can operate on some imaginary border between the experience of others and its representation. They do not necessarily deny that there is a world of lived experience, but they argue that it is impossible to represent such experience as it 'actually' is lived. This is so because language and speech create experience; hence, the very idea of having access to one's own experience as some kind of unmediated, direct lived 'happening' is chimerical because that very experience is discursively determined. Moreover, inquirers add another layer, so to speak, to such discursive constitution of experience because through their very acts of researching and writing they continuously create and transform the experience they seek to describe and map. Thus, there can only be inscriptions or retellings of experience.

In the phenomenological tradition that is the source of ideas for both *philosophical hermeneutics* and *deconstructionism,* the notion of experience is defined quite differently than in the empirical sciences (including many versions of qualitative inquiry). In the empirical sciences, there is a near exclusive preoccupation with the *epistemological* role of experience. The concern with validated knowledge leads to a standardization of experience and to a scientific conception of experience as an object, something that one might eventually validate as knowledge. In other words, knowledge and experience are distinguished. Experience is objectified as we take a third-person perspective toward our experience. In that way, experience becomes the world 'out there' that serves as the tribunal for testing and validating knowledge claims. In a similar way, the acts of understanding (knowing) and applying knowledge are separated. Knowledge is a product that the knower comes to possess about experience. In a separate step, this knowledge can then, if one chooses, be applied.

Particularly in the work of Gadamer, this scientific or empirical view of experience is found wanting because it strips experience of its *historicity*—its processual and dynamic character. In this tradition, experience is not a Baconian repository of sense data or a tribunal against which one tests a knowledge claim, nor is it something that is perfected and replaced by knowledge. Rather, experience has a processual, historical character; it is anticipatory and open. There is a knowing *within* experience. Gadamer explores these different senses of experience using the two German words for the notion: *Erlebnis* denotes experience as something one has, an event or adventure connected with a subject; it permits a plural 'experiences' that can be repeated by anyone. *Erfahrung* refers to experience as something one undergoes so that subjectivity is drawn into an 'event' of meaning; experience so understood is integrative, unfolding, dynamic, and hence singular. **See also CRISIS OF REPRESENTATION, INSCRIPTION, REPRESENTATION.**

Key References

Bruner, E. M., "Experience and Its Expressions," in V. M. Turner & E. M. Bruner, eds., *The Anthropology of Experience.* Urbana: University of Illinois Press, 1986.

Denzin, N. K., "Representing Lived Experience in Ethnographic Texts," in *Studies in Symbolic Interaction,* Vol. 12. Greenwich, CT: JAI, 1991.

Gubrium, J., & Holstein, J., *The New Language of Qualitative Method.* Oxford, UK: Blackwell, 1997.

Risser, J., *Hermeneutics and the Voice of the Other: Re-Reading Gadamer's Philosophical Hermeneutics.* Albany: State University of New York Press, 1997.

Van Maanen, J., *Tales of the Field.* Chicago: University of Chicago Press, 1988.

EXPERIMENTAL TEXT   This is a broad term for forms of writing qualitative studies that employ different literary and artistic genres (e.g., poems, stories, and performances). It also signals a commingling of journalistic, fictional, factual, and ethnographic accounts. Various forms of textual experimentation are often undertaken in an explicit bid to decenter the political and interpretive authority of the inquirer. *Testimonio,* for example, is both a research strategy and a form of textual presentation that has some affinity to both the novel and the autobiography but challenges those genres by giving voice to a previously anonymous and voiceless other. **See also AUTOETHNOGRAPHY, PERFORMANCE/ PERFORMATIVE/PERFORMATIVITY.**

Key References

Beverly, J., "Testimonio, Subalternity, and Narrative Authority," in N. K. Denzin & Y. S. Lincoln, eds., *Handbook for Qualitative Research*, 2nd ed. Thousand Oaks, CA: Sage, 2000.

Brady, I., *Anthropological Poetics*. Savage, MD: Rowman & Littlefield, 1991.

Clifford, J., & Marcus, G. E., *Writing Culture: The Poetics and Politics of Ethnography*. Berkeley: University of California Press, 1986.

Denzin, N. K., *Interpretive Ethnography: Ethnographic Practices for the 21st Century*. Thousand Oaks, CA: Sage, 1997.

EXPLANATION   In commonsense usage, to explain something is to make it intelligible or understandable. Generally, when we ask for an explanation, we are asking for an account of *why* something happened. Qualitative inquiry is often concerned not simply with what human actions mean but also with why they occur. Explanations of action take a variety of different forms. Perhaps the most common form is the *covering law model of explanation*, but other efforts to explain human *action* include Peter Winch's model of social action as meaningful, rule-governed behavior; functional explanations that account for social action in terms of the beneficial consequences that action has for the well-being or continuation of the larger social system; materialist explanations that construe human action (e.g., a social institution, political arrangement, particular social practice, group attitude, and ideology) in terms of the relation of that action to the material environment or culture of a society or group (topography, climate, social arrangements, technological factors, etc.); Foucault's *genealogy*, which aims to explain how subjects are constituted through discursive practices; Habermas's theory of communicative action; the efforts of *ethnomethodology* to explain actions in terms of their formal properties (i.e., *how* actors do things and what is being done); and historicist or *narrative explanation.*

One of the fundamental disputes in the broad field of qualitative inquiry centers on the issue of *nomological* versus historicist (i.e., narrative) accounts of human action. This dispute is often characterized as the quarrel between defenders of explanation (*Erklärung*) as the proper aim of the human sciences and those defending understanding (**Verstehen**) as the proper aim. Nomological explanations of the kind found in the natural sciences are characterized by their generality, universality, and atemporality. Defenders of *Verstehen* argue that if explanation means this natural science model of nomological, causal explanation, then explanation is not possible in the human sciences because human action is intentional and meaningful; it cannot be 'explained' in terms of general laws. In their view, human action can only be 'interpreted' by developing an understanding of its constitutive intersubjective meanings; by exploring the various forms that meaningful social action assume (e.g., ritual, practice, rule-following, and drama); by fashioning linguistic accounts showing how language is constitutive of action; or by describing some particular, temporal, circumstantial sequence of events that led up to the action to be accounted for (there is no implication that these events *always* lead to the action in question or that the events are subject to some lawful pattern). **See also** CAUSAL ANALYSIS/CAUSALITY, INTENTIONALISM, THEORY.

Key References

Bohman, J., *New Philosophy of Social Science*. Cambridge: MIT Press, 1991.

Fay, B., *Contemporary Philosophy of Social Science*. Oxford, UK: Blackwell, 1996.

Little, D., *Varieties of Social Explanation: An Introduction to the Philosophy of Social Science*. Boulder, CO: Westview, 1991.

EXTERNAL VALIDITY   See GENERALIZATION.

FACT   See **DESCRIPTION**.

FACT-VALUE DISTINCTION   This is the notion that we should not confuse claims about how things are (facts) with claims about how things should be (values). The empiricist David Hume (1711-1776) is well-known for his arguments that one cannot derive statements of value (the 'ought') from statements of fact (the 'is'). Influenced in part by Hume, the logical positivists argued that statements of value are not subject to reason because they are only expressions of preferences, attitudes, feelings, or assertions of will. Because they are claims of this kind, values are always subject to endless argument, and unlike claims of fact (or mathematics and logic) they can never be verified or falsified. Hence, value claims are not really knowledge claims at all and should not be allowed to intrude in the assessment of the truth or falsity of a scientific claim. (This is known as the emotivist theory of values or the doctrine of the radical undecidability of values.) This way of thinking about values—namely, that they are not subject to rational debate and cannot be justified and decided on in the same manner as facts—is particularly troublesome. If this is so, the determination of alternate courses of action in social policy or assessments of the merit of different social and educational interventions cannot be subject to warranted argument and rational deliberation.

Max Weber (1864-1920) is generally regarded as responsible for introducing the idea that the social scientist should be value neutral. That is, scientists should limit investigation to scientific explanation (i.e., the facts of the matter) and exclude their own political and moral (i.e., normative) judgments. The principle of value neutrality in social science derived from the fact-value distinction is often misunderstood. On the one hand, scientists do hold a set of 'internal' (disciplinary and epistemic) values in high regard. These epistemic values include public criticism (objectivity), consistency, testability, truth, fruitfulness, scope, and reliability. Of course, as the history of the development of scientific method shows, this set of values is not fixed once and for all but is debatable and changes over time. Nonetheless, it is in terms of this set of epistemic values or *criteria* that the truth or falsity (or warrantability) of claims (i.e., 'the facts of the matter') is settled. On the other hand, the work of the scientist is, without a doubt, also subject to influence by 'external' or 'extra-scientific' values, including institutional and personal social, political, and moral values. According to the principle of value neutrality, these external values should not be allowed to intrude in determining the truth or falsity of scientific claims. The inquirer should keep unconditionally separate the establishment of empirical fact and his or her own moral and political values. Stated somewhat differently, an inquirer should never confuse description and explanation with criticism and evaluation. The fact-value distinction is thus preserved.

Depending on one's point of view, this principle is either a dogma to be overcome or a regulative ideal to be upheld. For defenders of *naturalism,* value neutrality is an important methodological principle and the cornerstone of objectivity. For critical theorists and many feminist inquirers, among others, value neutrality must be exorcised to make way for a union of explanation and criticism in social theory. See also CONTEXT OF DISCOVERY/CONTEXT OF JUSTIFICATION, DISINTERESTED SOCIAL SCIENCE.

Key References

House, E. R., & Howe, K. R., *Values in Evaluation and Social Research.* Thousand Oaks, CA: Sage, 1999.

Phillips, D. C., *The Expanded Social Scientist's Bestiary.* Savage, MD: Rowman & Littlefield, 2000.

Root, M., *Philosophy of Social Science.* Oxford, UK: Blackwell, 1993.

Weber, M., *The Methodology of the Social Sciences,* E. Shils & H. Finch, eds. & trans. New York: Free Press, 1968.

FALLIBILISM   This is the doctrine that knowledge and beliefs are inherently uncertain, never conclusive, or beyond dispute. It is an epistemological stance that cautions against arrogance in the holding of cherished beliefs. Fallibilism is a statement about our epistemological limitations and not about the nature of the world per se. In other words, it is not a claim that the world is unknowable or that there is no world to be known; it simply means that our knowledge of that world is of a kind that is never certain. Fallibilists claim that we are content with our current (reasonably well-warranted) knowledge claims until some evidence comes along to challenge them and possibly cause us to revise or abandon them. The notion stands midway between dogmatism (the idea that we hold our beliefs to be true unquestionably and in the absence of any certainty) and radical *skepticism* (the idea that knowledge of any kind is impossible). The idea of a fallibilist epistemology was explained by Charles Sanders Peirce (1839-1914) as part of his detailed critique of Cartesian epistemology. It is also a key notion in Karl Popper's (1902-1994) philosophy of science. **See also FALSIFICATION, NONFOUNDATIONALIST EPISTEMOLOGIES, POSTEMPIRICISM, PRAGMATISM.**

Key Reference

Fay, B., *Contemporary Philosophy of Social Science.* Oxford, UK: Blackwell, 1996.

FALSIFICATION   Karl Popper (1902-1994) advanced the principle of falsification (or falsifiability) as a means of demarcating science from nonscience. He argued that the claims made by science are always, at least in principle, capable of being shown to be incorrect (i.e., falsified), whereas the claims of nonscientific pursuits are not. If a scientific claim withstands attempts to falsify it, it is then considered corroborated but not confirmed or verified. Popper was a fallibilist who strongly defended the (now widely accepted) view that scientific claims are never proved or conclusively justified. He believed that the growth of scientific knowledge is best characterized as a process of conjecture and refutation as shown in Figure F.1. In philosophy of science, falsification has been criticized as an untenable explanation for the growth of scientific knowledge, but it continues to serve as a practicable research principle in may forms of research. For example, the idea of seeking negative cases or disconfirming (vs. supporting) evidence for hypotheses in qualitative studies reflects this principle. The principle is also a key notion in the methodology for the human sciences defended in *naturalism.*

Problem identification

↘

Tentative solutions (conjectures)

↘

Error elimination through the testing of conjectures (refutation)

↘

Further conjectures

↘

Further refutations and so on

Figure F.1. A Popperian View of the Growth of Scientific Knowledge

Key References

Fay, B., *Contemporary Philosophy of Social Science.* Oxford, UK: Blackwell, 1996.

Phillips, D. C., *The Expanded Social Scientist's Bestiary.* Lanham, MD: Rowman & Littlefield, 2000.

Popper, K., *Conjectures and Refutations,* 2nd ed. New York: Basic Books, 1965.

FEMINIST EPISTEMOLOGIES   There is no single feminist epistemology. Discussions of epistemology by feminists simultaneously exhibit a wide range of ideas, including criticism of traditional epistemology (*rationalism* and *empiricism*), arguments that reason and objectivity are gendered concepts, tension with *postmodernism,* and alliances with ideas of *critical social science* and *participatory action research.* Three strands of feminist epistemology have been identified, although there is great variance within each:

1. Feminist empiricism: This is a defense of experiential or observational data as the only legitimate basis for the testing of hypotheses and theory. Feminist empiricists argue that these kind of data about women's experiences are traditionally missing from current medical, psychological, and sociological theory. They seek to rectify this situation by producing empirically more accurate pictures of social reality. Feminist empiricism, however, does not accept without question the methodological assumptions (e.g., detached objectivity, and neutrality) associated with empiricist epistemology.

2. Feminist *standpoint epistemologies:* Inquiry should begin in and be tested against the lived sociopolitical experiences of women because women have a more complete and less distorted vision of real social relations unavailable to men insofar as they benefit from the exploitation of women. These epistemologies often draw on Marxist and neo-Marxist analyses of class domination and the division of labor in society.

3. Feminist *postmodernism:* This is a catch-all phrase for an incredibly rich variety of perspectives that in one sense 'come after' the first two epistemologies noted previously. Postmodern epistemologies are in part characterized by debates between standpoint perspectives and defenders of *deconstructionism* and postmodern notions such as the suspicion of all universalizing claims, the rejection of truth as an oppressive illusion, and the relativizing of experience to local micropolitics. Some scholars view postmodernism and feminist theory as incompatible; others believe that insights of postmodernism—particularly its concerns with linking knowledge and power; its preoccupation with concrete, particular sites of struggles against oppression; its opening up of discourse to multiple voices; its critique of objectivity—actually serve to strengthen feminist epistemology.

Key References

Alcoff, L., & Potter, E., eds., *Feminist Epistemologies*. New York: Routledge, 1993.

Antony, L. M., & Witt, C., eds., *A Mind of One's Own: Feminist Essays on Reason and Objectivity.* Boulder, CO: Westview, 1993.

Harding, S., & Hintikka, M. B., eds., *Discovering Reality: Feminist Perspectives on Epistemology, Metaphysics, Methodology, and Philosophy of Science.* Dordrecht, The Netherlands: D. Reidel, 1983.

Nicholson, L. J., ed., *Feminism/Postmodernism.* New York: Routledge, 1990.

FIDELITY TO METHOD/FIDELITY TO PHENOMENON   This is another way of expressing the principle of *ethnographic naturalism.* This notion is said to distinguish qualitative field studies from the kinds of experimental studies conducted by psychologists. The claim is that qualitative studies are based on the presupposition of being faithful, in the first instance, to the phenomenon under investigation: The social world must be understood as it is in its 'natural' state. One should not attempt to structure or arrange the world of lived experience to meet some prior commitment to the requirements of scientific method (i.e., fidelity or faithfulness to methodological principles). **See also EMERGENT DESIGN, NATURALISTIC INQUIRY.**

Key Reference

Diesing, P., *Patterns of Discovery in the Social Sciences.* New York: Aldine, 1971.

FIELD   Traditionally, the field is the physical place or site where one goes to do *fieldwork.* For anthropologists, this has often been some foreign land with arrival on site dutifully noted in what is called an arrival tale in the report of the fieldwork. More generally, it is where your colleagues say you are when you are doing your research: "Where's Mary?" "She's in the field." The notion of 'field' as a place or situation in which some particular social *action* transpires whether or not the inquirer is present sets the notion apart from the idea of an 'artificial setting' (i.e., a laboratory experiment) in which some set of circumstances is especially contrived by the inquirer. Thus, the notion of the field is in part tied to the doctrine of *ethnographic naturalism.*

The notion of what constitutes 'being in the field' is currently under a great deal of reexamination. Traditionally, this notion meant being physically displaced from some comfortable familiar setting (i.e., the university) to some exotic, linguistically, and physically challenging remote place where one conducted a study. This traditional conception is less applicable as increasingly more field-workers undertake studies in nearby locales, including occasionally the field-worker's own work setting. More significantly, the idea of the field as a place 'out there' in which one studies is being challenged by claims such as the following: "The field is not so much a place as it is a particular relation between oneself and others, involving a difficult combination of commitment and disengagement, relationship and separation" (R. Lederman, "Pretexts for Ethnography: On Reading Fieldnotes," in R. Sanjek, ed., *Fieldnotes,* Cornell University Press, 1990, p. 88) and "The 'field' is not an entity 'out there' that awaits discovery and exploration by the intrepid explorer. The field is not merely reported in the texts of fieldwork: It is constituted by our writing and reading" (P. Atkinson, *The Ethnographic Imagination,* Routledge, 1992, p. 8). Other criticisms are directed at the notion of the field as a single site. Ethnographers point to the fact that globalization interpenetrates and structures notions of culture, politics, economy, and subjectivity. The site of culture is thus perhaps to be understood only in terms of connections, parallels, and contrasts among multiple, interrelated sites. Some qualitative inquirers influenced by poststructuralist thought offer a more radical critique. They argue that the concept of the field (events, actions, and contexts) as locatable in time and place should be replaced by the idea of a field as a multiplicity of images and reproductions characteristic of a cinematic society. In such a society, life is theater and the field is a staged social production. Hence, the traditional analytic vocabulary in which words such as the field, being in the field, fieldnotes, and field journal are used to frame the object and process of study is no longer applicable. One is no longer studying something real in a real field but rather images of the real (see also **HYPERREALITY**). **See also PARTICIPANT OBSERVATION.**

Key References

Burawoy, M., Blum, J. A., George, S., Gille, Z., Gowan, T., Haney, L., Klawiter, M., Lopez, S. H., O'Riain, S., & Thayer, M., *Global Ethnogra-*

phy: Forces, Connections, and Imaginations in a Postmodern World. Berkeley: University of California Press, 2000.

Denzin, N. K., *Images of Postmodern Society.* London: Sage, 1991.

Gubrium, J. F., & Holstein, J. A., *The New Language of Qualitative Method.* Oxford, UK: Oxford University Press, 1997.

Marcus, G. E., *Ethnography Through Thick and Thin.* Princeton, NJ: Princeton University Press, 1998.

Marcus, G. E., *Critical Anthropology Now: Unexpected Contents, Shifting Constituencies, Changing Agendas.* Santa Fe, NM: School of American Research Press, 1999.

Sanjek, R., ed., *Fieldnotes: The Makings of Anthropology.* Ithaca, NY: Cornell University Press, 1990.

FIELD JOURNAL   The field journal is a bound notebook that the field-worker carries into the *field* and in which is recorded observational notes, personal notes, sketches, ideas, lists of terms, and so on. In this journal are recorded what are often called jottings or jotted notes—phrases, key words, quotes, and so on that are later used as memory aids in the writing up of full *fieldnotes*. What exactly is contained in the field journal is a matter of research purpose, individual style, and need.

Key References

Lofland, J., & Lofland, L. H., *Analyzing Social Settings: A Guide to Qualitative Observation and Analysis,* 3rd ed. Belmont, CA: Wadsworth, 1995.

Sanjek, R., ed., *Fieldnotes: The Makings of Anthropology.* Ithaca, NY: Cornell University Press, 1990.

FIELDNOTES   Fieldnotes are a kind of *evidence* on which inquirers base claims about meaning and understanding. There is no standard definition of fieldnotes, their form, or content, however. Some field-workers define fieldnotes as 'raw' data or material—notes made in the *field* based on observations and conversations, rough diagrams and charts, lists of terms, and so on. Others contrast fieldnotes with data, defining fieldnotes more along the lines of daily entries made in a *field journal* to record thoughts, impressions, initial ideas, working hypotheses, issues to pursue, and so on. For some, fieldnotes include all those things collected in the course of *fieldwork*—the fieldwork journal, transcripts of conversations and interviews, photographs, audiotapes and videotapes, copies of documents, and artifacts. Others exclude some of these as not belonging to fieldnotes proper. This wide variation in defining fieldnotes is attributable to the fact these kinds of notes are very much prepared for an audience of one—the field-worker—and thus are individualistic and personal and reflective of the unique ways individual field-workers conduct fieldwork. Common wisdom also holds that the written product of fieldwork—the ethnography, case study, and so on—is based on fieldnotes. That is only partially correct, however, because field-workers come back from the field with both fieldnotes (however defined) and 'headnotes'—the former written down, and the latter continually evolving and changing. Written reports of fieldwork are a product of both of these kinds of notes.

Approaches to qualitative inquiry that place a premium on systematic, rigorous methods of generating and analyzing data will define fieldnotes as carefully prepared archives of data and documentation. Figure F.2 displays the traditional way of understanding the relationship of fieldnotes to the finished product of field research.

Fieldnotes are defined here as the 'real' data and distinguished from headnotes and from a record of reactions or a chronology of ideas found in a fieldwork journal. Data are tangible objects to be entered into files and records that can be manipulated and coded in various ways. (The logic of computer-assisted analysis of qualitative data seems to rest on this way of thinking about fieldnotes.) In this portrayal, fieldnote data are analogous to data in the form of responses to a survey or the results of the application of a psychometric measure. In summary, on a scientific conception of doing qualitative work, fieldnotes are linked to the production of the final report in something resembling a building-block model. Scientific analysis of qualitative data assumes that resulting interpretations or understandings of human action are capable of being found in or traced to discrete segments of data in the form of written notes on observations, typed transcripts, parts of documents, and so on.

The definition of fieldnotes and their relationship to fieldwork activity and written reports of fieldwork, however, is far more

Figure F.2. Traditional Conception of the Place of Fieldnotes

complex and problematic for several reasons. First, fieldnotes have a dynamic character: What one knows and records early on in fieldwork will be different than what one knows and records later. Second, preparing fieldnotes requires interpretive and textualizing practices. In other words, the making of fieldnotes is an interpretive practice and not merely a kind of recording. Third, although fieldnotes, broadly conceived, may indeed be the data that preserve the insights and understandings of field-workers forthcoming from their close and long-time encounter with that which they seek to understand, those fieldnotes 'become' the final written report through complex processes of translation. **See also ANALYZING QUALITATIVE DATA, THICK DESCRIPTION, INSCRIPTION, TRANSCRIPTION.**

Key References

Emerson, R. M., Fretz, R. I., & Shaw, L. L., *Writing Ethnographic Fieldnotes.* Chicago: University of Chicago Press, 1995.

Sanjek, R., ed., *Fieldnotes: The Makings of Anthropology.* Ithaca, NY: Cornell University Press, 1990.

FIELD RELATIONS   This is a shorthand way of referring to the complex set of logistical, procedural, ethical, and political dimensions of relating to informants, gatekeepers, respondents, and others in the *field* in which one studies. Included here are the responsibilities entailed in gaining access to settings, people, and documents; establishing and maintaining trust; negotiating a particular role in the setting; and departing the field. Confessional tales included in fieldwork reports often focus on some aspect of field relations and on the trials and tribulations of fieldwork more generally. **See also** ETHICS OF QUALITATIVE INQUIRY, FIELDWORK, PARTICIPANT OBSERVATION, RECIPROCITY.

Key References

Punch, M., *The Politics and Ethics of Fieldwork*. Beverly Hills, CA: Sage, 1986.

Shaffir, W. B., & Stebbins, R. A., eds., *Experiencing Fieldwork: An Inside View of Qualitative Research*. Newbury Park, CA: Sage, 1991.

Van Maanen, J., *Tales of the Field*. Chicago: University of Chicago Press, 1988.

FIELD STUDIES   This is a generic designation for all forms of social science research (e.g., *case study research* and *ethnography*) that involve direct, firsthand observation in naturally occurring situations or events and that rely principally on techniques of *participant observation* and *interviewing*. Field studies can involve the generation of both numeric and nonnumeric data. Not all qualitative studies are necessarily field studies because a qualitative inquirer could use existing texts, documents, or cultural artifacts as the data for analysis. **See also** FIELD, FIELDWORK.

Key Reference

Lofland, J., & Lofland, L. H., *Analyzing Social Settings: A Guide to Qualitative Observation and Analysis*, 3rd ed. Belmont, CA: Wadsworth, 1995.

FIELDWORK   This term refers to all those activities that one engages in while in the *field*, including watching, listening, conversing, recording, interpreting, dealing with logistics, and facing ethical and political dilemmas. It is an intensely personal and social process requiring both physical and intellectual stamina, political acumen, and moral sensitivity. *Participant observation* has traditionally been thought of as the *methodology* employed in fieldwork, but interview studies (including life-history work and oral history), case studies of various kinds, and coparticipative inquiries such as *action research* all entail some aspects of fieldwork as well. In the literature, the fieldwork process is often reconstructed into phases (e.g., gaining entry, negotiating access, maintaining *field relations,* collecting and analyzing data, and exiting the field) to address in some manageable way all the various skills, knowledge, and attitudes entangled in fieldwork activity. In practice, however, fieldwork rarely unfolds in any neatly linear fashion.

Fieldwork is often discussed more as a set of tool skills rather than as a way of being-in-the-world in relation to others. This is due, in part, to connotations associated with the term 'field*work' coupled with the lingering legacy of logical empiricism* that stresses the importance of *method* in defining scientific inquiry. In other words, fieldwork is traditionally defined as a particular kind of labor or work one engages in to produce results. This labor requires means-end knowledge—a set of procedural or tool skills (a kind of technical knowledge) used to solve the puzzle of understanding human action. This is not to deny that there is extensive literature on field relations and fieldwork ethics. This literature, however, is also often presented as a tool-like knowledge—a set of guidelines, procedures, and obligations entailed in the epistemo- logically responsible and ethically correct use of data-gathering and analysis tools. The notion of fieldwork as a tool skill set seems to be particularly prominent in the applied fields in which the discovery of qualitative inquiry is recent (e.g., health professions, social services administration, education, journalism, and telecommunications).

A reconceptualization of what fieldwork is and what fieldwork knowledge consists of, however, is at least suggested in ideas from *social constructionism, pragmatism, critical social science,* and *philosophical hermeneutics.* This different way of thinking does not mean abandoning notions of technical competence in skills of watching, listening, conversing, and recording. Rather, the shift in thinking about fieldwork means resetting those concerns within a different framework for knowledge and a different mode of the inquirer's engagement with the social world. When fieldwork is defined as *praxis* requiring a kind of *practical-moral knowledge,* emphasis shifts from a tool skill set to exploring the following ideas: the field-worker's way of being-in-the world; the difference between wisdom and knowledge; the moral and epistemological commitments to dialogue that fieldwork entails; the kind of knowledge of other people it requires; the incoherence, ambiguity, and contradictoriness of experience; and fieldwork as a kind of communicative action or practical discourse. **See also** **ETHICS OF QUALITATIVE INQUIRY, PARTICIPANT OBSERVATION.**

Key References

Wolcott, H. F., *The Art of Fieldwork.* Walnut Creek, CA: Altamira, 1995.

Wolf, D. L., ed., *Feminist Dilemmas in Fieldwork.* Boulder, CO: Westview, 1996.

FOUNDATIONALIST EPISTEMOLOGIES   These epistemologies assume the possibility and necessity of the ultimate grounding of knowledge claims. To be considered genuine, legitimate, and trustworthy (and not simply mere belief), knowledge must rest on foundations that require no further justification or interpretation. *Rationalism* and *empiricism* are foundationalist epistemologies. *Logical positivism* initially endorsed foundationalism (by attempting to establish that statements about sense perception were the foundation for all empirically meaningful claims) but eventually moved to a nonfoundationalist epistemology under the influence of Otto Neurath (1882-1945).

The term *objectivism* is often used as a synonym for foundation- alist epistemologies. For example, Richard J. Bernstein (1983) defines objectivism as

the base conviction that there is or must be some permanent, ahistorical matrix or framework to which we can ultimately appeal in determining the nature of rationality, knowledge, truth, reality, goodness, or rightness. An objectivist claims that there is (or must be) such a matrix and that the primary task of the philosopher is to discover what it is. (p. 8)

He argues that many scholars believe that the only alternatives to objectivism are *relativism* or radical *skepticism*, and he offers a fallibilistic *pragmatism* as a middle way. **See also NONFOUN-DATIONAL EPISTEMOLOGIES, FALLIBILISM.**

Key References

Bernstein, R. J., *Beyond Objectivism and Relativism: Science, Hermeneutics, and Praxis.* Philadelphia: University of Pennsylvania Press, 1983.

Grayling, A. C., "Epistemology," in N. Bunnin & E. P. Tsui-James, eds., *The Blackwell Companion to Philosophy.* Oxford, UK: Blackwell, 1996.

Rorty, R., *Philosophy and the Mirror of Nature.* Princeton, NJ: Princeton University Press, 1979.

FRANKFURT SCHOOL   This is the name given to members of the Marxist-oriented *Institut für Sozialforschung* (Institute for Social Research) founded in 1923 in Frankfurt, Germany. Because most of the institute's members were Marxists and Jews, the institute was forced into exile by the Nazis. In 1934, it formally moved to Columbia University. In this institute, a blend of explanatory social research, normative critique, and philosophical reflection divorced from the positivist and materialist inclinations of orthodox Marxism emerged that came to be called a critical theory of society by its members in the mid-1930s. Its most influential director was Max Horkheimer (1895-1973), and its first generation included the social theorists T. W. Adorno (1903-1969), Herbert Marcuse (1898-1979), Walter Benjamin (1892-1940), and Erich Fromm (1900-1980). Jürgen Habermas, a student of both Adorno and Horkheimer, is perhaps the most widely known member of the second generation of critical theorists to emerge from the institute after its return to Germany in 1950. **See also CRITICAL SOCIAL SCIENCE.**

Key References

Benhabib, S., *Critique, Norm, and Utopia: A Study of the Foundations of Critical Theory.* New York: Columbia University Press, 1986.

Bronner, S. E., & Kellner, D. K., eds., *Critical Theory and Society.* New York: Routledge, 1989.

Hoy, D. C., & McCarthy, T., *Critical Theory.* Oxford, UK: Blackwell, 1994.

FUNCTIONALISM   Functionalist theories or models aim to explain human behavior (e.g., rituals, customs, and ceremonies) and social-cultural institutions (e.g., family, church, and state) in terms of the functions they perform in a particular group, society, culture, or community. In sociology, functionalism is most often associated with the work of Emile Durkheim (1858-1917) and Talcott Parsons (1902-1979) and in anthropology with the work of Bronislaw Malinowski (1884-1942). A variation called structural functionalism was developed by the anthropologist Alfred Radcliffe-Brown (1881-1995), who distinguished between *structure* (a network of social relations and institutions comprising the permanent framework of society) and *function* (the way in which these relations and institutions contributed to the stable functioning of society). Functionalist explanations are also found in political science and systems theory. A common criticism of these kinds of explanations is that they assume stability and harmonious function of aspects of a society or culture and thus fail to address conflict. **See also EXPLANATION.**

Key References

Baert, P., *Social Theory in the 20th Century.* New York: New York University Press, 1998.

Giddens, A., "Functionalism: Aprés la lutté," in A. Giddens, ed., *Studies in Social and Political Theory.* London: Hutchinson, 1979.

GEISTESWISSENSCHAFTEN   A German term usually translated as "human sciences." **See also** SCIENCE, *VERSTEHEN*.

GENEALOGY   This notion originated with Nietzsche (1844-1900), who insisted on the interpretive character of all human thought. Nietzsche claimed that a particular kind of historical inquiry he called *genealogical inquiry*—an examination of the conditions under which various ways of interpreting and evaluating ourselves have arisen—was a valuable means of reevaluating interpretations of human life. Genealogical inquiry is thus a way of explaining our selves to our selves. Drawing on the work of Nietzsche, Foucault's (1926-1984) later work (e.g., *Discipline and Punish* and the three-volume *History of Sexuality*) employed a genealogical approach to understanding how we have been constituted as subjects in various systems of thought and bodies of knowledge that are intimately connected to systems of social control, domination, and, more broadly, the exercise of power. Moreover, Foucault strongly emphasized that these relations of power and knowledge that constitute social relations operate regardless of any particular individual's subjective awareness or intentions. The subject is constituted as a particular kind of subject through these discourses of power and knowledge. The purpose of engaging in genealogical inquiry is to disturb the taken-for-granted and allegedly self-evident character of our interpretations of 'subjects' as, for example, men, women, boys, girls, criminals, and adolescents. Baert (1998) captures the notion of genealogical inquiry as follows:

> The genealogist goes back in time to show that at some point radically new meanings were allocated to concepts. He or she then demonstrates that the emergence of these new meanings was due to power struggles or contingency. The new meanings were subsequently transmitted across generations, and so became part of the culture. These meanings gradually came to be experienced by people as self-evident, necessary, innocuous (if not honorable and consistent). Foucault's genealogy . . . aims at demonstrating that these meanings are neither obvious, necessary, harmless, honorable, or coherent. (p. 123)

Key References

Baert, P., *Social Theory for the Twentieth Century*. New York: New York University Press, 1998.

Foucault, M., *Discipline and Punish: The Birth of the Prison*. London: Allen Lane, 1977.

Foucault, M., "Nietzsche, Genealogy, History," in D. F. Bouchard, ed., *Language, Counter-Memory, Practice*. Ithaca, NY: Cornell University Press, 1977.

Geuss, R., "Nietzsche and Genealogy." *European Journal of Philosophy*, 1994, 2(3), 274-292.

GENERALIZATION   A generalization is a broad, encompassing statement or proposition made by drawing an inference from observation of the particular. Generalization is an act of reasoning from the observed to the unobserved, from a specific instance to all instances believed to be like the instance in question. Theories are thus generalizations because they explain some phenomenon across a variety of specific instances or cases of that phenomenon. Generalization or generalizability (also called external validity) is traditionally held to be one of the *criteria* for social scientific inquiry.

Broadly interpreted, generalization refers to the wider relevance or resonance of one's inquiry beyond the specific context in which it was conducted. Generalization is the process involved in moving from the specification of patterns, relations, processes, conditions, and meanings discerned in the data generated in the study of some particular event, person, institution, group, and so forth to a more general and abstract understanding of these aspects of human experience. This process is either empirical-statistical or theoretical-analytic, reflecting two different logics of sampling. Empirical generalizations are made by first carefully selecting a representative sample from a population of interest and then, by means of a statistical inference, calculating the probability that findings based on the sample are characteristic of the population. This is the least commonly used approach to generalization in qualitative studies. Theoretical or analytical generalizations do not rely on the logic of representative sampling. Rather, the selection of groups, units, cases, and so forth to study is made on the basis of their relevance to the theoretical account or explanation that the inquirer is developing. In other words, the criterion used to select cases from which one will generalize is not their representativeness. Rather, the criterion for deciding what cases to select for study is the extent to which they contribute to supporting and refuting the argument or explanation being developed by the inquirer.

G

The most well-developed version of this notion of theoretical elaboration or *analytic generalization* is discussed in *grounded theory methodology,* but it also is found in efforts to use qualitative studies to reconstruct social theory by means of the extended case method. Theoretical elaboration is also the notion underlying Clifford Geertz's efforts to connect the microscopic or situation-specific character of ethnography to more general understandings. Geertz (1983, p. 23) notes, "The important thing about the anthropologist's findings is their complex specificness, their circumstantiality." Specific cases, however, provide the context-specific material that makes it possible to think "realistically and concretely about" social scientific concepts and theories (e.g., modernization, stratification, legitimacy, integration, conflict, charisma, and structure) and to work "creatively and imaginatively with them."

There are several other positions on the desirability, possibility, and process of generalization within the broad field of qualitative inquiry. Robert Stake, for example, defends the importance of what he calls "naturalistic generalizations"—conclusions that both inquirer and reader arrive at through engagement in life or through vicarious experience—in contrast to formal, propositional generalizations. He argues that inquirers should assist readers in making naturalistic generalizations by developing interpretive accounts that are personal, narrative in structure, and richly detailed. Yvonna Lincoln and Egon Guba maintain that generalization is unrealizable, but, similar to Stake, they claim that extrapolation or *transferability* of findings from one specific *case* to another is possible. In their view, case-to-case transfer, an activity that is the responsibility of the reader of research, can be accomplished if the inquirer provides sufficient detail about the circumstances of the situation or case that was studied so that readers can engage in reasonable but modest speculation about whether findings are applicable to other cases with similar circumstances. Transferability, like theoretical elaboration, is a way to deal with the apparent paradox of qualitative work: its avowed focus on the particular and its simultaneous refusal to deny any interest whatsoever in the general. Likewise, Norman Denzin has promoted an affirmative postmodern approach to generalizing in interpretive studies. He holds the view that contextual, multivoiced, interactional, and interpretive texts contribute to theoretical understanding by illuminating interpretive theories already at work in the connections that frame the stories that are told. The inquirer engages in generalizing by making vivid and critically examining the connections between unique, uncommon lived experiences and the commonality of groups, social relationships, and culturally constructed images that partially define those experiences. The impossibility and undesirability of any and all attempts to generalize, however, is characteristic of some radical postmodernist approaches to qualitative study. These approaches are opposed to theory of any kind and look instead to the uniqueness of events and perspectives. They take an antitheoretical and antigeneralizing interest in the contingent and specific circumstances of everyday life events; they emphasize local narratives and local knowledge. **See also CROSS-CASE ANALYSIS, INFERENCE, SAMPLING LOGIC.**

Key References

Burawoy, M., "Reconstructing Social Theories" and "The Extended Case Method," in M. Burawoy, A. Burton, A. A. Ferguson, H. J. Fox, J. Gamson, N. Gartrell, L. Hurst, C. Hurzman, L. Salinger, J. Schiffman, & S. Ui, eds., *Ethnography Unbound: Power and Resistance in the Modern Metropolis.* Berkeley: University of California Press, 1991.

Denzin, N., *Interpretive Interactionism.* Newbury Park, CA: Sage, 1989.

Flick, U., *An Introduction to Qualitative Research.* London: Sage, 1998.

Geertz, C., "Thick Description: Towards an Interpretive Theory of Culture," in C. Geertz, ed., *The Interpretation of Cultures.* New York: Basic Books, 1983.

Lincoln, Y. S., & Guba, E. G., *Naturalistic Inquiry.* Beverly Hills, CA: Sage, 1985.

Stake, R., *The Art of Case Study Research.* Thousand Oaks, CA: Sage, 1995.

GENERATING DATA   It is a common mistake to think that data are somehow simply 'out there' and thus discovered and collected (i.e., gathered) like picking strawberries from the vine. On the contrary, what constitutes data depends on one's inquiry purposes and the questions one seeks to answer. Data are generated or constructed within conceptual schemes and by various means that are deemed appropriate to serving particular purposes and answering particular questions. **See also DESCRIPTION, THEORY-OBSERVATION DISTINCTION.**

Key Reference

Mason, J., *Qualitative Researching.* London: Sage, 1996.

GRAND NARRATIVE   Also called a master narrative or metanarrative, the term figures prominently in Jean-François Lyotard's (1924-1998) explanation of what the condition of postmodernity means. Lyotard claimed that modern science is characterized by the pursuit of absolute standards, grand theory, and universal categories. Moreover, the legitimation of science as a practice, as well as various other modern social and political practices, relied on metanarratives. Two prominent examples of the latter are the Enlightenment narrative of human progress through the advancement of scientific knowledge and the Marxist narrative of the triumph of socialism through class conflict and the revolution of the proletariat. For Lyotard, postmodernity meant the decline of the legitimating power of these grand narratives and the turn toward the acceptance of all knowledge as incomplete, tentative, local, perspectival, and resistant to all forms of unification. **See also GRAND THEORY, POSTMODERNISM.**

Key Reference

Lyotard, J.-F., *The Postmodern Condition: A Report on Knowledge.* Minneapolis: University of Minnesota Press, 1984.

GRAND THEORY   In the social sciences, grand theory refers to those efforts devoted to abstract, analytical theory building. It stands in contrast to empiricist approaches, which emphasize that knowledge of society is best acquired by accumulating empirical generalizations through improvements in methodology, and scientific approaches, which encourage the development of lawlike propositions and axiomatic theory. The work of Talcott Parsons (1902-1979) stands as an exemplar of grand theory in sociology. The period from approximately 1950 to 1970 in sociology was characterized by strong criticism of this kind of Parsonian theorizing from various viewpoints, including Robert Merton's defense of middle-range theory, Barney Glaser and Anselm Strauss's arguments for grounded theory, and C. Wright Mills and Alvin Gouldner's criticisms of abstract theory as a retreat from social action and practical reality. Grand theory experienced something of a resurgence in sociology in the late 1970s and early 1980s as represented, for example, in the structuration theory of Anthony Giddens, Jürgen Habermas's theory of communicative action, and Niklas Luhmann's system theory. More generally, there is a significant part of social theory that today is given to more speculative, less empirical, less scientific, and more all-encompassing social theorizing. These efforts are met by criticisms, on the one hand, from empiricists who are suspicious of any efforts to explain society that are seemingly 'merely philosophical' and, on the other hand, from postmodernist and poststructuralists who are deeply suspicious of all forms of grand theory and argue for the necessarily fragmented and incomplete character of all forms of knowledge. **See also POSTMODERNISM.**

Key Reference

Skinner, Q., ed., *The Return of Grand Theory in the Human Sciences.* Cambridge, UK: Cambridge University Press, 1985.

GROUNDED THEORY METHODOLOGY   This term is often used in a nonspecific way to refer to any approach to developing theoretical ideas (concepts, models, and formal theories) that begins with data. Grounded theory methodology, however, is a specific, highly developed, rigorous set of procedures for producing formal, substantive theory of social phenomena. This approach to the analysis of qualitative data simultaneously employs techniques of induction, deduction, and verification to develop theory. Experience with data generates insights, hypotheses, and generative questions that are pursued through further data generation. As tentative answers to questions are developed and concepts are constructed, these constructions are verified through further data collection.

G

Grounded theory methodology requires a concept-indicator model of analysis, which in turn employs the method of *constant comparison.* Empirical indicators from the data (actions and events observed, recorded, or described in documents in the words of interviewees and respondents) are compared, searching for similarities and differences. From this process, the analyst identifies underlying uniformities in the indicators and produces a coded category or concept. Concepts are compared with more empirical indicators and with each other to sharpen the definition of the concept and to define its properties. Theories are formed from proposing plausible relationships among concepts and sets of concepts. Tentative theories or theoretical propositions are further explored through additional instances of data. The testing of the emergent theory is guided by theoretical sampling. Theoretical sampling means that the sampling of additional incidents, events, activities, populations, and so on is directed by the evolving theoretical constructs. Comparisons between the explanatory adequacy of the theoretical constructs and these additional empirical indicators go on continuously until theoretical saturation is reached (i.e., additional analysis no longer contributes to anything new about a concept). In this way, the resulting theory is considered conceptually dense and grounded in the data.

Key References

Glaser B., & Strauss, A., *The Discovery of Grounded Theory.* Chicago: Aldine, 1967.

Strauss, A., *Qualitative Analysis for Social Scientists.* Cambridge, UK: Cambridge University Press, 1987.

Strauss, A., & Corbin, J., *Basics of Qualitative Research: Techniques and Procedures for Developing Grounded Theory,* 2nd ed. Thousand Oaks, CA: Sage, 1998.

HERMENEUTIC CIRCLE   As first developed in ancient rhetoric and then elaborated by Friedrich Schleiermacher (1768-1834) in nineteenth-century *hermeneutics,* this notion refers to the nature and means of interpreting a text. The circle signified a methodological process or condition of understanding, namely, that coming to understand the meaning of the whole of a text and coming to understand its parts were always interdependent activities. Construing the meaning of the whole meant making sense of the parts, and grasping the meaning of the parts depended on having some sense of the whole. For Schleiermacher, and for current versions of *conservative hermeneutics,* the hermeneutic circle indicates a necessary condition of interpretation, but the circularity of the process is only temporary—eventually the interpreter can come to something approximating a complete and correct understanding of the meaning of a text in which whole and parts are related in perfect harmony. In other words, the interpreter can, in time, get outside of or escape the hermeneutic circle in discovering the 'true' meaning of the text.

In the work of Heidegger (1889-1976) and Gadamer, the notion of the hermeneutic circle is given a stronger, more radical, and ontological interpretation. In their work, the circularity of interpretation is not simply a methodological principle but also an essential feature of all knowledge and understanding. In other words, the fact that every interpretation relies on other interpretations, and so on points to the finite and situated character of all understanding. The hermeneutic circle thus signifies the universality of hermeneutics: Interpretation is a ubiquitous and inescapable feature of all human efforts to understand; there is no special evidence, method, experience, or meaning that is independent of interpretation or more basic to it such that one can escape the hermeneutic circle. Moreover, all efforts to interpret (to understand) always take place within some background (e.g., historical tradition, web of belief, and practice) that cannot be transcended. In this sense, we always 'belong' to history. The image of the hermeneutic circle is thus transformed into a picture of how the interpreter is bound to a tradition and history, on the one hand, and to the particular object of interpretation, on the other hand. The notion is best captured in Figure H.1.

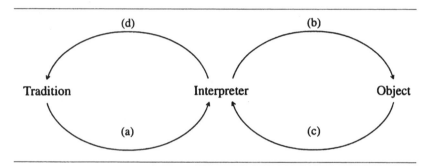

Figure H.1. The Hermeneutic Circle in Philosophical Hermeneutics
SOURCE: From S. Gallagher (1992), *Hermeneutics and Education*, p. 106. Reprinted by permission of the State University of New York Press, ©1992, State University of New York.

Gallagher explains that the anterior operation of tradition (a) as a fore-structure of understanding both conditions and suggests the fore-conceptions ('prior knowledge') (b) that the inquirer brings to interpret the object (a text or another human being). The feedback from the reading of the text (or from another human being's response in a conversation) motivates a new projection of meaning (interpretation). The relations (b) and (c) represent the hermeneutic circle; (d) indicates that in the process of interpreting, the inquirer's relation to a particular tradition can change; fore-conceptions (prior understandings) can be challenged and modified, and so on. The fact that there is no escaping the hermeneutic circle (no escaping the fact that we belong to history and to tradition) reveals its ontological character—that is, we are 'interpretive' beings. **See also HERMENEUTIC METHOD, PHILOSOPHICAL HERMENEUTICS.**

Key References

Hiley, D. R., Bohman, J. F., & Shusterman, R., eds., *The Interpretive Turn: Philosophy, Science, Culture*. Ithaca, NY: Cornell University Press, 1991.

Taylor, C., "Interpretation and the Sciences of Man," in C. Taylor, ed., *Philosophy and the Human Sciences, Philosophical Papers 2*. Cambridge, UK: Cambridge University Press, 1985. (Originally published in *Review of Metaphysics*, 1971, 25, 3-51)

HERMENEUTIC METHOD   Where the act of interpreting an utterance, text, or action is defined as a kind of exegesis (a clarification and subsequent explication of meaning that at first appears strange and puzzling), we imagine it to be a kind of critical analysis or explanation using the method of the *hermeneutic circle*. The *method* involves playing the strange and unfamiliar parts of an action, text, or utterance off against the integrity of the action, narrative, or utterance as a whole until the meaning of the strange passages and the meaning of the whole are worked out or accounted for. (Thus, for example, to understand the meaning of the first few lines of a poem, I must have a grasp of the overall meaning of the poem and vice versa.) In this process of applying the hermeneutic method, the interpreter's self-understanding and sociohistorical location neither affects nor is affected by the effort to interpret the meaning of the text or utterance. In fact, in applying the method, the interpreter abides by a set of procedural rules that help ensure that the interpreter's historical situation does not distort the bid to uncover the actual meaning embedded in the text, act, or utterance, thereby helping to ensure the objectivity of the interpretation.

When we speak of *verstehen* as the 'method' of the human sciences, it is this conception of hermeneutic method that is operative. In other words, defenders of *verstehen* as method argue that because human action is intentional it requires a special method to be understood (a method different from the method of explanation characteristic of the natural sciences). This idea that understanding proceeds by and is the result of the application of method—in this case, the hermeneutic method that is most appropriate to making sense of intentional speech or action—is repudiated in *philosophical hermeneutics* and *deconstructionism*. **See also HERMENEUTIC CIRCLE, INTENTIONALISM.**

Key References

Gallagher, S., *Hermeneutics and Education.* Albany: State University of New York Press, 1992.

Kerdeman, D., "Hermeneutics and Education: Understanding, Control, and Agency." *Educational Theory,* 1996, 48(2), 241-266.

HERMENEUTICS   This term refers generally to the art, theory, and philosophy of interpreting the meaning of an object (a *text,* a work of art, social *action,* the utterances of another speaker, etc.). There are several varieties of hermeneutics, however, behind which lay complex theoretical disputes. Friedrich Schleiermacher (1768-1834), who is generally recognized as a creator of modern hermeneutic theory, defined hermeneutics as the art of understanding practiced in reading classical, biblical, and legal texts. At the beginning of the twentieth century, Wilhelm Dilthey (1833-1911) extended the idea of hermeneutics to the epistemology and methodology of the human sciences. From Dilthey onward to the contemporary human sciences, hermeneutics has meant the theory of interpretation as a particular methodology. This interpretation, however, was challenged by Martin Heidegger (1889-1976), who understood hermeneutics to be the existential-phenomenological analysis of the constitution of *Dasein* ('existence' or 'Being-in-the-world'). He argued that hermeneutics ('understanding') is a fundamental concept of *ontology*—that is, a basic characteristic of human existence. Hans-Georg Gadamer developed Heidegger's ideas of hermeneutics (or 'understanding') as a primary and universal way of our being in the world and argued for hermeneutics as a kind of practical philosophy. Furthermore, because understanding is viewed as a linguistic event, Gadamer explored the centrality of language and dialogue to understanding. Inspired by both Heidegger and Nietzsche (1844-1900), Jacques Derrida and colleagues practice a form of radical or deconstructionist hermeneutics. Also, drawing on insights from Marx (1818-1883) and Freud (1856-1939) and ideas of the *Frankfurt School,* Jürgen Habermas in his early work developed a theory of critical or depth hermeneutics. Along with the tradition of *verstehende sociology,* the German tradition of hermeneutical thought serves as the major source of ideas for qualitative inquiry. **See also CONSERVATIVE HERMENEUTICS, CRITICAL HERMENEUTICS, DECONSTRUC-**

H

TIONISM, HERMENEUTICS OF SUSPICION, PHILOSOPHICAL HERME-
NEUTICS.

Key References

Bleicher, J., *Contemporary Hermeneutics: Hermeneutics as Method, Philoso-phy and Critique.* London: Routledge Kegan Paul, 1980.

Grondin, J., *Sources of Hermeneutics.* Albany: State University of New York Press, 1995.

Hekman, S., *Hermeneutics and the Sociology of Knowledge.* Notre Dame, IN: University of Notre Dame Press, 1986.

Palmer, R., *Hermeneutics: Interpretation Theory in Schleiermacher, Dilthey, Heidegger, and Gadamer.* Evanston, IL: Northwestern University Press, 1969.

HERMENEUTICS OF SUSPICION   This term was coined by Paul Ricoeur to characterize the hermeneutical philosophy of the more radical followers of Nietzsche (1844-1900), principally Derrida and Foucault (1926-1984). Also called radical or deconstructionist hermeneutics, this philosophy is profoundly suspicious of what-ever purports to be the truth; it argues that all interpretations are false and there is no escape from false consciousness. Its goal is to deconstruct—decipher, decode, or unmask—the reality or truth of the meaning of all notions or ideas that we take for granted and show these meanings to be entirely contingent and relative. Jürgen Habermas's *critical hermeneutics* shares this view to the extent that it seeks to unmask false consciousness. Because Habermas trusts in language and dialogue and holds out hope for the restoration of meaning and institutions, however, he also shares something with the *philosophical hermeneutics* of Gadamer and what is called the hermeneutics of trust. **See also DECONSTRUCTIONISM.**

Key References

Caputo, J., *Radical Hermeneutics: Repetition, Deconstruction, and the Herme-neutic Project.* Bloomington: Indiana University Press, 1987.

Caputo, J., *More Radical Hermeneutics: On Not Knowing Who We Are.* Bloomington: Indiana University Press, 2000.

Michelfelder, D. P., & Palmer, R. E., eds., *Dialogue and Deconstruction: The Gadamer-Derrida Encounter*. Albany: State University of New York Press, 1989.

HISTORICISM   This doctrine figured prominently in nineteenth-century German thought, most notably in the work of Dilthey (1833-1911), and is foundational to the development of *antinaturalism* and hence to much current thinking about qualitative inquiry. It is the view that we are historical beings or that there is an inescapably historical character to all of human existence such that all knowledge and understanding are inevitably interpretive, particular, perspectival, and contextual. As an epistemological doctrine, historicism developed in opposition to nomologicalism, which is the view that knowledge of society should be expressible in general laws offering universal, atemporal explanation.

Some confusion surrounds the use of the term that is attributable in large part to the fact that Karl Popper (*The Poverty of Historicism*, 1957) used the term to mean just the opposite of that defined previously. Popper argued that to be historicist meant to believe that history has a pattern, that that pattern can be captured in historical laws, and that the task of the social scientist is to discover these laws because they can be used to direct social action and policy. Popper was extremely critical of the view that there is a process of development working its way out through history. **See also NARRATIVE EXPLANATION.**

Key References

Fay, B., *Contemporary Philosophy of Social Science*. Oxford, UK: Blackwell, 1996.

Henderson, D. K., *Interpretation and Explanation in the Human Sciences*. Albany: State University of New York Press, 1993.

HISTORICITY   (Also historicality or *Geschichtlichkeit*) This is a notion that figures prominently in the phenomenological and hermeneutic traditions. It refers to a fundamental or essential feature of human existence, namely, that we are not merely *in* history but *belong* to history. History (or tradition), in other words, is not something external to us, objective, or past but a dynamic force that enters into all efforts to understand. Thus, our history (or tradition) is not something that can be overcome by a method that would make objective knowledge possible in the human sciences. The historical character of our being is not a limitation or restriction on our ability to know but the very condition or principle of understanding. Taken to its extreme, the notion of historicity is equivalent to radical relativism or universal perspectivism. **See also HERMENEUTIC CIRCLE, HISTORICISM, PHILOSOPHICAL HERMENEUTICS.**

Key References

Gadamer, H.-G., *Truth and Method*, 2nd rev. ed. J. Weinsheimer & D. G. Marshall, trans. New York: Crossroad, 1989.

Grondin, J. *Introduction to Philosophical Hermeneutics.* J. Weinsheimer, trans. New Haven, CT: Yale University Press, 1994.

HOLISM   A long-standing dispute in the social sciences concerns what is the proper level or means of explanation of social phenomena. Holism (also called methodological or metaphysical holism) is the view that explanation of social phenomena must proceed at the macroscopic level in terms of social 'wholes' (e.g., classes, groups, communities, societies, and states) and their properties. It assumes that the actions of individuals are a function of the place of these individuals within some social whole or system of meaning. Two prominent examples of explanations of social phenomena reflecting metaphysical holism are structuralism and Foucault's archaeology; in psychology, the Gestalt doctrine is an example of holistic explanation with respect to psychological phenomena. Holism denies that it is possible to reduce explanation of the 'whole' in question to more fundamental parts. Critics of holism call it metaphysical because they claim that social wholes, such as societies, groups, and states, are unobservable and hence nonempirical.

Holism is opposed to methodological individualism (also called explanatory reductionism). This doctrine holds that the basic units of social life are self-directing individuals, and that explanation of social phenomena must focus on the decisions, attitudes, actions, and so on of individuals. This view assumes that social wholes are reducible to, and capable of explanation in terms of, the activities of individuals that comprise those wholes.

It is often said that defenders of qualitative inquiry endorse holism and oppose efforts at reductionism. In this argument, however, the term "holism" seems to be used as a synonym for *contextualism*—that is, the view that the meaning of particular language and human *action* can only be understood in the specific context in which it unfolds. **See also REDUCTIONISM.**

Key References

Martin, M., & McIntyre, L. C., eds., *Readings in the Philosophy of Social Science*. Cambridge: MIT Press, 1994.

Phillips, D. C., *Holistic Thought in Social Science*. Stanford, CA: Stanford University Press, 1976.

HUMAN ACTION See ACTION.

HYPERREALITY This is a term coined by Jean Baudrillard to describe the condition of life in postmodernity. He argued that we live in an era of simulation brought on by technologies of information processing, media, and cybernetic control systems. These technologies implode the once taken-for-granted boundary between image/simulation and reality such that the very ground of the 'real' disappears. Models and simulations begin to replace 'real' life. Distinctions between what is 'real' and 'unreal' begin to blur, and 'hyperreal' signals that the real becomes artificially reproduced as real. Thus, the hyperreal is not unreal or surreal but more real than real. Hyperreality refers to the condition wherein models of the real replace the real as real. For example, when models of an ideal home, an ideal relationship, and an ideal physical body as portrayed in various media become determinant of a 'real' home, relationship, or body, the boundary between hyperreality and everyday life blurs and eventually disappears. Simulations come to constitute reality. The notion figures prominently in poststructuralist interpretive ethnography in discussions of what it means to represent social life in written accounts (see N. K. Denzin, *Interpretive Ethnography: Ethnographic Practices for the 21st Century*, Sage, 1997).

Key References

Baudrillard, J., *Simulations*. New York: Semiotext(e), 1983.

Best, S., & Kellner, D., *Postmodern Theory*. New York: Guilford, 1991.

HYPOTHETICO-DEDUCTIVE METHOD   The *covering law model of explanation* holds that human behavior is explained when the inquirer has discovered the relevant generalizations that 'cover' the case to be explained. This model of explanation uses the hypothetico-deductive method to form hypotheses, deduce implications, and test those hypotheses against experience. The following are steps in the ideal version of the method: (a) Theory provides the definitions, assumptions, and hypotheses about human behavior from which (b) predictions about behavior are logically deduced. (c) Those predictions are then tested through a process of empirical observation. (d) From the results of observations, the inquirer concludes either that the theory appears consistent with the facts (i.e., it explains the behavior) or that the theory is inconsistent with the facts. (e) If it is consistent, no further work is needed. If it is inconsistent, then the theory must either be discarded in favor of a better theory or modified to accommodate the newly required facts. For defenders of the antinaturalist stance of *interpretivism*, this method of explanation is regarded as inappropriate for making sense of human *action*. Interpretivists claim that action cannot be explained but must be understood; hence, they argue that the method of *verstehen* must be used in the human sciences.

Key Reference

Hollis, M., *The Philosophy of Social Science*. Cambridge, UK: Cambridge University Press, 1994.

IDEALISM   This philosophical doctrine holds that the world (reality and real objects) does not exist independently of minds. Idealist explanations of sociocultural and historical phenomena give priority to mental phenomena and thus contrast with materialist explanations that give primacy to material or physical phenomena and processes. Idealism stands in opposition both to *realism*, which defines the world (objects of knowledge) as a real structure that exists independently of our experience with it, our knowledge of it, and the conditions that allow us access to it, and to strict or direct *empiricism*, which claims the objects of knowledge are simply observable atomistic events. An idealist does not necessarily hold that the natural and social worlds are unreal or nonexistent but that there is no unmediated access to such worlds—that is, no direct understanding of the world. The world is always interpreted through mind. As is the case with any philosophical notion with a long history, idealism is a complicated view with many varieties. It is a philosophy that tries to say something about what lies behind or beyond experience, and in that sense early nineteenth-century German idealism (J. G. Fichte [1762-1814], F. W. J. Schelling [1775-1854], G. W. F. Hegel [1770-1831], all building on Immanuel Kant's [1724-1804] transcendental idealism) served as the fertile ground for the late nineteenth- and early twentieth-century reaction to *logical positivism*'s insistence on a strict empiricism. The spirit of idealism—its recognition of the importance of mind, life, emotion, and so forth—is a wellspring of qualitative inquiry, although not all so-called qualitative inquirers are necessarily philosophical idealists.

Key References

Bunge, M., *Finding Philosophy in Social Science*. New Haven, CT: Yale University Press, 1996.

Robinson, H., "Berkeley," in N. Bunnin & E. P. Tsui-James, eds., *The Blackwell Companion to Philosophy*. Oxford, UK: Blackwell, 1996.

IDENTITY   There is a long psychological and sociological tradition of examining this concept of sameness and unity of self amid change and diversity. The concept has received special attention from about the 1950s onward as notions of the loss of meaning in modern society and the accompanying search for identity began to collide with feminist, postmodernist, and cultural studies and their various examinations of the composition of the subject and the politics of identity. Currently, both the terms *identity* and *self* are widely discussed as projects or accomplishments rather than in terms of essences, substances, or categories. It is common to see examinations of an individual's multiple identities that are not simply attributable to individual intention or to classification in terms of familiar categories of race, class, and gender but the outcome of some collective practical activity or the result of the social construction of a moral-political order. Identities or various 'subject-positions' in society are thought to be constituted in the complex social interaction of language, gesture, bodily significations, desires, intents, and so forth. Identities are simultaneously epiphenomenal (derivative) in that they are socially bestowed, sustained, or transformed and phenomenal (material). Whether identities or subject-positions are capable of integration, endure, or have some kind of 'natural' basis behind or beneath them is widely debated. Some postmodernist thought erases the very idea of *an* identity, *a* subject, or *a* self arguing that individuals are 'sites' for competing cultural interpretations of the subject or self. In this view, identity (or the self) is always fragmented, never integrated, never fixed, and always being remade.

Key References

Bauman, Z., *Life in Fragments: Essays in Postmodern Morality*. Oxford, UK: Blackwell, 1995.

Butler, J., *Gender Trouble: Feminism and the Subversion of Identity*. New York: Routledge, 1990.

Lasch, S., & Friedman, J., eds., *Modernity and Identity*. Oxford, UK: Blackwell, 1992.

IDEOLOGY   Although the term has been employed in many ways, one common usage is to refer to a set of social, political, and moral values, attitudes, outlooks, and beliefs that shape a social group's interpretation of its behavior and its world. Following a usage established by Karl Marx (1818-1883), to label an outlook as ideological typically is to criticize it for obscuring or distorting the truth. Hence, ideologies must be unmasked or disclosed as Dorothy Smith (1990, pp. 42-43) explains: "Ideological practices ensure that the determinations of our everyday, experienced world remain mysterious by preventing us from making them problems for inquiry." She urges social inquirers to think ideologically, by which she means "to think in situationally determined modes since ideology deprives us of access to, hence critique of, the social relational substructure of our experience."

Key References

Burbules, N. C., "Forms of Ideology-Critique: A Pedagogical Perspective," in P. L. McLaren & J. M. Giarelli, eds., *Critical Theory and Educational Research*. Albany: State University of New York Press, 1995.

Smith, D., *The Conceptual Practices of Power*. Boston: Northeastern University Press, 1990.

Thompson, J. B., *Studies in the Theory of Ideology*. Cambridge, MA: Polity, 1984.

IDIOGRAPHIC INTERPRETATION   The German philosopher Wilhelm Windelband (1848-1915) developed the notion that the human or historical sciences aimed at idiographic explanation—a concern with particular instances or sociohistorically situated individual events—whereas the natural sciences were concerned with nomothetic (*lawlike*) explanation—the study of individual events for the purpose of forming general laws. The production of idiographic knowledge served the aims (values and interests) of human self-understanding and self-affirmation, whereas the pursuit of nomothetic knowledge served the aim of the mastery of nature. Windelband argued that any event could be studied either way (in other words, he did not posit a fundamental difference in the phenomena of the natural and human sciences), but that what distinguished human science was its concern with the method of idiographic interpretation.

This distinction between the individualizing approach of the human sciences and the generalizing approach of the natural sciences is preserved in the methodological traditions of biography, ethnography, and case study. Robert Stake's argument for the importance of what he calls "intrinsic case study"—studying a case because the case is of primary interest—is a current restatement of this idea.

Key References

Polkinghorne, D., *Methodology for the Human Sciences*. Albany: State University of New York Press, 1983.

Stake, R., *The Art of Case Study Research*. Thousand Oaks, CA: Sage, 1995.

INDEXICALITY   This is a central notion in *ethnomethodology;* many versions of qualitative inquiry, however, assume that language and action are indexical, which means that the meaning of language or action is dependent on the context in which it arises. The notion of indexical meanings or expressions challenges the idea that interpretive inquirers merely re-present what they hear and see—that is, simply observe and record speech and action. If meanings of speech and action are indexical, then interpreters must somehow come to understand and eventually portray the context in which meanings are situated. This notion of indexicality is apparent in Clifford Geertz's claim that the ethnographer's task is to "inscribe" (write down) social discourse, but that what he or she writes down is not the event of speaking itself (i.e., the language and actions that comprise the discourse) but the "said" of speaking—the meaning of the event and not the event as event. Writing about that context, about situated use, or about what Geertz refers to as the thought, gist, or content of speaking and acting is an act of interpretation and not mere representation. **See also CONTEXTUALISM, DESCRIPTION, INSCRIPTION, LANGUAGE, LANGUAGE GAMES, REPRESENTATION.**

Key References

Garfinkel, H., *Studies in Ethnomethodology*. Englewood Cliffs, NJ: Prentice Hall, 1967.

Geertz, C., "Thick Description: Toward and Interpretive Theory of Culture," in C. Geertz, ed., *The Interpretation of Cultures*. New York: Basic Books, 1973.

Heritage, J. C., *Garfinkel and Ethnomethodology*. Cambridge, MA: Polity, 1984.

INDUCTIVE ANALYSIS It is commonly said that qualitative studies are distinguishable by their commitment to inductive analysis, which usually is defined as working from the data of specific cases to a more general conclusion. This understanding of inductive analysis, however, is by no means unique to qualitative work—much of probability theory and statistics is part of this logic of induction. There is something of a half-truth in the claim that qualitative studies are inductive. Qualitative analysis often does indeed begin with the data of specific cases, but that simply means that its efforts at analysis are grounded in data and not speculative or abstract. Qualitative analysis often (but not always) seeks to construct hypotheses by mucking around for ideas and hunches in the data rather than by deriving those hypotheses in the first instance from established theory. Typically, however, qualitative analyses employ some combination of inductive and deductive analyses. The claim that qualitative studies are inductive may actually be a way of saying that they reject the *hypothetico-deductive method* of the natural sciences. **See also EXPLANATION, INFERENCE.**

Key Reference

Strauss, A., *Qualitative Analysis for Social Scientists.* Cambridge, UK: Cambridge University Press, 1987.

INDUCTIVE-STATISTICAL EXPLANATION See **EXPLANATION.**

INFERENCE To make an inference is to draw a conclusion from particular premises. Three kinds of rules or procedures for making inferences are deductive, inductive, and abductive. In *deduction*, the conclusion must follow from the premises (in other words, it is logically impossible for the conclusion to be false if the premises are true). A common principle of deductive inference (or a legitimate deductive argument) employed in social science is modus tollens, which takes the following form:

Modus Tollens	
Premise 1:	If p then q
Premise 2:	Not q
Inference:	Therefore, not p.

Inductive inferences (and arguments) are more typical in social scientific inquiry. One kind of inductive inference relies on the principle of enumeration to reach a general conclusion about a group or class of individuals or events from observations of a specific set of individuals or events. The inference-making process is as follows: I have observed a suitable number of *A*s in a reasonably wide variety of circumstances and have seen that they are *B*s; hence, I infer that *all A*s are *B*s. In other words, I generalize the conclusion derived from my sample of *A*s to all *A*s. (Of course, the potential threat to the integrity of the inference here is how to determine what constitutes a suitable number of observations and a reasonably wide variety of circumstances.) A second kind of inductive inference is a statistical argument that also depends on the principle of enumeration but in which the conclusion is stated in probabilistic terms such as "most," "many," "rarely," and "some," rather than "all" or "always."

An *abductive* inference (or abductive reasoning) is also called an inference to the best explanation. Imagine that you are examining a set of evidence and have devised a number of possible hypotheses that might explain the evidence. Inference to the best explanation is selecting that one hypothesis that provides the best explanation of the available evidence. The kind of inference making that takes place here assumes that inquiry is a kind of puzzle that requires speculation and best guesses. Abductive inference is explained by C. S. Peirce (1839-1914), but it also bears some similarity to Karl Popper's (1902-1994) conception of science as a process of conjectures and refutations. **See also GENERALIZATION, VALIDITY.**

Key Reference

Polkinghorne, D., *Methodology for the Human Sciences*. Albany: State University of New York Press, 1983.

INFORMANT   This is one of several terms—including participant, subject, actor, respondent, collaborator, interviewee, and the observed—used to identify the individuals that a researcher studies. Each term at least implies a different kind of ethical, political, and pedagogical relationship between the researcher and those he or she studies. Anthropological and sociological field-workers often make use of informants. Informants are knowledgeable insiders and assist the field-worker in gaining and maintaining access, developing an insider's understanding (or learning the actor's point of view), and checking emerging understandings. They act as a *fieldwork* assistant, debriefer, and guide and often provide the field-worker with information on what he or she cannot experience.

A researcher-informant relationship reflects the assumption that the field-worker is in a position of learning about a culture or group, and the informant serves as a special kind of teacher, guide, and facilitator. This relationship and role is often cultivated by the field-worker; an informant is identified, selected, and trained to the role. Informants often become the confidant and trusted adviser of the field-worker, developing a special bond of trust. Whereas rapport characterizes the field-worker's relationship with most participants in a given study, friendship is more likely with informants.

The increasing interest in the politics of fieldwork and the purpose of studying others' ways of life is causing reexamination of the forms of the researcher-researched relationship in several ways. First, although not denying that participants in a particular social setting have their own special perspectives on the action in that setting, postmodern ethnographers are questioning whether the idea of informant is not yet another way to objectify the Other or to use the Other as an extension of the imperialist gaze of the ethnographer. Second, advocates of participatory approaches to research aim to recast all parties to a study as coparticipants rather than classify them as respondents, informants, researchers, and so on. This is more than a semantic distinction; it signals a democratic impulse underlying the inquiry and a different goal of the inquiry process. Third, some feminist researchers, particularly those committed to action research and participatory inquiry, argue for identification with those one studies and putting the researcher "on the same plane" as the respondent.

Key References

Dean, J. P., Eichorn, R. L., & Dean, L. R., "Fruitful Informants for Intensive Interviewing," in *An Introduction to Social Research*, 2nd ed., J. T. Doby, ed. New York: Appleton-Century-Crofts, 1967.

Wolcott, H., *The Art of Fieldwork*. Walnut Creek, CA: Altamira, 1995.

INSCRIPTION   Literally, this term means to "write down," but its connotations in contemporary fieldwork are more profound and suggest that writing down what one sees and hears is not so simple or innocent an act. Clifford Geertz was among the first to challenge the idea that a field-worker merely observes and records. He argued that the correct answer to the question "What does the ethnographer do?" is "He or she writes." *Postmodern ethnography,* however, challenges the centrality of inscription as the origin of realistic description in fieldwork. Inscription signals that writing down (and this includes photographing, videotaping, or audiotaping) is far from mere mechanical recording. The act of writing requires prior focus, selection, and interpretation. Furthermore, inscription signals an interruption in the field-worker's attention to the flow of social discourse (speech and action). The field-worker as participant observer turns away from that discourse to make a note (mental or written, long fieldnote or scratch note). Hence, inscription is not some orderly process of data 'gathering' but an act of selective attention—a particular kind of practice whereby data are generated, undertaken in the midst of other activity. **See also DESCRIPTION, FIELDNOTES, REPRESENTATION, THICK DESCRIPTION, TRANSCRIPTION.**

Key Reference

Clifford, J., "Notes on (Field)Notes," in R. Sanjek, ed., *Fieldnotes: The Makings of Anthropology.* Ithaca, NY: Cornell University Press, 1990.

INSIDER/OUTSIDER PERSPECTIVE   This is one way of thinking about the difference in the *epistemology* of *interpretivism* versus *naturalism* or the difference between *understanding* and *explanation.* An internalist or insider perspective holds that knowledge of the social world must start from the insider or social actor's account of what social life means. To know the world of human *action* is to understand the subjective meanings of that action to the actors. In contrast, an externalist or outsider perspective argues that knowledge of the social world consists in causal explanations of human behavior. The social world (much like the natural world) can (and should) be viewed with a spectator's detachment.

In fact, the externalist argues that this kind of outside objective stance is necessary to develop explanations (much like the explanations fashioned in the natural sciences) that are grounded in either empirical regularities or underlying causes, mechanisms, and necessities (scientific *realism*). **See also INTENTIONALISM.**

Key Reference

Smith, J. K., *The Nature of Social and Educational Inquiry: Empiricism Versus Interpretation.* Norwood, NJ: Ablex, 1989.

INSTRUMENTALISM   At least three senses of this term are found in the literature on the foundations of qualitative inquiry. First, in the philosophy of science, instrumentalism is an antirealist view of theories and theoretical terms. The *logical positivists* were instrumentalists (and, not, as is often claimed, realists). They regarded theories and concepts as nothing more than tools, devices, or instruments allowing scientists to move from a set of observation statements to another set of predicted observations. In this sense, logical positivists privileged observation statements over theoretical terms or reduced the latter to the former. Second, a critique of instrumentalism or instrumental rationality as a defining interest of the empirical-analytic sciences figures prominently in the work of critical theorists, postmodernists, poststructuralists, feminists, and contemporary writers on philosophical hermeneutics. Here, the term means something like means-end thinking and is associated with *scientism* and technicism. The argument is that empirical-analytic sciences serve an interest in the prediction and instrumental control of nature. When this interest is extended to the social or human sciences, it results in the manipulation of social relations, the attempt to transform what are essentially moral-political matters into technical problems to be solved, the support of dominant political and social classes and their agendas, and the impoverishment of democratic political discussion. Third, in the pragmatic epistemology of John Dewey, instrumentalism signifies that the truth (warranted assertability) of all concepts and actions resides in the extent to which they function successfully to direct, integrate, and control our interactions with the social and natural world. **See also PRAGMATISM.**

Key References

Fay, B., *Social Theory and Political Practice*. London: Allen & Unwin, 1975.

Thayer, H. S., *Meaning and Action: A Critical History of Pragmatism*, 2nd ed. Indianapolis, IN: Hackett, 1981.

INTENTIONALISM   All qualitative inquiry at least implicitly assumes that human action is intentional—that is, it reflects the motives, beliefs, attitudes, desires, and so on of actors. Intentionalism is the name for the doctrine that claims that understanding the meaning of human action requires understanding intentions. Moreover, the doctrine assumes that meaning is a kind of fixed entity or object independent of the inquirer that *resides or is located within* action and is discoverable (hence, the doctrine is often called meaning realism). To understand intentions, the inquirer has two related options. The first is to discover the intentions of the actor by getting inside the actor's head, so to speak, to discern motives, beliefs, attitudes, and so on. The second is to attempt to discover the intention in the act by locating it within some network of actions, language, or practices that give the act its meaning. Intentionalism is one version of *antinaturalism*, but its view of meaning is radically at odds with the conception of meaning in *philosophical hermeneutics*. **See also ACTION, EXPLANATION, INTERPRETIVISM, MEANING.**

Key References

Fay, B., *Contemporary Philosophy of Social Science*. Oxford, UK: Blackwell, 1996.

Roth, P. A., *Meaning and Method in the Social Sciences: A Case for Methodological Pluralism*. Ithaca, NY: Cornell University Press, 1987.

INTENTIONALITY   This notion originated in scholastic philosophy but came to prominence in the work of the nineteenth-century German philosopher Franz Brentano (1838-1917). It is a central principle of all phenomenological approaches to human inquiry, and its meaning derives from the Latin root *intendo* (to aim at or to extend toward); thus, it does not refer to intentions in the ordinary sense of doing something on purpose. The doctrine is also spoken of as engagement with the world and claims that our consciousness or mental states are always 'about' something. It stands in sharp contrast to a Cartesian conception of human agency, which holds that the individual mind, consciousness, or being (human existence) faces a pregiven world on which it 'operates.' The agent or knowing subject is distinct from the object to be known. Individual consciousness takes on a project of theoretical contemplation of this pregiven world.

Intentionality is the view that individual consciousness or individual historical being is already 'there' before individual awareness of same. In other words, consciousness or being is part of the pregiven *life-world*—consciousness or being is already engaged (i.e., historical, temporal, and social). Thus, intentionality stresses the fundamental interaction of mind and world, subject and object. Although we can distinguish subject from object, intentionality means that our experiences of the natural and social world are not a separate sphere of subjective reality that stands in contrast to the sphere of objective reality of the world 'out there.' 'Being' and experience are already in the world; subject and object are always united.

Intentionality calls our attention to the fact that as humans we are in the first instance (i.e., fundamentally and essentially) beings who are engaged with the world. We are related to the world we experience and live in through structures of meaning and significance. This way of understanding our being or agency as humans stands in sharp contrast to the everyday and scientific assumption that we can experience and engage in the social and natural worlds 'in themselves.' This kind of objectifying stance of disengagement, this view of our agency as subjects standing over and against the world we experience, is secondary or derivative. We are first and foremost engaged beings, hence the expression being-in-the-world. Scholars in the phenomenological tradition (including Merleau-Ponty, Husserl, Heidegger, Gadamer, and Taylor) argue in various ways that the modern ascendance of the objectifying stance of science (*scientism*) has led to our losing sight of the way in which we as humans are fundamentally engaged with the world, and this in turn has led us to feel alienated from both self and world. **See also BODY, PHILOSOPHICAL HERMENEUTICS, SUBJECT-OBJECT RELATIONSHIP.**

Key References

Cooper, D., "Modern European Philosophy," in N. Bunnin & E. P. Tsui-James, eds., *The Blackwell Companion to Philosophy*. Oxford, UK: Blackwell, 1996.

Crotty, M., *The Foundations of Social Research*. London: Sage, 1998.

Taylor, C., *Philosophical Arguments*. Cambridge, MA: Harvard University Press, 1995.

INTEREST   This notion plays an important role in Habermas's critical theory of society. To Habermas, interests are not individual preferences but cognitive or knowledge-constitutive ideas, which means that they determine what counts as knowledge. These interests are also defined as basic or fundamental, meaning they are not just part of an *epistemology* or way of knowing the world but also rooted in human nature or particular aspects of social life. Habermas described three primary cognitive interests—technical, practical, and emancipatory—and identified each with a different form of social science. The *technical* interest requires the isolation of objects and events to examine them empirically and form theoretical explanations of them. The empirical-analytic disciplines are informed by this technical interest and by a conception of social life as purposive-rational or instrumental action (or simply "work," i.e., the ways in which we manipulate and control our world to survive and thrive in it). *Nomological* knowledge is essential to this conception. The *practical* interest is concerned with developing intersubjective understanding and agreement on values, meanings, and practices. The historical-hermeneutic disciplines are guided by this interest and by the assumption that human life is characterized by interaction or communicative action through which we establish consensual norms for behavior and mutual understanding of intentions and obligations. The *emancipatory* interest is an effort to provide an account of the genesis of meanings, values, and practices and how they are reflections of changing social structures. Critically oriented social sciences are grounded in this interest and in the assumption that reflection about interests is central to social life. Reflection requires free, open communication and the material conditions that permit this kind of communication to determine how our meanings, practices, and values may be ideologically frozen or distorted. Habermas regarded the emancipatory interest as the most basic interest. **See also CRITICAL SOCIAL SCIENCE, THEORY.**

Key Reference

Habermas, J., *Knowledge and Human Interests*. J. J. Shapiro, trans. Boston: Beacon, 1971.

INTERPRETATION   This is the act of clarifying, explicating, or explaining the meaning of some phenomenon. The claims of both the natural and the human or social sciences are interpretations in this sense. The terms *interpretivism,* interpretive (or interpretative) social science, and the *interpretive turn,* however, carry a somewhat narrower or more specific meaning. These terms all signal a fundamental difference between the two sciences: The natural sciences explain the behavior of natural phenomena in terms of causes, and the human sciences interpret or understand the meaning of social *action.* In these terms, the notion of interpretation refers to ways of conceiving of the aim and method of the human sciences as informed by the traditions of *hermeneutics* and **Verstehende** *sociology.*

Key Reference

Rabinow, P., & Sullivan, W. M., eds., *Interpretive Social Science: A Second Look.* Berkeley: University of California Press, 1987.

INTERPRETIVE ANTHROPOLOGY   This term describes many developments in concepts of culture and the method of ethnography that transpired in the late 1960s and early 1970s in anthropology. Interpretive anthropologists understand culture not in terms of social structures and behaviors but in terms of meanings, symbols, and ideas. They view ethnography as a method whereby culture can be read and interpreted as *text* and its meaning(s) inscribed in the accounts prepared by the ethnographer.

Key References

Geertz, C., *The Interpretation of Cultures.* New York: Basic Books, 1973.

Geertz, C., *Local Knowledge: Further Essays in Interpretive Anthropology.* New York: Basic Books, 1983.

Marcus, G. E., & Fischer, M., *Anthropology as Cultural Critique*. Chicago: University of Chicago Press, 1986.

INTERPRETIVE TURN   This is a term designating a widespread interest in the epistemological, political, and moral aspects of the nature, origin, and justification of interpretations across a wide variety of disciplines, including philosophy, literary criticism, cultural anthropology, jurisprudence, and sociology. It also includes the study of interpretations as an activity in the natural sciences.

Key References

Hiley, D. R., Bohman, J. F., & Shusterman, R., eds., *The Interpretive Turn: Philosophy, Science, Culture*. Ithaca, NY: Cornell University Press, 1991.

Mitchell, W. J. T., ed., *The Politics of Interpretation*. Chicago: University of Chicago Press, 1982.

INTERPRETIVISM (or the interpretivist tradition)   This term is occasionally used as a synonym for all qualitative inquiry, blurring important distinctions in intellectual traditions. More accurately, the term denotes those approaches to studying social life that accord a central place to *verstehen* as a method of the human sciences, that assume that the meaning of human action is inherent in that action, and that the task of the inquirer is to unearth that meaning. **See also ETHNOGRAPHIC NATURALISM, INTENTIONALISM, MEANING, NATURALISTIC INQUIRY, *VERSTEHENDE* SOCIOLOGY.**

Key Reference

Giddens, A., *New Rules of Sociological Method*, 2nd ed. Stanford, CA: Stanford University Press, 1993.

INTERSUBJECTIVITY   Literally, this means occurring between or among (or accessible to) two or more separate subjects or conscious minds. Thus, intersubjective criticism and agreement are regarded as one means of establishing the *objectivity* of a claim.

For many qualitative inquirers, the term signals both the character or nature of the *life-world* and social constitution of the self. The everyday world is made up of our individual interpretations of experience, behavior, action, meaning, and so forth. These interpretations, however, are not simply subjective (i.e., the perspectives of individual subjects), and we could not understand shared or common interpretations by somehow summing up or averaging the interpretations of all subjects. Our interpretive schemes, our ways of making meaning of experience, are essentially intersubjective, socially constituted through symbolic interaction. Hence, intersubjectivity lies at heart of subjectivity.

Key References

Mead, G. H., *Selected Writings*, A. J. Reck, ed. New York: Bobbs-Merrill, 1964.

Taylor, C., "Interpretation and the Sciences of Man," in C. Taylor, ed., *Philosophy and the Human Sciences, Philosophical Papers 2*. Cambridge, UK: Cambridge University Press, 1985. (Originally published in *Review of Metaphysics*, 1971, 25, 3-51)

INTERTEXTUALITY   See TEXT.

INTERVIEWING   There are at least three (interrelated) ways to examine the practice of interviewing within qualitative studies. First, interviewing can be examined as a set of techniques for generating and analyzing data from structured, group, and semi- and unstructured interviews with respondents, participants, or *informants*. Concerns include the logistics and mechanics of arranging and conducting interviews, the costs and benefits of various interview strategies, and the methods of analyzing textual data. Generally, qualitative studies make greatest use of unstructured, open-ended, informal interviews because these allow the most flexibility and responsiveness to emerging issues for both respondents and interviewees. The use of structured open- (and closed-) ended interviews, however, is not uncommon in field studies in which time is limited or where it is desirable to obtain some specific or focused information from a large number of people or both. Different research interests and approaches influence the means chosen to analyze transcripts of interviews (compare, for example, the painstaking transcription and fine-grained analysis performed by conversational analysts to the semantic and thematic analysis often undertaken in ethnographic interviews). Second, interviewing can also be studied as a particular kind of person-to-person encounter between researcher and researched that entails ethical considerations involving the researcher's role, the consequences of the use of information, confidentiality, anonymity, and so on. Feminist interview research, for example, explores the consequences of close versus distant relations with interviewees, hierarchical researcher-respondent relationships, believing and being trusted, advocacy, and self-disclosure that are attendant on the particular circumstances in which open-ended, in-depth interviews are used. Third, interviewing can also be examined from the perspective of what one is doing when interviewing. Here, there are two primary perspectives. The first, and perhaps most common, is to regard interviews as a means of gaining direct access to an interviewee's experience. In this perspective, the interview is a behavioral event; it is spoken of as verbal behavior, a verbal exchange, or pattern of verbal interaction. Using the logic of stimulus-response (question and answer), the interviewer aims to ask the right questions so as to elicit responses in the form of authentic feelings and meanings of the interviewee. The interview situation is isolated from cultural and situational norms and frameworks of meaning. The second perspective views interviews as a particular kind of discursive, narrative, or linguistic event unfolding in a specific sociopolitical context. In this event, the meanings of questions and responses are contextually grounded and jointly constructed by interviewer and respondent. What transpires in this view of interviewing is the active joint construction of plausible stories or accounts of social life. **See also BIOGRAPHY, TRANSCRIPTION.**

Key References

Holstein, J. A., & Gubrium, J. F., *The Active Interview*. Thousand Oaks, CA: Sage, 1995.

Kvale, S., *InterViews: An Introduction to Qualitative Research Interviewing*. Thousand Oaks, CA: Sage, 1996.

Mishler, E., *Research Interviewing: Context and Narrative*. Cambridge, MA: Harvard University Press, 1986.

Reinharz, S., *Feminist Methods in Social Research*. Oxford, UK: Oxford University Press, 1992.

JUDGMENT   A judgment is a considered, deliberate opinion based on good reasons. As a means of reaching a decision or resolving disagreements, judgment is often contrasted with algorithmic, technical, rule-bound, or procedural decision making. Judgment is also distinguished from the expression of mere opinion or taste. Judgment requires an ability to unite general principles, standing commitments, and established conventions or rules with the specifics of the situation at hand. Knowing how to make good judgments is essential in every aspect of being an researcher.

A common mistake in the education of inquirers is that of confusing the development of methodological prowess in the form of knowledge of procedures and technique with the acquisition of the ability to make good judgments. Two examples should suffice to make the point: A researcher can be adept at procedures for the statistical design and analysis of quasi-experiments, but no amount of procedural knowledge will help that researcher determine which rival hypotheses are most important to consider in a given research situation and what is the best way to rule them out. Likewise, a field-worker can have a thorough grasp of all the principles involved in conducting a "good" interview—including design of the interview, knowledge of appropriate interviewer behaviors, and knowledge of the ethical principles of informed consent, confidentiality, and protecting the rights of informants—but be incapable of offering good reasons for a sound judgment in response to the question, "How will you approach the interview with Bob on Monday?" **See also** *PHRONESIS*.

Key References

Barber, B., *The Conquest of Politics.* Princeton, NJ: Princeton University Press, 1988.

Bernstein, R. J., *Beyond Objectivism and Relativism: Science, Hermeneutics, and Praxis.* Philadelphia: University of Pennsylvania Press, 1983.

Larmore, C. E., *Patterns of Moral Complexity.* Cambridge, UK: Cambridge University Press, 1987.

JUSTIFICATION OF A CLAIM   See EVIDENCE.

J

KNOWLEDGE   One of the primary reasons that the field of qualitative inquiry is so diverse and broad is that it is a site in which metatheoretical debates about the nature of knowledge and its production are being played out. Although it is most likely that the majority of practitioners of the various kinds of qualitative inquiry do not actively entertain or engage in these debates, the issues nonetheless foreground their work. In the brouhaha that often surrounds efforts to label this view or that as postpositivist, empiricist, postmodernist, interpretivist, feminist, poststructuralist, and so forth, it is easy to lose sight of the fact that all varieties are struggling with a set of issues concerning the nature of knowledge and its justification. These issues can very roughly be captured as follows: (a) What is knowledge?—Is knowledge the search for foundations or is it about dismantling taken-for-granted foundations? Is it characterized by a quest for certainty or by acceptance of fundamental fallibility? Are knowledge, values, and politics inevitably intertwined, or should they be kept separate? (b) Who is the 'knower'—a single, solitary, disengaged critically reflective mind or an engaged, embodied, dialogical self? (c) What are we attempting to know in the human sciences—meanings, processes, accomplishments, causes, structures, or forces? (d) How do we generate knowledge—via method, intuition, reason, or sensory experience? (e) What is the scope of a claim to know—general, universal, atemporal or particular, individual,

K

and temporal? and (f) What form should knowledge take—discursive, narrative, practical, tacit, or propositional?

At one time or another in the history of our thinking about the form and function of knowledge, strong arguments have been assembled for all the possible answers to the questions listed previously. Despite these different ways of thinking, however, there is something of a working consensus in Anglo-American thought about what knowledge is. What is being played out in the arena of qualitative inquiry, at least as it is broadly defined in the second edition of the *Handbook of Qualitative Research* (N. K. Denzin & Y. S. Lincoln, eds., Sage, 2000), is a set of manifold criticisms of the following most fundamental assumptions concerning knowledge across the disciplines, as explained by Elizabeth Grosz (1993):

1. The centrality and neutrality of *method* to the production of knowledge: Methods, procedures, and techniques used to generate socially legitimate knowledge are assumed to be transparent and neutral instruments or intellectual tools that contribute to the growth of knowledge but do not constitute the object of knowledge. Any contribution or influence that these tools might have on what it is that we seek to know can be calculated and distinguished from the object of knowledge. These tools are not integral to our understanding of what knowledge is but only convenient for it; thus, they do not distort, manipulate, or constrain (in ways beyond calculation) that which we seek to know.

2. The scope and limits of knowledge are set by boundaries within and between the disciplines of the human and natural sciences: For example, psychology deals with the 'interior' of subjects and sociology with the 'exterior'; philosophy deals with the universal and history with the particular. Grosz claims that "although the boundaries are not *immutable*, enabling some cross-fertilization between disciplines, nevertheless each defines and is defined by both a mainstream or core and a periphery or margins. These margins and the *spaces between disciplines* are unable to be theorized in the terms of the core—that is, within the discipline itself" (p. 190).

3. Shared assumptions about the *criteria* according to which knowledge is judged to be valid or true: These criteria include

clarity, precision, the capacity to be verified or falsified, parsimony, communicability, and translatability. Grosz claims that "underlying these [criteria] is a belief that the object of investigation, whether a text, human behavior, or social interactions, exists independently of knowledge of it, presuming a 'reality' resistant to false or invalid methods, misinterpretation, or misrepresentation" (p. 191).

4. The presumption that knowledge is atemporal and transgeographic: Although knowledge is produced at specific times and in specific places, the genesis of knowledge is considered irrelevant to its nature; "Knowledges do not carry the index of their origins" (p. 191).

5. The presumption that genuine knowledge is neither personal or idiosyncratic: "The knowing subject who produces knowledge is, as it were, bracketed off from the knowledges thus produced" (p. 191).

See also EPISTEMOLOGY, PARADIGMATIC KNOWLEDGE CLAIM.

Key Reference

Grosz, E., "Bodies and Knowledge: Feminism and the Crisis of Reason," in L. Alcoff & E. Potter, eds., *Feminist Epistemologies*. New York: Routledge, 1993.

K

LANGUAGE Underlying virtually all contemporary versions of qualitative inquiry is the belief that language is central to conceptions of meaning and being. This belief, in turn, rests on an important distinction between two different families of language theories. One family is variously called empiricist, representational, referential, designative, descriptive, or the picture theory of language; the other family includes theories of the pragmatics of language, the 'use' theory of language, and the expressivist-constitutive theory of language.

The picture theory of language assumes that the mind contains concepts and ideas that presumably represent an external reality (the way things are). Knowledge consists of having ideas that reliably and accurately represent reality. The words in our language are given meaning by being attached to (depicting) the things being represented via our ideas that represent them. In other words, the way things are shapes the way we (perceive and) conceive them, and this, in turn, is expressed in the language we use. Thus, the meaning of words and sentences is explained by the way they depict or represent the world. In this theory, language is an instrument or tool at our disposal by which we gain objective knowledge of the world. Because the picture theory of language is primarily about how language represents the world, two kinds of concerns dominate. The first is understanding the syntactical relations of language—its logical structure; the second is defining the semantic relations of a language—the way in which words are linked with observations.

In pragmatic and expressivist-constitutive views of language, the relationship of language to world is reversed. These theories assume that our language shapes what we see and how we see it, and those things shaped by language constitute reality. [Note: One must be careful here in making sense of the notion of 'constitutes.' A radical interpretation of this notion, found in some versions of *social constructionism* and *poststructuralism,* is linguistic idealism—the thesis that there is nothing more to reality than our symbolic interpretations, or that reality is a product of our linguistic practices. A more moderate interpretation concedes that indeed there is a language-independent reality but that our awareness and understanding of that reality is mediated by interpretation and language. In other words, there is no direct, language-free cognition.] In these views, language is a range of activities in which we express and realize a certain way of making sense of and being in the world. The meaning of words and sentences cannot be simply explained by their ability to designate or depict something. Rather, the meaning of words and sentences is also explained by their relation to other words and sentences and how they are used.

Two different kinds of concerns (often, but not always, interrelated) are characteristic of this family of theories. The first is a practical interest—understanding the different ways in which words and sentences are used to accomplish something (e.g., to give an order, to tell a joke, and to make a description). This interest is readily apparent in the centrality of the notion of *indexicality* in *ethnomethodology* and *conversation analysis*. It also underlies those versions of *social constructionism* concerned with the way in which meaning is generated in language. The second is an ontological and phenomenological interest—understanding how it is that language constitutes being. Here, language is not regarded as a tool at our disposal but as itself constituting a framework in which we have purposes, behaviors, meanings, and so forth. Notions such as "we are language beings" and "language does not belong to us, we belong to language" stem from this interest. This interest in 'linguisticality' (in the idea that language constitutes being) stands in opposition to a central doctrine in modern versions of humanism that underlie empiricist epistemology, namely, the autonomous, self-actualizing, atomistic self. In this doctrine, knowledge and meaning arise within the subject, the individual knower. Human *agency* is decidedly 'monological.' In the expressivist-constitutive view, however, language is a background or framework that we belong to, not a practice we partake in, or a tool that we as individual knowing agents choose to use. Thus, human agency is engaged and 'dialogical'; we are always already participating in practices and understandings that are not located in me or in you as individuals but in the common spaces between us. The linguistic (or discursive) nature of being figures prominently, albeit in quite different ways, in the *genealogy* of Foucault, Heidegger's existential *phenomenology*, Gadamer and Taylor's *philosophical hermeneutics*, and Derrida's *deconstructionism*. See also DISCOURSE/DISCOURSE ANALYSIS, LANGUAGE GAMES, MEANING, SEMIOTICS.

Key References

Shapiro, M. J., *Language and Political Understanding: The Politics of Discursive Practices.* New Haven, CT: Yale university Press, 1981.

Taylor, C., *Philosophical Arguments.* Cambridge, MA: Harvard University Press, 1995.

LANGUAGE GAMES   This notion originates in Ludwig Wittgenstein's (1889-1951) later writings, particularly *Philosophical Investigations* (1952). Here, in an apparent rejection of his earlier views, Wittgenstein advanced the notion that words and sentences do not have meanings because they designate, refer to, or depict reality. Rather, words and sentences acquire their meanings because they are used in some rule-governed, self-contained practice like a game. As examples of language games, Wittgenstein mentioned giving orders and obeying them, describing the appearance of an object, forming and testing a hypothesis, reporting an event, and making a joke or telling a joke. Thus, the notion of language games as forms of life (combinations of intentions, motivations, speech, action, interests, etc.) was used to direct attention away from language as designation to language as activity.

The picture theory of language and its concern with what and how terms designate or represent was a principal preoccupation in Wittgenstein's earlier work and a central concern of the philosophy of logical positivism. Thus, the significance and meaning of concepts such as truth and knowledge were to be found in a logical analysis of language and in efforts to develop a theory of semantic rules linking concepts with observations. Wittgenstein's later work turns away from this concern with linking meaning of words to the syntactic and semantic properties of statements and propositions and toward an understanding of how the meaning of words arises within and is fixed by different linguistic practices.

The philosopher Peter Winch linked the notion of language games to the notion of *Verstehen* and argued that understanding the meaning of language and action is possible only if one understands the different language games or social practices in which that language and action occur. Variations on this idea of how linguistic practices shape social reality are foundational to pragmaticist, phenomenological, constructionist, hermeneutic, and poststructural theories.

For example, a radical interpretation of the notion of language games leading to the view that all meanings are relative to some particular culture, way of life, group, or social practice is found in some versions of social constructionism. This view unfolds as follows: Taking their cue from Wittgenstein's notion of language games (as elaborated by Winch), some radical social constructionists begin with the premise that language is embedded in social practices or forms of life. They then argue that different language games or different forms of life are incommensurable. In other words, the rules that govern a particular form of life circumscribe and close that form of life off to others. Hence, it is only within and with reference to a particular form of life that the meaning of words and actions can be deciphered, described, and understood. Thus, standards for rationally evaluating beliefs are completely dependent on the particular language game or form of life in which those beliefs arise. No evaluation of beliefs *across* different forms of life is possible. Hence, this is epistemological relativism.

Another radical interpretation of the notion of language games called linguistic idealism—the notion that reality is nothing but the product of linguistic convention—is drawn by some postmodernists and poststructuralists. John Patrick Diggins (*The Promise of Pragmatism: Modernism and the Crisis of Knowledge and Authority,* University of Chicago Press, 1994) provides a brief and not particularly charitable summary of this view as "the conviction that all human cognition is inescapably verbal or textual and consists of a web of unstable, dancing signifiers having no reference to a reality beyond the text; words full of sound and fury signifying not nothing but almost everything, as though the script were out of control; philosophers assuming they are looking for truth and waking up to realize they are only writing words about words, manipulating metaphors, alternating verbal images" (p. 435).

See also LANGUAGE, MEANING.

Key References

Bernstein, R. J., *The Restructuring of Social and Political Theory*. Philadelphia: University of Pennsylvania Press, 1976.

Turner, S. R., *Sociological Explanation as Translation*. Cambridge, UK: Cambridge University Press, 1980.

Winch, P., *The Idea of a Social Science and Its Relation to Philosophy*. London: Routledge Kegan Paul, 1958.

LAWLIKE GENERALIZATION   Lawlike does not mean almost a law; rather, the terms *lawlike, nomological,* or *nomothetic* are meant to distinguish generalizations that have the force of laws from those that are merely accidental. Generalizations that have lawlike force state what *must* be the case. I might claim "All the books on the bookshelf in my office are published in the United States." (A generalization because it is in the form "All *X's* are *A's.*") That may in fact be true, but its truth is accidental; the statement is not a lawlike generalization because it does not possess the quality of unrestricted necessity. **See also GENERALIZATION.**

Key Reference

Little, D., *Varieties of Social Explanation: An Introduction to the Philosophy of Social Science*. Boulder, CO: Westview, 1991.

L

LEBENSWELT   See LIFE-WORLD.

LIFE-HISTORY METHODOLOGY   See BIOGRAPHY.

LIFE-WORLD   The everyday world or the life-world (*Lebenswelt*) is the intersubjective world of human experience and social action; it is the world of commonsense knowledge of everyday life. It is constituted by the thoughts and acts of individuals and the social expressions of those thoughts and acts (e.g., laws, institutions). The life-world (and its phenomena) is regarded as the primary object for study by the human sciences. Describing what the life-world consists of—that is, the structures of experience and the principles and concepts that give form and meaning to the life-world—has been the project of *phenomenology*. Edmund Husserl (1859-1938) claimed that the life-world was the basis for meaning in every science; in all natural and social science (as well as logic and mathematics), the life-world is presupposed and pregiven. Husserl's transcendental phenomenological philosophy sought to explain the existence and meaning of the life-world. He distinguished between the "natural attitude," characteristic of our being in the life-world—our everyday relatively unproblematic involvement with people, things, and the world—and the "phenomenological attitude," the philosophical act of pure reflection in which we suspend, distance ourselves from, or bracket all the intentions, awareness, and convictions characteristic of the natural attitude. This posture Husserl called the transcendental *epoché* (*transcendental* meaning literally to get beyond or transcend the limits of ordinary experience). Husserl argued that by making the phenomenological reduction (***bracketing***)—moving back from the natural attitude to the phenomenological attitude —we are capable of recognizing the true nature and meaning of the life-world, its ultimate transcendental ground that, in Husserl's view, was the transcendental ego (a quite complex notion in Husserl's philosophy).

Building on Husserl's work, but relinquishing somewhat the attachment to phenomenological psychology and transcendental philosophy, Alfred Schutz (1899-1956) developed a descriptive phenomenology of the life-world or a *phenomenological sociology*. Schutz analyzed the concepts of subjective meaning, action, experience, intentionality, behavior, and intersubjectivity and thereby sought to develop a theory that explained the life-world. (For a brief summary and critique of some of Schutz's major ideas as they relate to defining the aim of social inquiry, see R. J.

Bernstein, *The Restructuring of Social and Political Theory*, Part 3, University of Pennsylvania Press, 1976.)

Philosophical hermeneutics is also concerned with understanding the principles and organization of the life-world but from a somewhat different perspective. Rather than portray the structures or features of the life-world, philosophical hermeneutics is concerned with understanding how we are part of or engaged with that world and how conditions of our engagement (e.g., language and the nature and structures of communication) make interpreting that world an inescapable feature of our existence. **See also ACTION, MULTIPLE REALITIES.**

Key References

Husserl, E., *The Crisis of European Sciences and Transcendental Phenomenology*. D. Carr, trans. Evanston, IL: Northwestern University Press, 1970.

Schutz, A., *The Phenomenology of the Social World*. G. Walsh & F. Lehnert, trans. Evanston, IL: Northwestern University Press, 1967.

Schutz, A., *Collected Papers*, Vol. 1. M. Natanson, trans. The Hague, The Netherlands: Martinus Nijhoff, 1967.

LITERARY TURN (IN SOCIAL SCIENCE)   This phrase refers to the increasing interest in recent decades in examining the literary or rhetorical features of the texts produced by social inquirers. It does not simply point to a form of literary criticism concerned only with tropes, narrative strategies, and other textual devices, however. Rather, it reflects the assumption that writing is central to what social inquirers do both in the field and after, and that writing about others is part of the complex process of social construction and reconstruction of reality. The literary turn introduced the idea that sociological and anthropological texts are fiction—that is, made or crafted by the inquirer—and thus shaped by rhetorical, political, institutional, and disciplinary conventions.

The examination of fieldwork texts as literature is intimately linked to the issue of *representation*. It challenges naive *ethnographic realism* and assumptions about transparency of representation and the immediacy and authenticity of field experience. Within the literary turn, the examination of written texts becomes a means of addressing questions about the methodology, epistemology, politics, authority, and ethics of the activity of social inquiry. Literary processes (e.g., metaphor, figuration, and narrative) at work in texts are explored to understand how they help constitute the inquirer-as-author and the human *action* and people he or she seeks to represent. **See also TEXT, VOICE, WRITING STRATEGIES.**

Key References

Atkinson, P., *The Ethnographic Imagination: Textual Constructions of Reality.* London: Routledge, 1990.

Geertz, C., *Works and Lives: The Anthropologist as Author.* Stanford, CA: Stanford University Press, 1988.

Hunter, A., ed., *The Rhetoric of Social Research Understood and Believed.* New Brunswick, NJ: Rutgers University Press, 1990.

LITERATURE REVIEW   See **REVIEW OF LITERATURE.**

LIVED EXPERIENCE   See **EXPERIENCE.**

LOGICAL EMPIRICISM   This mid-twentieth-century more moderate version of *logical positivism* informs contemporary mainstream thinking in the philosophy of social science. It is represented in the work of Ernest Nagel (1901-1985), Hans Reichenbach (1891-1953), Rudolph Carnap (1891-1970), Carl Hempel (1905-1997), and, to some extent, Karl Popper (1902-1994) in *The Logic of Scientific Discovery* (1958). Three ideas central to this view are (a) the *covering law model of explanation,* (b) the unity of sciences thesis, and (c) the distinction between the *context of discovery* and the *context of justification.* Logical empiricists hold that the aim of science is the development of theoretical explanations, and that legitimate explanations, in turn, take the form of general (covering) laws; events to be explained are subsumed under covering laws. The controversy regarding what constitutes a legitimate scientific explanation and whether there can be laws in social science centers around the defense and critique of this central logical empiricist idea (see, for example, the collection of papers in Part 2 of *Readings in the Philosophy of Social Science,* eds. M. M. Martin & L. C. McIntyre, eds., MIT Press, 1994). Logical empiricists also argue for the unity of the sciences, claiming that both natural and social sciences have the same aim and that there are no basic methodological differences between the two. They believe that philosophers such as Wilhelm Dilthey (1833-1911), Max Weber (1864-1920), Alfred Schutz (1899-1956), Peter Winch, and others who claimed that there was a fundamental difference between explanation and understanding as goals of the natural and social sciences, respectively, were mistaken. In their view, the idea of pursuing an understanding of the 'meaning' of human action was a residue of metaphysical thinking. Finally, logical empiricists also draw a sharp line between the process involved in creating a theory or hypothesis (context of discovery) and the process required for testing that theory or hypothesis (context of justification). This distinction along with the covering law model of explanation and the naturalism of logical empiricism are the foils for hermeneutic and phenomenological approaches to social inquiry. Despite a variety of criticisms of various features of this philosophy of science, the generalized picture of logical empiricism has become something of a vision of what the social sciences should be (see, for example, D. C. Phillips, *The Expanded Social Scientist's Bestiary*, Rowman & Littlefield, 2000). **See also NATURALISM.**

Key References

Brown, H. I., *Perception, Theory and Commitment: The New Philosophy of Science*. Chicago: University of Chicago Press, 1977.

Hempel, C., *Philosophy of Natural Science*. Englewood Cliffs, NJ: Prentice Hall, 1966.

Nagel, E., *The Structure of Science: Problems in the Logic of Scientific Explanation*. London: Routledge Kegan Paul, 1961.

Reichenbach, H., *The Rise of Scientific Philosophy*. Berkeley: University of California Press, 1951.

LOGICAL POSITIVISM   From approximately 1922 to 1940, a group composed largely of philosophers and scientists that came to be known as the Vienna Circle developed a philosophy of science they called logical positivism. This philosophy enjoyed an approximately 30-year life before the weight of criticisms of these doctrines caused its internal collapse. It developed into a more moderate philosophy called *logical empiricism*. Logical positivism is a particular species of analytic or linguistic philosophy preoccupied with scientific philosophy, that is, it aimed to solve a special set of problems arising out of the activity and claims of the natural sciences. Its method was that of the analysis of scientific language—analyzing concepts, propositions, and scientific sentences to develop a transparent linguistic framework modeled on formal logic. It sought to discover the uniform logical structure of language and thus establish the foundation for all knowledge claims about the world.

From the positivist philosophy of Auguste Comte (1798-1857) and the *empiricism* of David Hume (1711-1776), the logical positivists appropriated the idea of a strong critique of *metaphysics* and a devotion to the value of empirical observations. From the analytic philosophers Ludwig Wittgenstein (1889-1951) (*Tractatus Logico-Philosophicus*, which first appeared in 1921), Bertrand Russell (1872-1970) (*Introduction to Mathematical Philosophy*, 1919), and Alfred North Whitehead (1861-1947) (coauthor with Russell of the three-volume *Principia Mathematica*, 1910-1913), the logical positivists developed the idea of constructing a logically correct language that would readily distinguish between meaningful and meaningless scientific propositions. (Note, however, that Wittgenstein, Russell, and Whitehead were not positivists and rejected the scientistic, empiricist philosophy of the Vienna Circle.)

This philosophy rested on the central notion that there are only two legitimate forms of scientific inquiry that yield genuine knowledge: logical analysis and empirical research. Although there was not complete unanimity in the outlook of the group, generally they endorsed three central doctrines:

1. The verification theory of meaning: To be considered genuine, legitimate, and meaningful, a knowledge claim about the world must be capable of verification.

2. The doctrine of meaningful statements: Only two kinds of statements are of any value in scientific knowledge—the analytic statements of mathematics and logic that are knowable a priori and synthetic or contingent statements that are knowable a posteriori based on verification through observation. Statements that are not capable of expression in either of these forms are

not verifiable and, therefore, at best irrelevant to scientific knowledge and at worst meaningless. Hence, logical positivism was extremely hostile to theological and metaphysical speculation about the world. In fact, the logical positivists disdained the appellation 'positivists' because they believed that August Comte's philosophy of science was entirely too metaphysical.

3. A foundationalist epistemology: All justified belief ultimately rests on noninferential self-evident observations (protocol statements or observation statements).

See also POSITIVISM.

<u>Key References</u>

Ayer, A. J., ed., *Logical Positivism.* New York: Free Press, 1959.

Friedman, M., *Reconsidering Logical Positivism.* Cambridge, UK: Cambridge University Press, 1999.

LOGOCENTRISM   See **DECONSTRUCTIONISM.**

MARGINAL NATIVE   See **PARTICIPANT OBSERVATION.**

MATERIALIST EXPLANATION   See **EXPLANATION.**

MEANING   A taken-for-granted assumption in qualitative inquiry is that it studies meaningful social *action*. What does it mean, however, to say that human or social action is meaningful or has meaning? Minimally, human action is considered meaningful in the sense that it cannot be adequately described in purely physical terms. Consider, for example, witnessing the identical physical movement of raising one's right hand above one's shoulder as performed by a woman on a busy city street as she steps to the curb, by a third-grader in a classroom, and by a witness stepping to the stand in a court room. In all three instances, the same physical phenomenon is observed, but in each instance the meaning of the action is different. Moreover, the significance of the action cannot be adequately explained in terms of a behaviorist stimulus-response model. What comprises the meaning of this action (and more complicated social actions, such as teaching, bargaining, trusting, and worshipping) and how to understand that meaning is subject to a variety of different interpretations in the philosophical traditions that foreground qualitative inquiry.

The interpretivist tradition embraces two different views of what meaning is and how it is to be grasped or understood. First, the meaning of an action resides in the consciousness of the actor (her or his intentions, motivations, desires, attitudes, and beliefs) and, hence, the inquirer must use some method of psychological

153

reenactment (i.e., empathy) that facilitates tapping into the actor's own description of the action. The aim here is to understand the meaning of the action in terms of the actor's intentions. (This view of meaning is also operative in *conservative hermeneutics*, in which the aim is to understand the author's intended meaning.) Second, an action has meaning not by virtue of the actor's intention but because it is part of some larger web or system of actions. This web is variously interpreted as a system of action-guiding norms or action-constituting rules. Here, the aim is to understand the intention of the act by locating it within some comprehensive scheme of communication or of institutionalized values and norms. In both of these views as defined in the interpretivist tradition, it is assumed that the meaning of action is fixed, finished, and complete and thus, in principle, determinable or discoverable by the inquirer.

The hermeneutic tradition (which includes the different hermeneutic philosophies of Gadamer, Habermas, and Derrida) introduces a different way of conceiving of meaning and the understanding of meaning. In this tradition, meaning resides neither in the intentions of the actor nor in the act itself. Meaning is undecidable, never fixed or complete, and exists only in 'reading' an action (or text) such that meaning is always meaning for someone. In Gadamer's hermeneutics, meaning occurs in the mediation or dialogue that occurs between the action (or text) to be understood and the interpreter in the context of the tradition in which the interpreter stands. Meaning thus is created or constructed each time one seeks to understand; hence, understanding meaning is never complete. The deconstructionist hermeneutics of Derrida shares this view of the incompleteness of meaning with one very important difference. For Gadamer, interpretation (understanding meaning) is a process of dialogue and listening in which the living word of conversation is privileged. In this process, the meaning of text, speech, or action is disclosed as it 'speaks' to the interpreter situated in her or his own tradition and cultural horizon. For Derrida, interpretation (understanding meaning) is also dialogic, but the dialogue privileges the sign (the 'word,' something that stands for something else) and reveals the irreducible equivocation, the continual breakup, and continual deferral (rather than disclosure) of meaning (what the sign stands for or is a sign of). **See also HERMENEUTIC METHOD, INTENTIONAL-ISM, INTERPRETIVISM, LANGUAGE.**

Key References

Collin, F., *Social Reality*. London: Routledge, 1997.

Fay, B., *Contemporary Philosophy of Social Science*. Oxford, UK: Blackwell, 1996.

Giddens, A., *New Rules of Sociological Method*, 2nd ed. Stanford, CA: Stanford University Press, 1993.

Habermas, J., *On the Logic of the Social Sciences*. S. W. Nicholsen & J. A. Stark, trans. Cambridge: MIT Press, 1988.

Outhwaite, W., *Understanding Social Life: The Method Called Verstehen*. London: Allen & Unwin, 1975.

MEANING REALISM   See INTENTIONALISM, OBJECTIVISM.

MEMBER CHECK   Also called member or respondent validation, this is a sociological term for soliciting feedback from respondents on the inquirer's findings. It is often claimed to be an important procedure for corroborating or verifying findings or of ensuring they are valid and meet the criterion of *confirmability*. Many researchers, however, view it as a problematic notion in several respects. First, on epistemic grounds, it is not entirely clear how the procedure actually helps establish the truth of findings. Suppose, for example, that a member check yields a difference of opinion between the inquirer and respondents and that respondents disagree with some or all aspects of the inquirer's findings or interpretations or both. The inquirer must then do further checking to explore the nature of the disagreement; for example, are respondents disagreeing to protect something—do they actually accept that the findings are correct but do not wish them to be made public because the findings somehow cast respondents in a bad light or are unbalanced, slanted in favor of something negative or positive; are respondents ambivalent or unconcerned because they have not actually taken the time to inspect the findings; are respondents disagreeing because the inquirer made an error in interpretation (if so, what kind of error and how can it be remedied); and so on? Hence, rather than being some sort of simple corroboration or act of validation by respondents, member checking seems but one more opportunity to gather data about the integrity of the inquirer's findings. Second, implementing member checking may be coupled with the assumption that researcher effects must be minimized. In this view, the researcher must guard against doing anything in the field that would influence respondents or change their behaviors or opinions. This, of course, assumes that the inquirer must stand apart from the world he or she studies. Thus, in doing member checking the inquirer must somehow guard against introducing bias. Member checking, however, assumes a quite different character and meaning to the extent that the inquiry becomes a more participative and dialogical undertaking and less the monological activity of the lone field-worker doing research *on* respondents. Third, member checking may be more of an ethical act than an epistemological one. In other words, it may simply be the civil thing to do for those who have given their time and access to their lives to give them the courtesy of knowing (or to honor their right to know) what the inquirer has to say about them. The consensus seems to be that member checking is not profitably viewed as either an act of validation or refutation but is simply another way of generating data and insight. **See also TRIANGULATION, VALIDITY.**

Key References

Bloor, M., "Notes on Member Validation," in R. M. Emerson, ed., *Contemporary Field Research.* Prospect Heights, IL: Waveland, 1983.

Fielding, N. G., & Fielding, J. L., *Linking Data.* Newbury Park, CA: Sage, 1988.

MEMOING　　This analytic procedure was suggested by Barney Glaser for explaining or elaborating the coded categories that a field-worker develops in analyzing data. Memos are conceptual in intent, vary in length, and are primarily written to oneself. The content of memos can include commentary on the meaning of a coded category, an explanation of a sense of pattern developing among categories, or a *description* of some specific aspect of a setting or phenomenon. Memos capture the thoughts of the inquirer while he or she is engaged in the process of analysis. Typically, the final analysis and interpretation are based on integration and analysis of memos. **See also ANALYZING QUALITATIVE DATA.**

Key References

Glaser, B., *Theoretical Sensitivity: Advances in the Methodology of Grounded Theory*. Mill Valley, CA: Sociology Press, 1978.

Miles, M., & Huberman, A. M., *Qualitative Data Analysis*, 2nd ed. Thousand Oaks, CA: Sage, 1994.

Strauss, A., *Qualitative Analysis for Social Scientists*. Cambridge, UK: Cambridge University Press, 1987.

METAETHNOGRAPHY   This is a term coined by George Noblit and R. Dwight Hare for the process of creating new interpretations from the synthesis of multiple field studies. Although this idea is something of a qualitative analog to the notion of statistical meta-analysis, the authors emphasize that metaethnographic inquiry is interpretive and not aggregative or analytical. They describe three strategies for analysis: reciprocal translation of one study into the terms of another; refutational synthesis—opposing the claims of two or more studies; and lines-of-argument synthesis in which the interpreter engages in something like grounded theorizing combining parts of various studies into an integrated whole. **See also CROSS-CASE ANALYSIS, REVIEW OF LITERATURE.**

Key Reference

Noblit, G., & Hare, R. D., *Meta-Ethnography: Synthesizing Qualitative Studies*. Newbury Park, CA: Sage, 1988.

METANARRATIVE   See **GRAND NARRATIVE.**

METAPHYSICS   This is the study of reality, of being, of the real nature of whatever is, and of first principles. Sometimes called ontology (although some philosophers define ontology as a branch of metaphysics), it is concerned with understanding the kinds of things that constitute the world. For example, Platonism is a theory of metaphysical dualism: There is the world of matter—appearances, everyday life, and the senses—and the world of mind—true realities and the objects of the intellect. Cartesian metaphysics posits a somewhat different mind-body dualism: Human beings are composed of the mental and the material. Much contemporary psychology assumes a metaphysical distinction between an inner mental life and outer physical behavior, although Descartes (1596-1650) never proposed the distinction in this way. *Idealism* is a metaphysics as well. One version of idealism holds that nothing exists but minds and their content, the experience of minds. Another version acknowledges that there are material things in the world as well as minds but seeks to reduce matter to mind by arguing that the universe is constituted by mind. Martin Heidegger's (1889-1976) metaphysics, central to the work of Hans-Georg Gadamer and *philosophical hermeneutics*, is aimed at understanding *Dasein* or human-being-in-the world. Edmund Husserl's (1859-1938) *phenomenology*, a metaphysics concerned with the essential structures of conscious experience, strongly influenced Alfred Schutz (1899-1956), whose work in turn provides the philosophical basis for *phenomenological sociology* and *ethnomethodology*. The logical positivists were openly hostile to metaphysics—to any philosophical claims about reality, truth, or being. They argued that metaphysical statements were incapable of being judged as true or false and thus of no consequence for increasing scientific knowledge of the world. Thus, it is not incorrect to say that contemporary postpositivistic philosophy of human and social sciences is marked by a return of the metaphysical, if by that phrase we mean a renewed concern with the nature, constitution, and structure of being and social reality and how knowledge of same plays a role in our claims to know social reality.

Key Reference

Blackburn, S., "Metaphysics," in N. Bunnin & E. P. Tsui-James, eds., *The Blackwell Companion to Philosophy*. Oxford, UK: Blackwell, 1996.

METHOD   This term encompasses many different connotations that are relevant to the practice of qualitative inquiry:

1. In the everyday, ordinary usage of the term in qualitative studies (and social inquiry more generally), method denotes a procedure, tool, or technique used by the inquirer to generate and

analyze data. Typically, three classes or types of tools are used to generate qualitative data: *interviewing* (listening, talking, conversing, and recording), *observation* (watching and video-taping), and *document analysis* (reading and photographing). Tools for analyzing qualitative data are equally varied and include displays, taxonomies, typologies, constant comparison, enumeration, analytic induction, content analysis, and univariate and bivariate statistical analyses. This cornucopia of methods available to qualitative inquirers does not simply point to eclecticism of method. Rather, it signals the fact that qualitative inquiry is not defined by a preoccupation with a particular method: There is no one method or set of methods that if adopted render a particular inquiry as precisely *qualitative.*

2. Method is also conventionally understood in purely instrumental terms. In other words, as a tool, method contributes to the generation and growth of *knowledge* but is itself transparent or neutral, or at least the effects of a method on the object of understanding are determinable and controllable. In the conventional understanding of method, the question "How does this method *constitute* its object?" is considered irrelevant. This feature of method is the subject of considerable criticism in feminist and critical theory approaches to social understanding.

3. It is often said that qualitative inquiry eschews the use of the scientific method, but just what that claim means is not always clear. In the philosophy of science, it is generally acknowledged that there is no operational definition of what is commonly called scientific method. Rather, this term signals a broad approach to or logic of inquiry (also called the *hypothetico-deductive method*) that includes the identification and clarification of problems, the formulation of tentative solutions, the practical or theoretical testing of these solutions, and the elimination of those solutions deemed not successful in solving the problem. Precisely how these activities are conducted varies widely given different research designs, research questions, tools, and so forth. There are many qualitative studies that follow this logic; there are others that object to the underlying assumptions of this logic, most notably the assumption that the logic is applicable to understanding social *action.*

4. A modern, Cartesian, or Enlightenment conception of method also assumes a subject-object dichotomy. It begins from the belief that we should separate the mind (the subject, knower, and consciousness) from the thing (that which is to be known, the object of consciousness). In this way of thinking, the function of method is to bracket *bias* or *prejudice* and keep the object of understanding at arm's length, where it can be observed safely with disinterest and lack of involvement. Thus, it is not the subjectivity of the inquirer that produces knowledge but the method. Defenders of this idea argue that it is precisely because method functions in this way that we are able to acquire an objective, rational *explanation* of the way the world really is (i.e., the truth about the world) free of the predilections, eccentricities, prejudices, and characteristics of age, social location, race, class, gender, and ethnicity that define the inquirer. In other words, genuine, legitimate knowledge is limited to methodically self-conscious knowledge. This understanding of method is alive and well in some versions of *Verstehende sociology* and *phenomenological sociology.*

5. A variety of criticisms are aimed at undermining or overthrowing the central place that method occupies in a modern or Cartesian conception of what constitutes knowledge in human affairs. For example, defenders of *philosophical hermeneutics* model knowledge and understanding on practical reason, dialogue, and interpretation as fundamental activities of being human. They challenge the idea that understanding our social world is to be determined by method, and that knowledge is the product of methodical consciousness. Likewise, many feminist epistemologies challenge the idea of method as requiring disengaged, detached objectivity. Postmodernists offer a more radical critique. Because, as Lyotard once noted, *postmodernism* sets out to change the meaning of the word knowledge, and it challenges the very idea of an inquirer as knowing subject, postmodernist approaches generally reject all claims that methods (or inquirers) produce knowledge. A postmodernist inquirer may employ a 'strategy' such as deconstruction but never a method. These strategies are used to further the paradox of multiple meanings and to play with an infinite variety of

M

interpretations. **See also HERMENEUTIC METHOD, KNOWL-EDGE, METHODOLOGY, MIXED METHODS.**

Key References

Kaplan, A., *The Conduct of Inquiry*. New York: Harper & Row, 1964.

Phillips, D. C., *The Expanded Social Scientists Bestiary*. Lanham, MD: Rowman & Littlefield, 2000.

Tuana, N., ed., *Feminism & Science*. Bloomington: Indiana University Press, 1989.

METHODOLOGY   This is a theory of how inquiry should proceed. It involves analysis of the assumptions, principles, and procedures in a particular approach to inquiry (that, in turn, governs the use of particular methods). Methodologies explicate and define the kinds of problems that are worth investigating; what comprises a researchable problem, testable hypothesis, and so on; how to frame a problem in such a way that it can be investigated using particular designs and procedures; how to understand what constitutes a legitimate and warranted explanation; how to judge matters of generalizability; how to select and develop appropriate means of generating data; and how to develop the logic linking problem-data generation-analysis-argument.

A methodology is a particular social scientific discourse (a way of acting, thinking, and speaking) that occupies a middle ground between discussions of method and discussions of issues in the philosophy of social science. This two-way relationship is displayed in Figure M.1. There is no direct, unbroken, logically necessary link between various positions on issues in the philosophy of social science, methodologies, and methods. For example, two researchers could each be committed to scientific realism and to the notion of disinterested social science but employ different methodologies (e.g., participant observation and quasi-experimentation). Likewise, a single methodology (e.g., life-history methodology or participant observation methodology) can be quite differently defined in interpretive ethnography, symbolic interactionism, critical social science, cultural studies, postmodern ethnography, and feminist inquiry, depending on a researcher's perspectives on critical issues in philosophy of social science (e.g., the nature of knowledge generated via that methodology, the meaning of 'experience' and 'subjectivity,' the meaning of 'culture,' the relationship of descriptive and normative concerns of social science, and the ethical obligations of the inquirer).

ISSUES IN THE PHILOSOPHY OF SOCIAL SCIENCE

E.g., causation, explanation, historicism, nomologicalism, subject-object relation, fact-value distinction, intentionalism, structure vs. agency, the nature of meaning, relation of self-other, value-neutrality, scientific realism, justification, theory of language.

↑↓

METHODOLOGIES

E.g., quasi-experimental/experimental methodology, survey resarch methodology, participant observation methodology, naturalistic inquiry, symbolic interactionism, ethnomethodology

↑↓

METHODS

E.g., procedures for generating qualitative and quantitative data—structured and unstructured interviews, structured and unstructured observations, types of document analysis, psychometric and sociometric measures; procedures for analyzing data of various kinds—descriptive and inferential statistics, constant comparison method, coding, analytic induction, conversational analysis, narrative analysis

---

Figure M.1. Interrelationships of Methods, Methodologies, and Issues in the Philosophy of Social Science

Methods and methodology display a synergetic relationship: A particular method (or set of methods) is employed (and given meaning) within a methodology that defines the object of study and determines what comprises an adequate reconstruction of that object. This relationship is illustrated in Table M.1, which reveals how various kinds of qualitative data (textual data, transcripts, observations, etc.) are generated in different ways and ac-

M

Table M.1   Illustration of Relationships Between Methodologies
and Methods in Qualitative Inquiry

Methodology	Methods of Generating Qualitative Data	Object of Understanding and Theorizing Reconstructed by Method
Social phenomenological	Registering methods (e.g., audiotape- and video-transcribed documents); methods of contextual description	The social or everyday life (the life-world) understood from the perspective of interaction or the interaction order; the social accomplishment of reality
Ethnographic and naturalistic	In-depth, ethnographic (semantic) and unstructured interviews; life-history interviews; participant observation	The social or everyday life (the life-world) understood from the actor's perspective, knowledge, experience, intentions, interpretations, etc.
Narrative and interpretive interactionist	'Active' and narrative interviews	The dialogic process of communication; the 'exchange process' and the joint construction of accounts of social life in conversation and reflection
Objectivist hermeneutics	Exegesis; hermeneutic method	Author's intended meaning of the text

NOTE: For the idea of this illustration, I am indebted to a lecture by Dr. Bettina Dausein of the Universität Bielefeld given at the International Symposium on Lifelong Learning and Experience at Roskilde University, Denmark, August 1999.

quire different meaning in light of different methodologies. **See also METHODS, MIXED METHODS.**

Key Reference

Kaplan, A., *The Conduct of Inquiry*. New York: Harper & Row, 1964.

METHODS OF TEXT ANALYSIS   See **TEXTUAL ANALYSIS.**

MICROETHNOGRAPHY   This is an approach to field study specifically concerned with exhaustive, fine-grained examination of a very small unit within an organization, group, or culture (e.g., a particular classroom in a school); a specific activity within an organizational unit (e.g., how physicians communicate with elderly patients in an emergency room); or ordinary everyday conversation. **See also** ETHNOMETHODOLOGY.

Key Reference

Spindler, G., ed., *Doing the Ethnography of Schooling: Educational Anthropology in Action.* New York: Holt, Rinehart & Winston, 1982.

MISUNDERSTANDING   See UNDERSTANDING.

MIXED METHODS   This is the notion of using multiple methods to generate and analyze different kinds of data in the same study —for example, combining a narrative analysis of in-depth interviews with a content analysis of questionnaire responses or conducting an ethnographic study simultaneously with a quasi-experimental study of the same social phenomenon. The notion has received considerable attention in the field of social and educational program evaluation, in which discussions unfold about mixing methods at both 'technical' levels (i.e., generating different kinds of data via different procedures) and 'philosophical' and 'paradigmatic' levels.

Underlying the notion appears to be the pragmatic assumption that to judge the value of an educational or social program or policy, an evaluator should employ whatever methods will best generate evidence of the warranted assertability of the value of that program or policy. This is a relatively noncontroversial assumption in a variety of social science research endeavors. For example, it is not uncommon for an ethnographer who is investigating the relationship of schools to their communities or one who is studying household decision making regarding the allocation of educational resources to boys and girls to engage in substantial periods of intense participant observation and also to conduct a more structured household or community survey. It is also not unusual for a social policy analyst to design a study to determine the success of policy implementation that uses both measured variables and interviews with key participants involved in the implementation. In both cases, the object of study is framed by a particular purpose and set of questions, and different kinds of *evidence* generated via multiple, or mixed, methods is deemed relevant to addressing the purpose of the study and answering the questions.

Beyond this common understanding and practice of combining methods and types of data, it is not readily apparent what 'mixing' so-called paradigms or philosophies means or how that might be accomplished. Several preliminary questions must be answered. First, just what are the likely candidates for 'philosophies' or 'paradigms,' and what does each entail? Second, what does it mean to "apply" that philosophy or paradigm to the study of some problem or phenomenon? Third, what does the verb "to mix" mean in this circumstance—just what is it that is being mixed when applying different philosophical frameworks? Consider an example at the level of methodologies. For the sake of argument, assume that *ethnomethodology* and *naturalistic inquiry/ethnography* are candidates for different 'paradigms.' What would it mean to "mix" the ethnomethodologist's concern with understanding *how* social life is accomplished in talk-in-interaction with the interpretivist's concern with the meaning of social life or with understanding *what* is happening? Each defines the object of the study quite differently and employs different means to generate and analyze different kinds of data. Surely, each kind of study provides a different perspective on social life, but what would it mean to "mix" these perspectives? Consider, again for the sake of argument, that Gadamer's hermeneutics and Derrida's deconstructionism are candidates for 'philosophies' and suppose they are "applied" to the analysis of texts. It will become immediately apparent that they are not compatible because they make a host of different assumptions about what reading a text means and what such a reading yields. Both philosophies, however, share some central concerns—for example, the undecidability of the meaning of a text and a strong criticism of method as the path to knowledge. Thus, just what it might mean to mix philosophies is not obvious.

Perhaps advocacy for the notion of mixed methods is an implicit endorsement of pluralism in social science. It might be a way of saying that our understanding of social life should not be driven by either-or thinking—for example, structure versus agency, historicism versus nomologicalism, and meaning versus cause. Rather, we should accept that different ways of framing and studying social phenomena yield different kinds of understandings. Also, these different understandings should be engaged with one another and not simply tolerated as different. **See also** **METHODOLOGY, PARADIGM, PLURALISM.**

Key Reference

Greene, J. C., & Caracelli, V. J., eds., *Advances in Mixed-Method Evaluation: The Challenges and Benefits of Integrating Diverse Paradigms*, New Directions for Evaluation No. 74. San Francisco: Jossey-Bass, 1997.

MULTIPLE REALITIES   A central insight of the *interpretive turn* in the social and natural sciences is that the meaning of human action and language can only be grasped in relation to some specific context or frame of reference (see **INDEXICALITY**). For example, Thomas Kuhn (1922-1996) (*The Structure of Scientific Revolutions*, 2nd ed., University of Chicago Press, 1970) argued that paradigms were such a frame of reference in the natural sciences, and Peter Winch (*The Idea of a Social Science*, Routledge Kegan Paul, 1958) held that social action can only be understood in the context of particular forms of life or *language games* (concepts he borrowed from Ludwig Wittgenstein's [1889-1951] philosophy). Another notion that shares this basic premise is multiple realities. Originating in the psychology of William James (1842-1910), a theory of multiple realities was developed by Alfred Schutz (1889-1956) as part of his phenomenology of the *life-world* or social world in which we live. Schutz used the idea of multiple realities or "finite provinces of meaning" to clarify the relationship between the reality of the world of everyday life and the world of scientific, theoretical contemplation. He explained that the paramount reality or primary world in which we live is the intersubjective world of daily life. It possesses a specific set of characteristics that mark its unique "cognitive style." For example, we do not doubt its existence; in it we experience a particular form of sociality, in it we have a specific time perspective, and so on. We also live our lives, however, in other worlds or finite provinces of meaning on which, in Schutz's words, we "bestow the accent of reality." These include the world of dreams, art, and religion, the play world of the child, the world of scientific contemplation, and the world of the insane. Each of these provinces of meaning has its own "cognitive style," and as we alter attention from one finite province to another we experience a "shock" of breaking through the "system of relevances" unique to one province of meaning to shift to the system of relevances unique to the other. Schutz emphasized that these different provinces of meaning were not literally different realities. He wrote,

> The finite provinces of meaning are not separated states of mental life in the sense that passing from one to another would require a transmigration of the soul. . . . They are merely names for different tensions in one and the same consciousness, and it is the same life, the mundane life, unbroken from birth to death, which is attended to in different modifications. (p. 232)

Turning to the finite province of meaning called scientific contemplation, Schutz explained that its distinctive cognitive style centered on the attitude of the "disinterested observer" who turns the world into an object of contemplation. This attitude, in turn, is indispensable to scientific theorizing about the world. The scientific attitude means that the scientist puts his or her bodily existence, subjectivity, social relationships, and so on in brackets so as to adopt an attitude of total disinterested contemplation. The scientist suspends the cognitive style and the concerns that dominate his or her everyday life. Thus, the same individual acting in the finite province of meaning of the everyday world adopts a radically different set of relevant concerns, attitudes, and interests when acting in the finite province of meaning of scientific contemplation.

Key Reference

Schutz, A., *Collected Papers*, Vol. 1. M. Natanson, trans. The Hague, The Netherlands: Martinus Nijhoff, 1967.

NAÏVE REALISM   See **REALISM.**

NARRATIVE   Several senses of this term figure prominently in many versions of qualitative inquiry. Generally, the term refers to any spoken or written presentation, but it is primarily used in a more narrow sense to mean a form or genre of presentation organized in story form. Story, in turn, refers to a kind of writing that describes a sequence of actions or events with a plot (a beginning, middle, and end) arranged in temporal order. The term may be used to indicate a particular kind of data; for example, a narrative interview is specifically designed to elicit narrative data—an informant's or respondent's story. Narrative data or stories can be of two kinds: A personal experience story relates the teller to some significant episode, event, or personal experience, and a personal history or the reconstruction of a life is a more encompassing and involved account. Narrative may also refer to a discourse form of research reporting that is distinct from an argumentative form. In an argument, a conclusion is compelled because of the form of the argument. Moreover, the argument form in research reporting is typically synchronic (focuses on a limited set of events in a specific time period). A story form for research reporting, however, is typically diachronic (dealing with a phenomenon as it changes over time). It contains surprises, coincidences, embellishments, and other rhetorical devices that draw the reader in and hold attention in a different manner. **See also NARRATIVE INQUIRY.**

Key References

Polkinghorne, D., *Narrative Knowing and the Human Sciences.* Albany: State University of New York Press, 1988.

Polkinghorne, D., "Reporting Qualitative Research as Practice," in W. G. Tierney & Y. S. Lincoln, eds., *Representation and the Text: Re-framing the Narrative Voice.* Albany: State University of New York Press, 1997.

NARRATIVE ANALYSIS   This term refers to a variety of procedures for interpreting the narratives or stories generated in research. It includes formal and structural means of analysis (e.g., examining how a story is organized, how it is developed, and where it begins and ends), functional analyses of what a story is 'doing' or what is being told in the story (e.g., telling a moral tale, a cautionary tale, a success story, and a chronicle of trials and tribulations), and analyses of stories as a particular kind of oral performance. **See also NARRATIVE INQUIRY.**

Key References

Coffey, A., & Atkinson, P., *Making Sense of Qualitative Data.* London: Sage, 1996.

Mishler, E. G., "Models of Narrative Analysis." *Journal of Narrative and Life History,* 1995, 5(2), 87-123.

Polkinghorne, D., "Narrative Configuration in Qualitative Analysis." *Qualitative Studies in Education,* 1995, 8(1), 5-23.

Riessman, C. K., *Narrative Analysis.* Newbury Park, CA: Sage, 1993.

NARRATIVE CRITERIA   See **VERISIMILITUDE.**

NARRATIVE ETHICS   Also called virtue ethics, this approach to ethical reasoning emphasizes the connection between a substantive conception of human nature (i.e., a concept of the 'good' or purpose of human life) and its connection to personal identity and the virtues (excellences of character). It views morality as a telling

N

and living of individual and collective stories in which conceptions of the purpose of human life and virtues are given intelligibility. The centrality of stories or narratives to this view of ethics emphasizes the moral order and unity of life and the moral self as integrated (moral identity and moral purpose are linked over time). Narrative ethics is highly critical of ethical theories that view morality in terms of a series of episodic decisions disconnected from identity and human purpose. **See also** ETHICS OF QUALITATIVE INQUIRY.

Key References

MacIntyre, A., *After Virtue*. Notre Dame, IN: University of Notre Dame Press, 1981.

Newton, A. Z., *Narrative Ethics*. Cambridge, MA: Harvard University Press, 1995.

NARRATIVE EXPLANATION   (also called narrative constructivism or historical constructivism) Narrative explanations are stories (historical narratives) constructed about past events that give an accounting of and an account for those events. There is a long-standing controversy in the discipline of history over whether constructing stories about past events actually *explains* the occurrence of those events. The debate unfolds between defenders of *covering law model of explanation* applied to history, on the one hand, and proponents of a unique form of narrative understanding, on the other hand. Thus, the debate echoes the more general argument in the human sciences over whether explanation or understanding is its proper aim. **See also** HISTORICISM, NARRATIVE REALISM.

Key References

Hempel, C., "The Function of General Laws in History." *Journal of Philosophy*, 1942, 39, 35-48.

Mandelbaum, M., *The Anatomy of Historical Knowledge*. Baltimore, MD: Johns Hopkins University Press, 1977.

Mink, L., "The Autonomy of Historical Understanding." *History and Theory*, 1965, 5, 24-47.

Roth, P., "Narrative Explanations: The Case of History." *History and Theory*, 1988, 27, 1-13.

NARRATIVE INQUIRY   This is a broad term encompassing the interdisciplinary study of the activities involved in generating and analyzing stories of life experiences (e.g., life histories, narrative interviews, journals, diaries, memoirs, autobiographies, and biographies) and reporting that kind of research. Narrative inquiry or research also includes examination of the methodology and aim of research in the form of personal narrative and *autoethnography*.

Key References

Ellis, C., & Bochner, A., eds., *Composing Ethnography: Alternative Forms of Qualitative Writing*. Walnut Creek, CA: AltaMira, 1996.

Josselson, R., & Liebech, A., eds., *Interpreting Experience: The Narrative Study of Lives*. Thousand Oaks, CA: Sage, 1995.

Lieblich, A., Tuval-Mashiach, R., & Zilber, T., *Narrative Research: Reading, Analysis, Interpretation*. Thousand Oaks, CA: Sage, 1998.

NARRATIVE PSYCHOLOGY   Narrative has been proposed as a particular cognitive function, way of thinking, or rationality. For example, Jerome Bruner argued that there are two distinctive ways in which we order experience. The two are complementary but not reducible to one another: the paradigmatic or logicoscientific mode and the narrative mode. The former leads to the well-formed argument that seeks to convince us of its truth through "tight analysis, logical proof, sound argument, and empirical discovery guided by reasoned hypothesis," whereas the latter leads to good stories that seek to convince us of their lifelikeness. Each mode of thought has different criteria for evaluating its outcome. Bruner has written about the psychology of narrative thought, particularly how it is that we construct the world through narrative. Narrative psychology also includes examinations of how narratives are central to the construction of self-identity.

Key References

Bruner, J., *Actual Minds, Possible Worlds*. Cambridge, MA: Harvard University Press, 1986.

Sarbin, T., *Narrative Psychology: The Storied Nature of Human Conduct*. New York: Praeger, 1986.

NARRATIVE REALISM   (also called narrative ontology) This is a doctrine concerned with the storied nature of being or how narrative is the very 'lived' character of human existence. (*Narrative explanation,* however, is concerned with narrative as the 'told' character of existence.) The expression 'we lead storied lives' expresses this concern. There are many strands of thought entailed here, but generally narrative realism holds that narrative structures exist in the human world and not simply in the stories that people tell about that world. Narrative is regarded as a temporal structure inherent in our way of living and acting.

Key References

Carr, D., *Time, Narrative, and History.* Bloomington: Indiana University Press, 1986.

Ricoeur, P., *Time and Narrative,* 2 vols. K. McLaughlin & D. Pellauer, trans. Chicago: University of Chicago Press, 1984-1986.

NATIVE'S POINT OF VIEW   This is one of the methodological innovations marking the emergence in the 1920s of participant observation as the scientific approach of ethnography. The accounts of earlier interpreters—missionaries, government administrators, traders, travelers, and the like—of the native life of indigenous peoples generally failed to offer the perspective and the practices of the members of the group (i.e., 'the natives'). By placing increased emphasis on powers of observation of events in daily life and on the collection of first-person, native, or insider accounts, the methodology of *participant observation* sought to establish a firmer scientific basis for anthropological understanding. **See also EMIC/ETIC, ETHNOGRAPHIC NATURALISM, OTHER (THE OTHER, OTHERNESS).**

Key Reference

Stocking, G. W., Jr., ed., *Observers Observed: Essays on Ethnographic Fieldwork.* Madison: University of Wisconsin Press, 1983.

NATURALISM   This is one of four basic approaches to the study of social phenomena (the others are *antinaturalism, critical social science,* and *pluralism*). The naturalist holds that the social or human sciences should approach the study of social phenomena with the same aim and methods as the natural sciences approach the study of natural (physical) phenomena (hence the phrase "naturalistic interpretation of the social sciences"). In other words, the social sciences should have as their goals both prediction and causal, nomological *explanation* of human behavior. Naturalists such as Karl Popper (1902-1994) and Ernest Nagel (1901-1985) admit that the search for lawlike explanations (or explanatory theory) in the social sciences may be more difficult due to the nature of the subject matter. They insist, however, that there are no fundamental differences in kind in the explanatory goals of the natural and social sciences. **See also LOGICAL EMPIRICISM.**

Key References

Bernstein, R. J., *The Restructuring of Social and Political Theory.* Philadelphia: University of Pennsylvania Press, 1976.

Little, D., *Varieties of Social Explanation.* Boulder, CO: Westview, 1991.

Phillips, D. C., *The Expanded Social Scientists Bestiary.* Lanham, MD: Rowman & Littlefield, 2000.

NATURALISTIC INQUIRY   In the social sciences literature, naturalism or naturalistic inquiry is the name for a particular methodology that emphasizes understanding and portraying social *action* (i.e., the meaning, character, and nature of social life) from the point of view social actors. It emphasizes that this kind of understanding can be forthcoming only from firsthand, eyewitness accounts of 'being there.' It aims at faithful, authentic reproduction or representation of others' ways of life. The following are notable examples of the use of this term: In 1969, two psychologists, Edwin Willems and Harold Rausch, edited a collection of papers titled *Naturalistic Viewpoints in Psychology,* in which they defined naturalistic inquiry as "the investigation of phenomena within and in relation to their naturally occurring contexts." In 1971, sociologist Norman Denzin published the paper "The Logic of Naturalistic Inquiry," in which he explained that the naturalist inquirer resists using methods that oversimplify the complexity of everyday life. In 1978, Egon Guba published the monograph *Toward a Methodology of Naturalistic Inquiry in Educational Evaluation,* in which he identified the characteristics of naturalistic inquiry and

N

compared it with what he called more conventional (experimental and quasi-experimental) inquiry. Several years later, Guba and Yvonna Lincoln published *Naturalistic Inquiry* (Sage, 1985), in which they contrasted postpositivist and naturalist paradigms on philosophical and methodological dimensions. (In a subsequent formulation of their approach to qualitative studies that appeared in *Fourth Generation Evaluation* [Sage, 1989], Guba and Lincoln renamed their approach constructivist.) What these various methodologies sharing the same name have in common is a commitment to studying human action in some setting that is not contrived, manipulated, or artificially fashioned by the inquirer; hence, the setting is said to be "natural" or "naturally occurring."

Some confusion surrounding the term stems from the fact that in philosophy of social science, *naturalism* or *naturalistic* refers to efforts to define the aim of the social sciences as the same aim as the natural sciences (see NATURALISM). One who rejects those efforts (i.e., rejects the naturalistic interpretation of the social sciences) is an *anti*naturalist. Thus, to the philosopher, those qualitative inquirers who call themselves naturalistic inquirers are actually antinaturalists. To state it more concretely, the philosopher might say that a better title for Guba and Lincoln's book is "Antinaturalistic Inquiry." **See also** ETHNOGRAPHIC NATURALISM.

Key Reference

Gubrium, J., & Holstein, J., *The New Language of Qualitative Method*. Oxford, UK: Blackwell, 1997.

NATURALISTIC INTERPRETATION OF THE SOCIAL SCIENCES See NATURALISM.

NATURAL SETTING   See ETHNOGRAPHIC NATURALISM, NATURALISTIC INQUIRY.

NATURWISSENSCHAFTEN   This is a German term usually translated as "natural sciences." **See also** SCIENCE, *VERSTEHEN.*

N

NEGATIVE CASE   This is an instance or case that refutes or challenges a developing hypothesis. This notion is central to the logic of testing hypotheses as explained under *analytic induction*. The idea of using negative case analysis to establish the *credibility* of a researcher's conclusions has also been discussed as a key feature of *naturalistic inquiry.*

Key References

Fielding, N. G., ed., *Actions and Structure*. London: Sage, 1988.

Lincoln, Y. S., & Guba, E. G., *Naturalistic Inquiry*. Beverly Hills, CA: Sage, 1985.

NOMOTHETIC KNOWLEDGE   Nomothetic knowledge comprises knowledge claims that have the character of a *lawlike generalization*. Compare to *idiographic interpretation*. **See also COVERING LAW MODEL OF EXPLANATION, EXPLANATION.**

NONFOUNDATIONAL EPISTEMOLOGIES   The leading version of nonfoundationalist epistemology is *coherentism,* which is the view that the justification of a belief involves an assessment of the degree of coherence of that belief within a system of beliefs. Nonfoundationalist epistemology stands in opposition to foundational epistemology, which claims that justification is a matter of relating a belief to some kind of foundational beliefs (i.e., beliefs that are fundamental, basic, or 'brute' and hence in need of no additional justification). For the foundationalist, justification is like a building, with foundational beliefs at the base and all other beliefs supported by that foundation. For the nonfoundationalist, justification is more like a raft in which each plank (i.e., belief) is supporting every other. Some beliefs (like some planks) can, over time, be found to be unreliable and are replaced without dismantling the entire raft. This latter image, also called Neurath's boat, was developed by the logical positivist Otto Neurath (1882-1945). **See also FOUNDATIONALIST EPISTEMOLOGIES.**

Key Reference
Grayling, A. C., "Epistemology," in N. Bunnin & E. P. Tsui-James, eds., *The Blackwell Companion to Philosophy*. Oxford, UK: Blackwell, 1996.

O

OBJECTIVISM   There are multiple senses of this term:

1. It is a synonym for *foundationalist epistemologies.*

2. It can be used as another term for metaphysical (or ontological) realism—the doctrine that there is an independently existing world of objective reality that has a determinate nature that can be discovered.

3. It is a notion equivalent to the epistemological doctrine of meaning realism—the view that human *action* is an 'object' in which meaning resides independently of consciousness and experience; with the right methods, that meaning can be discovered (see **INTENTIONALISM**).

4. It is a belief in a particular metaphysical and epistemological relation of subject to object. For example, Pierre Bourdieu (1990) defines objectivism as the "theoretical relation" to the world. In that relation, the social world is "a spectacle offered to an observer who takes up a 'point of view' on the action and who . . . proceeds as if it were intended solely for knowledge" (p. 52). For Bourdieu, the important contrast is between the theoretical relation to the world with its attendant attitude of objectification and a "practical relation" to the world. A similar view is discussed by Charles Taylor, who criticizes an epistemology that privileges disengagement and control and assumes that

one does not live in or through one's experience but treats experience as an object (see also **INTENTIONALITY**).

5. It is a term that designates a complex set of interlocking beliefs about the nature of reality (metaphysical realism), the manner in which that reality can be known and knowledge claims justified (logical positivist or representationalist epistemology), the role of the scientist (an axiology of disinterest), and the Enlightenment belief in the unquestioned power (and authority) of science to shape society (**See also OBJECTIVITY**).

Key References

Bernstein, R. J., *Beyond Objectivism and Relativism: Science, Hermeneutics, and Praxis*. Philadelphia: University of Pennsylvania Press, 1983.

Bourdieu, P., *Logic of Practice*. Stanford, CA: Stanford University Press, 1990.

Fay, B., *Contemporary Philosophy of Social Science*. Oxford, UK: Blackwell, 1996.

OBJECTIVIST HERMENEUTICS   See **CONSERVATIVE HERMENEUTICS**.

OBJECTIVITY   In everyday usage, objectivity can refer to *a property or quality of a claim*—for example, a claim is objective if it is supported with reasons and evidence (or warrantable and supportable); *a characteristic of a person*—for example, the objective person is unbiased and unprejudiced; or *an aspect or characteristic of a process* or means by which a claim is warranted—for example, the enterprise of science is objective because the claims of scientists are subject to public scrutiny and intersubjective criticism.

In the literature on social science methodology and philosophy, there are several interrelated but distinct senses of this term that are all broadly related to the question of justifying a claim:

1. An absolute or ontological sense reflecting a belief in metaphysical realism: The objectivity of science refers to its ability to know things as they really are.

2. A disciplinary or critically intersubjective sense: Objectivity refers to the process of inquiry, the ability to reach consensus within some specialized disciplinary community through dialogue, debate, reasoned argument.

3. A mechanical sense: Objectivity means following the rules or procedure because these are a check on subjectivity and restrain idiosyncrasy and personal judgment.

4. A moral-political sense: Objectivity is fairness and impartiality, the absence of self-interest or prejudice that distorts judgment.

Some criticisms originating in qualitative inquiry (and in all social science more generally) are directed at the notion of objectivity as a regulative ideal for inquiry in the first sense noted previously—that is, the belief in an ability to know things as they really are. Other kinds of criticisms are aimed at objectivity as a stance or posture from which an inquirer allegedly can view social life unencumbered by prejudices and personal characteristics. Still other kinds of criticisms, specifically those raised in feminist epistemologies, are often simultaneously political and epistemological. For example, putatively objective science has a sexist bias; a concern with scientific objectivity has imposed a hierarchical and controlling relationship on the researcher-researched pair; and holding to objectivity as a regulative ideal has meant excluding personal, subjective knowledge from consideration as legitimate knowledge. **See also** BIAS, OBJECTIVISM, SUBJECTIVITY.

Key References

Fay, B., *Contemporary Philosophy of Social Science*. Oxford, UK: Blackwell, 1996.

Harding, S., *Whose Science? Whose Knowledge?* Ithaca, NY: Cornell University Press, 1991.

Megill, A., ed., *Rethinking Objectivity*. Durham, NC: Duke University Press, 1994.

Natter, W., Schatzki, T. R., & Jones, J. P., III, eds., *Objectivity and the Other*. New York: Guilford, 1995.

Rescher, N., *Objectivity: The Obligations of Impersonal Reason*. Notre Dame, IN: Notre Dame University Press, 1997.

OBSERVATION   Direct firsthand eyewitness accounts of every-day social action have always been regarded as essential to answering the classic fieldwork question, "What's going on here?" Extended periods of observation in the field define both anthropological work dating from the 1920s and fieldwork sociology originating in the Chicago school tradition of the 1930s. Observation as a method of generating data about human experience is characterized by the following traits: (a) Events, actions, meanings, norms, and so on are viewed from the perspective of people being studied; (b) a premium is placed on attention to detail; (c) events and actions can only be understood when they are set within a particular social and historical context; (d) social action is regarded as processual and dynamic and not as a set of discrete events; and (e) efforts are made by the observer to avoid premature imposition of theoretical notions on participants' perspectives, although some general theoretical framework initially shapes the making and interpretation of observations (e.g., symbolic interactionism, semiotic conception of culture, structural-functionalism, and ethnomethodology).

This view of observation as method and its underlying epistemological assumptions are subject to strong criticisms in postmodern and poststructural theories that, in part, reflect Dewey's (1859-1952) critique of the spectator theory of knowledge. Dewey argued that modernist conceptions of knowing regarded it as a passive recording of facts about the world, wherein the accuracy of knowing was to be judged as a matter of correspondence between our beliefs and those facts. Dewey viewed knowing as doing—as a constructive activity. Knowledge was not passive but instrumental in that it guided our dealings with the world we experience. The criterion that constituted knowledge was not correspondence but warranted assertability.

Postmodern and poststructuralist approaches to qualitative inquiry radicalize Dewey's criticisms of the knower as a neutral spectator. They claim that observation is part of the 'gaze' of an 'ocular epistemology' that privileges visual representations and (wrongly) assumes a relatively seamless link between textual *representations* (videotapes, transcriptions of audiotapes, and photographs) and the way the world really is. They maintain that experience is composed or constructed and hence never stable and determinate such that it can be grasped in visual representations. Representations are always textual reconstructions and not literal images. They argue that if knowledge is equated to visual perception (knowing through seeing), then (a) understanding is excluded because, unlike seeing, understanding is processual, changing, and dynamic; and (b) the conscious knower or subject is excluded from the act of knowing because he or she is simply looking in or looking at the experience of others—the one looking and not also the one who is being looked at. These criticisms thus make problematic both epistemological and political dimensions of the traditional conception of the participant-as-observer who is peripherally involved or only marginally participates in the scene that he or she studies. They invite examination of collaborative approaches to social inquiry that introduce the idea of active participation of the inquirer in the setting and sharing the role of researcher with participants. **See also KNOWLEDGE, PARTICIPANT OBSERVATION.**

Key References

Bryman, A., *Quantity and Quality in Social Research*. London: Unwin Hyman, 1988.

Denzin, N. K., *The Cinematic Society: The Voyeur's Gaze*. London: Sage, 1995.

Lonergan, B., "Consciousness and the Trinity," in W. J. Ong, ed., *Interfaces of the Word*. Ithaca, NY: Cornell University Press, 1977.

OCULAR EPISTEMOLOGY   See **OBSERVATION**.

ONTOLOGICAL HERMENEUTICS   See **PHILOSOPHICAL HERMENEUTICS.**

ONTOLOGY   See **METAPHYSICS.**

OTHER (THE OTHER, OTHERNESS)   In a broad sense, the goal of all forms of human inquiry is to understand 'the Other' (another person, tradition, history, ancestors, being, etc.). Anthropological and sociological studies, in particular, aim to understand other people and their language, culture, community, norms, values, beliefs, ways of life, traditions, and so on. Also, although the notions of 'same' and 'other' date to Plato's philosophy, it was not until the mid- to late twentieth century that scholars in anthropology and sociology, among other fields, began to engage in serious criticism of the interlocking epistemological, moral, and political dimensions of the posture through which inquirers of one culture studied another. Where once it was commonplace to read of studying the 'natives,' understanding the 'native's point of view,' or fears of 'going native' (losing one's supposed objective stance and becoming part of the very others one was attempting to study), it is now recognized that racist and colonialist assumptions often were embedded in such language. One of the strongest and oft-quoted contemporary statements of the colonizing and racist gaze of scholars was Edward Said's *Orientalism,* in which he argued that orientalists (scholars of the East) represented the interests of old colonial powers in viewing the East as 'other'—foil and prey of the civilizing and, ultimately, triumphant West. Historical studies indicate that orientalism accompanied the rise and subsequent development of the Western nation-states from the sixteenth century onward, and contemporary studies further revealed how this kind of racism has been not only an academic disposition but also institutionalized in a variety of agencies and endeavors that promote Western education and economic and political growth and development to help the 'underdeveloped' other.

Overlapping and, in some ways intersecting with, this kind of moral-political reconsideration of what it means to study other peoples and their ways of life is the broad critique of Cartesian subject-centered reason and its accompanying will to mastery of situations and closure to alternatives that seems to characterize modernity. This critique informs a variety of positions, including (a) the 'decentering of the subject' characteristic of the *poststructuralism* of Jacques Derrida; (b) the shift from a monological method-driven conception of knowledge of others to the view that understanding others requires being prepared for the other to speak to us (thus treating the other as a being to be met and not an object to be viewed, tolerated, or disregarded) and recognizing that dialogue and conversation (not method) are the conditions in which understanding emerges. These views are elaborated in the *philosophical hermeneutics* of Hans-Georg Gadamer and in Martin Buber's (1878-1965) I-Thou philosophy; and (c) the concern with the primacy of the ethical over the ontological as found in the work of Paul Ricoeur and Emmanuel Levinas (1906-1993) and elaborated in the postmodern ethics of Zygmunt Bauman. These positions on what it means to engage the other have, in turn, influenced scholarship in feminist thought, anthropology, gay and lesbian theory, postcolonial studies, multicultural studies, and other fields. **See also ETHNOCENTRISM, PLURALISM, POLITICS OF RESEARCH, UNDERSTANDING.**

Key References

Bauman, Z., *Postmodern Ethics*. Oxford, UK: Blackwell, 1993.

Davis, C., *Levinas: An Introduction*. Notre Dame, IN: University of Notre Dame Press, 1996.

di Leonardo, M., ed., *Gender at the Crossroads of Knowledge: Feminist Anthropology in the Postmodern Era*. Berkeley: University of California Press, 1991.

Friedman, M., ed., *Martin Buber and the Human Sciences*. Albany: State University of New York Press, 1996.

Levinas, E., *Otherwise Than Being or Beyond Essence*. A. Lingis, trans. The Hague, The Netherlands: Martinus Nijhoff, 1981.

Ricoeur, P., *Oneself as Another*. K. Blamey, trans. Chicago: University of Chicago Press, 1992.

Said, E., *Orientalism*. London: Routledge Kegan Paul, 1978.

PARADIGM   In Thomas Kuhn's (1922-1996) monograph *The Structure of Scientific Revolutions* (1962), the term paradigm played a significant role in his argument about the rationality of scientific inquiry. In the years following that publication (and its subsequent 1970 revision), it was particularly fashionable to talk about the qualitative versus quantitative 'paradigm debate' in the social sciences (although Kuhn's book did not discuss the social sciences). The term offered a convenient conceptual shorthand for pointing to apparently significant differences in methodologies. It was not always entirely clear, however, what the term actually meant in this context. Difficulty with the use of the term stems from Kuhn's own lack of conceptual clarity. Among the many uses of the term, he singled out two quite distinct definitions in responses to his critics. On the one hand, a paradigm refers to a type of cognitive framework—an exemplar or set of shared solutions to substantive problems used by a very well-defined, specific community of scientists (e.g., radio astronomers, protein chemists, and solid-state physicists) both to generate and to solve puzzles in their field. Kuhn argued that the essential activity of puzzle solving could be carried out only if the community of scientists shared these concrete exemplars because scientists solved problems by modeling them on previous puzzle solutions. Using this definition, it is doubtful that social scientists have similar kinds of paradigms that guide their work. On the other hand, Kuhn also used the term to mean a disciplinary matrix—commitments, beliefs, values, methods, outlooks, and so forth shared across a discipline. This sense of paradigm as a worldview or general perspective is generally what social scientists appear to have in mind when they use the term. The following are critical issues: (a) What actually comprises different methodological paradigms or disciplinary matrices in social inquiry? What are the beliefs, assumptions, and values about the aim of social inquiry, self, society, human agency, method, and so forth shared by inquirers committed to postmodern versus interpretive ethnography, for example, or those committed to feminist theory or philosophical hermeneutics? (b) In what way do similar concerns and commitments cut across or overlap paradigms or disciplinary matrices that are often regarded as distinct? and (c) How are these paradigms actually accomplished, enacted, or constituted socially and politically? **See also METHODOLOGY.**

Key References

Guba, E. G., ed., *The Paradigm Dialog.* Newbury Park, CA: Sage, 1990.

Guba, E. G., & Lincoln, Y. S., "Competing Paradigms in Qualitative Research," in N. K. Denzin & Y. S. Lincoln, eds., *Handbook of Qualitative Research.* Thousand Oaks, CA: Sage, 1994.

Gutting, G., *Paradigms & Revolutions: Applications and Appraisals of Thomas Kuhn's Philosophy of Science.* Notre Dame, IN: University of Notre Dame Press, 1980.

PARADIGMATIC KNOWLEDGE CLAIM   This notion refers to a typical instance, specimen, archetype, or exemplary form of a knowledge claim. What is the exemplary form of a knowledge claim in social inquiry? What kind of knowledge does social inquiry aim to produce? These questions are explored by the feminist philosopher Lorraine Code. She argues that in a *logical empiricist* framework a simple observational statement about an object—for example, "the door is open" and "that square object is red"—is regarded as paradigmatic and fundamental for what it means to know. More complex claims are built from these simple observational statements. She contends, however, that knowing other people is at least as worthy a candidate for paradigmatic status as is knowledge of objects. She maintains that the former kind of knowledge is qualitatively different from simple observational claims in the following ways: (a) It assumes a different subject-object relation; (b) these claims to know are open to negotiation between knower and 'known'; (c) the process of knowing other people requires constant learning—how to be with them, respond to them, and act toward them; and (d) this kind of knowledge is never complete or finished—even if one knew all the facts about someone (or about one's self), that would not guarantee that one would know that person as he or she is.

The issue of what constitutes a specimen (paradigmatic) knowledge claim is important for conceiving of the various aims of qualitative inquiry. Forms of qualitative inquiry wedded to empiricist assumptions generally regard simple observational claims as most important. Code, however, argues for forms of feminist inquiry that take seriously the notion of knowing other people as defining what it means to seek knowledge. Approaches to qualitative inquiry that draw on *philosophical hermeneutics* echo a similar view in arguing for practical-moral knowledge or knowledge of *praxis*. Some social constructionists also hold this view. For example, John Shotter argues that social inquiry must shift its focus from efforts to understand objects to understanding human beings—from an interest in epistemology to an interest in practical hermeneutics. Practical hermeneutics, in turn, examines what Shotter variously refers to as knowledge-in-practice, knowledge-held-in-common with others, or the kind of knowledge one has from within a situation, group, social institution, or society. **See also EPISTEMOLOGY, KNOWLEDGE.**

Key References

Code, L., *What Can She Know? Feminist Theory and the Construction of Knowledge*. Ithaca, NY: Cornell University Press, 1991.

Shotter, J., *Conversational Realities*. London: Sage, 1993.

PARTICIPANT OBSERVATION   The notion of 'being there,' of witnessing social action firsthand, emerged as a professional scientific norm in cultural anthropology in the early twentieth century. As a methodology for ethnographic *fieldwork*, participant observation is a procedure for generating understanding of the ways of life of others. It requires that the researcher commit to some relatively prolonged period of engagement in a setting (e.g., community, group, and classroom), take some part in the daily activities of the people among whom he or she is studying, and reconstruct their activities through the processes of *inscription, transcription,* and *description* in *fieldnotes* made on the spot or soon thereafter. Broadly conceived, participant observation is a methodology that includes activities of direct observation, interviewing, document analysis, reflection, analysis, and interpretation. It encompasses logistical, ethical, and political concerns involved in entering the world of those one studies, gaining their trust, developing empathy, and understanding their ways of talking about and acting in their world. Participant observation is also an epistemology, a way of knowing. It is a way of gaining access to the meaning of social action through empathetic identification with those one is observing, through witnessing how the behaviors of actors acquire meaning through their connection to linguistic or cultural systems of meanings or forms of life, or both.

Participant observation is a means whereby the researcher becomes at least partially socialized into the group under study to understand the nature, purpose, and meaning of some social action that takes place there. It has been commonplace to insist that the participant observer adopt the stance of a marginal native or professional stranger. In this role, the field-worker always maintains some respectful distance from those studied—cultivating empathy but never sympathy, rapport but never friendship, and familiarity but never full identification (i.e., 'going native'). This critical distance is required for creating an objective account of what is being studied. Hence, the participant observer is advised always to maintain something like dual citizenship—having primary allegiance to an academic culture or disciplinary home although taking up temporary residence in the culture or group being studied.

Postmodern ethnography is characterized by a variety of criticisms of the foregoing account of participant observation as a methodology and epistemology. Criticisms are directed at assumptions about the nature and purpose of researcher-actor interaction; what counts as legitimate, credible, and authentic knowledge that allegedly results from firsthand, eyewitness accounts;

what the field-worker is actually doing when he or she claims to be 'recording' observations of interactions and utterances and 'documenting' the lived realities of others; what constitutes the *authority* of the participant observer; and so on. Other criticisms of participant observation are offered by feminist ethnographers, who argue *for* closeness, friendship, and mutual identification with women being studied, and by participatory researchers, who advocate for a form of research *with* and not *on* the people being studied. See also ETHNOGRAPHIC NATURALISM, ETHNOGRAPHY, INTENTIONALISM, OBSERVATION.

P

Key References

Clifford, J., "On Ethnographic Authority." *Representations,* 1983, 1(2), 118-146.

Stocking, G., ed., *Observers Observed: Essays on Ethnographic Fieldwork.* Madison: University of Wisconsin Press, 1983.

PARTICIPATORY ACTION RESEARCH (PAR)   This is a broad designation for several kinds of *action research* that place a premium on the politics and power of knowledge production and use. Participatory action researchers typically work with groups and communities experiencing or subject to control, oppression, or colonization by a more dominant group or culture. Three characteristics appear to distinguish the forms of this practice from other forms of social inquiry: (a) its participatory character—cooperation and collaboration between the researcher(s) and other participants in problem definition, choice of methods, data analysis, and use of findings. (Note: There are various ways of participating or collaborating, including participants-as-researchers, participants networked to share knowledge, participants as problem formulators, researcher-as-colleague, and researcher-as-participant.); (b) its democratic impulse—PAR embodies democratic ideals or principles, but it is not necessarily a recipe for bringing about democratic change; and (c) its objective of producing both useful knowledge and action as well as consciousness raising—empowering people through the process of constructing and using their own knowledge. PAR is also marked by tension surrounding the simultaneous realization of the aims of participant involvement, social improvement, and knowledge production. Some advocates of

PAR disavow all efforts to produce general or theoretical knowledge and focus instead on the improvement of particular practices.

Key References

Fals-Borda, O., & Rahman, M. A., eds., *Action and Knowledge: Breaking the Monopoly With Participatory Action Research.* New York: Intermediate Technology/Apex, 1991.

Freire, P., *Pedagogy of the Oppressed.* New York: Herder & Herder, 1970.

McTaggart, R., ed., *Participatory Action Research: International Contexts and Consequences.* Albany: State University of New York Press, 1997.

Reason, P., *Participation in Human Inquiry.* London: Sage, 1994.

Whyte, W. F., ed., *Participatory Action Research.* Newbury Park, CA: Sage, 1991.

PEER DEBRIEFING   In this procedure, a field-worker confides in trusted and knowledgeable colleagues and uses them as a sounding board for one or more purposes. The field-worker may wish to recount ethical or political dilemmas encountered in the field and solicit colleagues' reactions or simply have colleagues serve as good listeners. Peer debriefing can also involve sharing ideas about procedures and logistics in the field to get advice and to check the dependability of ways of proceeding. Also, it can involve sharing one's evolving attempts at describing and analyzing qualitative data to achieve some kind of consensual validation.

Key Reference

Lincoln, Y. S., & Guba, E. G., *Naturalistic Inquiry.* Beverly Hills, CA: Sage, 1985.

PERFORMANCE/PERFORMATIVE/PERFORMATIVITY   These terms appear with increasing frequency in the extensive literature on qualitative inquiry—for example, the performance of identities, the performance (scripting and enactment) of research—and reflect the following several interrelated but distinct ideas:

1. In the 1960s, as part of a broad critique of behaviorist psychology, Erving Goffman (1922-1982) used the sociology of the theatre or *sociology of performance* to describe social interactions and relations in public.

2. The term *performative* was used by the philosopher J. L. Austin (1911-1960) to refer to a written or spoken utterance that affects action. According to Austin, there is a class of utterances that do not describe, report, or merely say something; neither are they true or false. Rather, these kinds of utterances perform or are part of an action (the classic example used by Austin is the utterance "I do" spoken in a wedding ceremony). Austin's notion of a performative, and, more broadly, his theory of how we accomplish things with language, has been influential in *ethnomethodology, conversation analysis, deconstructionism,* some feminist scholarship, and poststructuralist theory.

3. *Performativity*, a term introduced by Lyotard (1924-1998), refers to the state of affairs that characterize modernity. Modernity values and desires performativity (i.e., efficiency, completion, perfection, and measurement); consider, for example, the keen interest in performance management and performance assessment in virtually all aspects of social life. Performativity is a particular form of legitimation arising in modern capitalism and producing a bleak state of affairs that Lyotard called "a generalized computerization of society."

4. Used in a somewhat different sense, partially influenced by Austin's notion of a performative, *performativity* can also refer to the notion that language 'performs' (produces) identity. For example, Judith Butler argues that gender identity is not an attribute of self, but that one comes to be 'gendered' through a performative combination of sex, gender, sexual practice, and desire.

5. *Performance* often refers to an act or event. In the case of *performance texts* (experimental texts that are dialogical, multivoiced, etc.) or *performance art*, the term signals a different genre or form of telling, reporting, or portraying. As an event or act, a performance belies the notion of a 'real' experience or performance; performance texts or art are often ironic in that they undercut the meaning of a performance as complete, certain, and perfect.

Presence and reproduction, hallmarks of a 'real' performance, are replaced by experience and re-presentation in a performance text. Performance texts in postmodern and feminist ethnography may also be viewed as a genre in which the formerly silenced are given *voice*.

6. The notion of a *performance aesthetic* evident in rhetorical strategies of both writing and performing reflects some of the notions discussed previously. This is an aesthetic of no completion, no perfection, and no complete realization or 'carrying out' of things. It emphasizes a serious playful mood. This, in turn, is related to the notion of a *performance ethic*—a way of relating to others that cautions against the dangers of taking *the other* for granted and of ways of understanding that close down rather than open up change and difference.

Key References

Austin, J. L., *How to Do Things With Words*. Oxford, UK: Oxford University Press, 1962.

Butler, J., *Excitable Speech: A Politics of the Performative*. New York: Routledge, 1997.

Denzin, N. K., *Interpretive Ethnography: Ethnographic Practices for the 21st Century*. Thousand Oaks, CA: Sage, 1997.

Denzin, N. K., "Performance Texts," in *Representation and the Text: Re-Framing the Narrative Voice*, W. G. Tierney & Y. S. Lincoln, eds. Albany: State University of New York Press, 1997.

Lyotard, J.-F., *The Postmodern Condition: A Report on Knowledge*. Minneapolis: University of Minnesota Press, 1984.

Parker, A., & Sedgwick, E. K., eds., *Performativity & Performance*. New York: Routledge, 1995.

Turner, V., *The Anthropology of Performance*. New York: PAJ, 1986.

PHENOMENOLOGICAL SOCIOLOGY This social theory aims to describe the structures of experience or the *life-world*. Its principal architect was Alfred Schutz (1899-1956), who built on the *phenomenology* of Edmund Husserl (1859-1938) to develop a phenomenological foundation for Weber's idea of meaningful *social action*. Schutz aimed to explain how it is that the life-world is actually produced and experienced by individuals. He sought to explain the essence of what he called the 'natural attitude'—the fact that we do not doubt the existence of the everyday world and its intersubjective, social character. Schutz argued that to effectively study the everyday world, the social inquirer must bracket or suspend one's taken-for-granted attitude toward its existence; the inquirer must assume the attitude of a disinterested observer. Schutz's work was an early influence in the development of Garfinkel's *ethnomethodology*. See also MULTIPLE REALITIES, PHENOMENOLOGY, *VERSTEHEN*.

Key References

Giddens, A., *New Rules of Sociological Method,* 2nd ed. Stanford, CA: Stanford University Press, 1993.

Schutz, A., *The Phenomenology of a Social World.* Evanston, IL: Northwestern University Press, 1967.

Schutz, A., *Collected Papers,* 3 vols., M. Natanson, ed. The Hague, The Netherlands: Martinus Nijhoff, 1973.

PHENOMENOLOGY   This complex, multifaceted philosophy defies simple characterization because it is not a single unified philosophical standpoint. It includes the transcendental phenomenology of Edmund Husserl (1859-1938), the existential forms of Maurice Merleau-Ponty (1908-1961) and Jean-Paul Sartre (1905-1980), and the hermeneutic phenomenology of Martin Heidegger (1889-1976). Generally, phenomenologists reject scientific *realism* and the accompanying view that the empirical sciences have a privileged position in identifying and explaining features of a mind-independent world. Phenomenologists are opposed to the empiricist idea that genuine legitimate knowledge can only be had by rejecting the way we perceive the world of everyday life as 'mere appearance.' Hence, phenomenologists insist on careful description of ordinary conscious experience of everyday life (the *life-world*)—a description of 'things' (the essential structures of consciousness) as one experiences them. These things we experience include perception (hearing, seeing, etc.), believing, remembering, deciding, feeling, judging, evaluating, and all experiences of bodily action. Phenomenological descriptions of such things are possible only by turning from things to their meaning, from what is to the nature of what is. This turning away can be accomplished only by a certain phenomenological reduction or *epoché* that entails 'bracketing' or suspending what Husserl calls the "natural attitude," which is the everyday assumption of the independent existence of what is perceived and thought about.

The two major variants of phenomenology that are manifest in contemporary qualitative methodologies are the hermeneutic and the existential. The former, perhaps best known through the work of Hans-Georg Gadamer and Paul Ricoeur, tends to focus on the collective or intersubjective features of moral-political life as evident in a primary concern with issues of language and the nature and structure of communication. The latter variant is perhaps best known to social scientists through the work of the phenomenological sociologist Alfred Schutz (1899-1956)—a colleague of Husserl—who considerably influenced the social constructionist views of Peter Berger and Thomas Luckmann (*The Social Construction of Reality*, Anchor, 1967) and the development of *ethnomethodology* by Harold Garfinkel and Aaron Cicourel. This kind of phenomenology is oriented more toward describing the experience of everyday life as it is internalized in the subjective consciousness of individuals.

The use of the term phenomenology in contemporary versions of qualitative inquiry in North America tends to reflect a subjectivist, existentialist, and noncritical emphasis not present in the Continental tradition of phenomenology represented in the work of Husserl and Heidegger. The latter viewed the phenomenological project, so to speak, as an effort to get beneath or behind subjective experience to reveal the genuine, objective nature of things and as a critique of both taken-for-granted meanings and subjectivism. Phenomenology, as it is commonly discussed in accounts of qualitative research, emphasizes the opposite: It aims to identify and describe the subjective experiences of respondents. It is a matter of studying everyday experience from the point of view of the subject, and it shuns critical evaluation of forms of social life. **See also** LIFE-WORLD, PHENOMENOLOGICAL SOCIOLOGY.

Key References

Crotty, M., *The Foundations of Social Research*. London: Sage, 1998.

Hammond, M., Howarth, J., & Keat, R., *Understanding Phenomenology*. Oxford, UK: Blackwell, 1991.

PHILOSOPHICAL HERMENEUTICS   Also called ontological *her-meneutics*, this is a philosophy of the humanities (or of the self-understanding of the humanities as historical sciences) attributable to Hans-Georg Gadamer, who built on the hermeneutic philosophy of Martin Heidegger (1889- 1976) and drew on Aristotle's theory of practical knowledge. Because philosophical hermeneutics is not a methodology, and cannot be transformed into one without making it into something other than it is, its relevance for qualitative inquiry is not easily grasped. Moreover, the vast majority of approaches to qualitative inquiry are informed by thinking characteristic of the empirical sciences and not the humanities.

Gadamer was sharply critical of Dilthey's (1833-1911) view that hermeneutics was a *method* for generating knowledge in the human sciences. Philosophical hermeneutics is neither a method nor a methodology for obtaining knowledge and is not based on a traditional *subject-object relationship*. It aims to explicate a way of understanding (or a mode of experience in which we understand) through which a truth is disclosed and communicated—a truth that is not a matter of verification through methodical procedures of the empirical sciences. Understanding is an event or process that one participates in versus a process that is constructed by the knower (subject) to make sense of (discover the meaning of) an object (action, text, etc.).

Philosophical hermeneutics assumes that understanding an object (a *text*, a work of art, *human action*, another speaker, etc.) and interpreting it are essentially the same undertaking. Following Heidegger's lead, Gadamer argues that hermeneutics is ontological, universal, and conversational: It is ontological because 'understanding' is our very mode of being in the world, universal because understanding underlies all human activity, and conversational because the interpretation of an object is always a dialogical encounter—as interpreters we participate in, open ourselves to, share in, and listen to the claims that the object is making on us. Understanding is always open and anticipatory; one never achieves a final, complete interpretation. This is so because we are always interpreting in light of 'prejudice' (or prejudgment or preconception) that comes from the tradition of which we are part. This tradition does not stand apart from our thought but constitutes the 'horizon' in which we do our thinking. Furthermore, lan-

guage is the medium of all understanding in philosophical hermeneutics. Language is not understood as an instrument or tool but
as an activity that, like play, reflects an intentionality and allows
for both the constitution of meaning and the instability of meaning. Philosophical hermeneutics has also been characterized as a
hermeneutics of trust because it reflects the belief that meaning or
truth will be found through interpretation modeled on dialogue
and conversation. It is thus often contrasted with *deconstructionism* or the *hermeneutics of suspicion*. **See also EXPERIENCE,
HERMENEUTIC CIRCLE, PLAY, PRAXIS.**

Key References

Gadamer, H.-G., *Truth and Method*, 2nd rev., ed. & trans. J. Weinsheimer &
D. G. Marshall. New York: Crossroad, 1989 (Original work published
in German in 1960; first English translation 1975)

Risser, J., *Hermeneutics and the Voice of the Other: Re-reading Gadamer's
Philosophical Hermeneutics*. Albany: State University of New York
Press, 1997.

PHRONESIS   See *PRAXIS*.

PLAY   As signifying a drama analogy, this notion relates broadly
to the dramaturgical sociology of Goffman (1922-1982) and his interest in studying actors in sociopolitical situations. Play as a metaphor for life or experience, however, is also centrally important
in both *philosophical hermeneutics* and *deconstructionism*. Both
philosophies share the view that play is a kind of event, encounter,
or movement that has no goal, that renews and repeats itself, and
in which players (if they are truly playing) lose themselves. Play is
not trivial but serious. The seriousness, however, belongs to the
event and not the player, in the sense that the play is a kind of fasci-
nation with the world that takes over the player. Playing is a kind
of being-played. Thus, the primacy of the event (play) is emphasized over the conscious reflection and control of the player.

In Gadamer's philosophical hermeneutics, play is a dialectic of
transcendence and appropriation. On the one hand, as one gives
oneself to play, one becomes fascinated with the world and loses

oneself in the game or play. The play takes over determining possibilities and moving the player into the unknown. On the other hand, play affects a kind of self-discovery; it reveals possibilities to the player and thus is a kind of self-transformation. For Gadamer, being at play (or the event of play) is like being in a genuine conversation or dialogue with a text or with another person. Play is thus an analogy for the event of understanding. Both activities share the following features: There is a back-and-forth movement; each player or party to the conversation is exposed, vulnerable, and at risk; and in each event, one player recognizes that other players or dialogue partners have something to say, and this requires not the subjectivity of a distanced onlooker but participation and involvement in the play or conversation. Gadamer argues that it is in this kind of encounter that a kind of disclosure takes place, a recognition of meaning (although this is not recognition as recollecting an original meaning). The deconstructionism of Jacques Derrida makes use of this conceptualization of the metaphor of understanding as play but with one important difference. Deconstructionism does not agree that meaning unfolds or is disclosed through play, or that there can be such a thing as a continuity of meaning across encounters. For the deconstructionist, play reveals only the radically ambiguous nature of meaning, the continual play of indeterminate meanings. **See also POSTSTRUCTURALISM.**

Key References

Gallagher, S., *Hermeneutics and Education.* Albany: State University of New York Press, 1992.

Michelfelder, D. P., & Palmer, R. E., eds., *Dialogue and Deconstruction: The Gadamer-Derrida Exchange.* Albany: State University of New York Press, 1989.

PLURALISM   This is one of four basic approaches to the study of social phenomena (the others are *antinaturalism, naturalism,* and *critical social science*). Pluralists maintain that antinaturalistic and naturalistic approaches to the study of social life are complementary or compatible. They see no real difficulty with a social science that seeks both to explain human action and to interpret its meaning. A common view is that explanatory (naturalis-

P

tic) and interpretive (antinaturalistic) approaches are compatible because each illuminates a different aspect of human *action* necessary for a complete understanding.

More broadly, pluralism is a type of reaction to the variety of traditions, philosophic orientations, methodologies, political perspectives, cultural views, values, and so on that characterize not simply the current scene in social science but also life more generally. A central theme in much postmodernist thought and in philosophical hermeneutics and pragmatism is that as humans we face an inherently contingent, ambiguous, and pluralistic world. Bernstein (1991, pp. 335-336) argues that how one responds to this 'pluralization' can take several forms: (a) fragmenting pluralism —one communicates only with one's own 'group' and sees no need to engage with others outside this small circle; (b) flabby pluralism—"where our borrowings from different orientations are little more than glib superficial poaching"; (c) polemic pluralism —the existence of plural points of view does not signify a genuine willingness to listen and learn from others but becomes an "ideological weapon to advance one's own orientation"; (d) defense pluralism—a form of tokenism in which one pays lip service to the fact that others do their own thing, but one is already convinced that there is nothing to be learned from them; and (e) engaged fallibilist pluralism, which means

> taking our own fallibility seriously—resolving that however much we are committed to our own styles of thinking, we are willing to listen to others without denying or suppressing the otherness of the other. It means being vigilant against the dual temptations of simply dismissing what others are saying by falling back on one of those standard defensive ploys where we condemn it as obscure, wooly, or trivial, or thinking we can always easily translate what is alien into our own entrenched vocabularies. (pp. 335-336)

See also MIXED METHODS.

Key References

Bernstein, R. J., *The New Constellation: The Ethical-Political Horizons of Modernity/Postmodernity*. Cambridge: MIT Press, 1991.

Braybrooke, D., *Philosophy of Social Science*. Englewood Cliffs, NJ: Prentice Hall, 1987.

Fay, B., *Contemporary Philosophy of Social Science*. Oxford, UK: Blackwell, 1996.

Roth, P., *Meaning and Method in Social Science: A Case for Pluralism*. Ithaca, NY: Cornell University Press, 1987.

P

POIESIS   See *PRAXIS*.

POLITICS OF RESEARCH   Topics in the politics of qualitative inquiry include examination of the political forces that operate *on* the enterprise of research from the outside, so to speak, to influence the choice of questions, topics, methods, and so on; the micropolitics of relating to the people studied in field settings; the sociopolitical stance of individual inquirers; and the politics that act *through* the enterprise of inquiry. How these concerns are addressed depends, in large part, on how one conceives of the proper relationship between explanatory (descriptive) and normative (critical) interests of the social sciences.

Two long-standing political-ethical images of the inquirer based on the belief in value neutrality in social science are (a) the image of the liberal scholar who is committed to the ideal of knowledge for knowledge's sake and (b) the ideal of the disinterested social scientist who views his or her task as that of developing and testing empirical explanations of the social world and not changing that world. Scholars from a variety of philosophical persuasions maintain that value neutrality in the social sciences is an impossibility. They aim to restore (in a variety of ways) normative criticism to a proper place in social theorizing and, in so doing, seek ways to reunite theory and practice.

One way in which this kind of criticism of the politics and ethical aims of social research unfolds is through efforts to theorize the activity of social inquiry not simply in epistemological terms but as a kind of social agency. Hence, critics explore social inquiry as an economic, political, and social institution (practice) that accrues and exercises power to define the sociopolitical world. For example, Dorothy Smith (1990b, p. 2) identifies sociology as one of the "ruling apparatuses of society—those institutions of administration, management, and professional authority and of intellectual and cultural discourses which organize, regulate, lead, and direct capitalist societies." A similar view is expressed by the sociologist Zygmunt Bauman in his analysis of expertise in modern societies. Likewise, Charles Lindbloom argues that contemporary industrialized societies tend to be scientifically guided societies that look to the expertise of social scientists for social problem solving, social betterment, and guided social change.

Social scientists participate in the construction of ruling relations not by exercising social authority to command obedience or control decisions about policy but by virtue of the epistemological or cognitive authority that society invests in their discipline or profession. This role for social science in society leads to what Dorothy Smith calls a conceptual practice of power—a power to define the sociopolitical world through objectified knowledge. This power is exercised not simply in the scientific pronouncements (theories and claims) of social science professionals but also through the metaphysical commitments that are reflected in social scientific activity. In other words, social scientists do not simply teach us their scientific views, they also convey their beliefs about the sociopolitical world.

Scholars concerned with the ways in which politics act through the institution of social science often argue that social inquiry has been depoliticized: To depoliticize a practice of cognitive authority is to close the question of authority in favor of the experts, whereas to politicize the expertise of social science professionals is to open the question of cognitive authority to the critical scrutiny of society at large. Sandra Harding explains that the kind of politics that act less visibly and less consciously through the dominant institutional structures, priorities, practices, and languages of science paradoxically function as a kind of depoliticalization. A depoliticized practice, in Harding's (1992, pp. 568-569) view, "certifies as value-neutral, normal, natural, and *not political at all* the existing scientific policies and practices through which powerful groups can gain the information and explanations that they need to advance their priorities." **See also DISINTERESTED SOCIAL SCIENCE, ETHICS OF QUALITATIVE RESEARCH, FACT-VALUE DISTINCTION, OTHER (THE OTHER, OTHERNESS), (THE) PROBLEM OF THE CRITERION, THEORY.**

Key References

Bauman, Z., *Intimations of Postmodernity*. London: Routledge, 1992.

Fuller, S., *Social Epistemology*. Bloomington: Indiana University Press, 1988.

Haan, N., Bellah, R. N., Rabinow, P., & Sullivan, W. M., *Social Science as Moral Inquiry*. New York: Columbia University Press, 1983.

Harding, S., "After the Neutrality Ideal: Science, Politics, and 'Strong Objectivity.' " *Social Research*, 1992, 59(3), 567-587.

Lindbloom, C., *Inquiry and Change*. New Haven, CT: Yale University Press, 1990.

Smith, D., *The Conceptual Practices of Power*. Boston, MA: Northeastern University Press, 1990a.

Smith, D., *Texts, Facts, and Femininity: Exploring the Relations of Ruling*. New York: Routledge Kegan Paul, 1990b.

P

POSITIVISM   This is a term coined by August Comte (1798-1857) indicating a philosophy of strict empiricism—the only genuine or legitimate knowledge claims are those founded directly on experience. Comte sought to advance the project of 'positive knowledge' by distinguishing this kind of dependable empirical knowledge from claims made by theology and *metaphysics.* He divided history into three stages—the theological, the metaphysical, and the positive. In the last stage, metaphysical speculation is dissolved by science. He developed a unified hierarchical conception of the sciences and argued that the goal of science was prediction accomplished by identifying laws of succession. Sociology, in his view, should aim at identifying the laws that govern the development of society. The term is often used as shorthand for *logical positivism* or more generally to designate any approach that applies *scientific method* to the study of human *action.* **See also EMPIRICISM, LOGICAL EMPIRICISM.**

Key Reference

Hollis, M., *The Philosophy of Social Science: An Introduction*. Cambridge, UK: Cambridge University Press, 1994.

POSTEMPIRICISM   This is the name for a collection of ideas and arguments in the philosophy of science that followed the demise of the strict *empiricism* of *logical positivism.* Postempiricist philosophers include Popper (1902-1994), Quine, Hanson, Lakatos, Feyerabend (1924-1994), Kuhn (1922-1996), and Toulmin. Postempiricism is a *nonfoundationalist epistemology* that accepts fallibilism but does not relinquish the idea that evidence is necessary for judging the truth or falsity of scientific claims. The following are central ideas of the postempiricist view: (a) Data are not detachable from theory; (b) the language of science is irreducibly metaphorical and inexact; (c) meanings are not separate from facts but, in some sense, determine facts; (d) scientific theories can never be either conclusively verified or conclusively refuted by data alone; and (e) science consists of research projects or programs structured by presuppositions about the nature of reality. Ironically, many contemporary defenders of qualitative approaches to inquiry do not attack this postempiricist epistemology but, rather, a long-since-abandoned strict empiricism. **See also POSTPOSITIVISM, THEORY-OBSERVATION DISTINCTION.**

Key References

Brown, H. I., *Perception, Theory and Commitment: The New Philosophy of Science.* Chicago: University of Chicago Press, 1977.

Hesse, M., *Revolutions and Reconstructions in the Philosophy of Science.* Bloomington: Indiana University Press, 1980.

POSTMODERN ETHNOGRAPHY   This term signifies the postmodern critique of ethnographic practices both in classical and in *interpretive anthropology.* Postmodern ethnography criticizes classical ethnography for privileging participant observation, for its tendency to assume a smooth link between 'being there' and understanding the lived experience of others, and for its effort to develop seamless, comprehensive descriptions of common material culture and perspectives. Interpretive ethnography is criticized for privileging *thick description* and for assuming that the ethnographer's understanding can unproblematically reflect the viewpoint of the 'other.' Central concerns in the postmodern ethnographic critique include the connections between authorship, *authority, representation,* and rhetoric and an effort to experiment with textual forms for ethnography that decenter the monologic voice of the ethnographer in favor of dialogic or polyphonic texts. **See also** ETHNOGRAPHIC REALISM, PARTICIPANT OBSERVATION, POSTMODERNISM.

Key References

Clifford, J., & Marcus, G., *Writing Culture: The Poetics and Politics of Ethnography.* Berkeley: University of California Press, 1986.

Denzin, N. K., *Interpretive Ethnography: Ethnographic Practices for the 21st Century.* Thousand Oaks, CA: Sage, 1997.

POSTMODERN FEMINISM.   See FEMINIST EPISTEMOLOGIES.

POSTMODERNISM   Although this term and *poststructuralism* are often used interchangeably, postmodern theory or postmodernism is generally regarded as a more encompassing notion. The term originated as a description of a particular architectural style opposed to modernist architecture and eventually was applied to graphic arts, literature, and the contours of social and political life. Broadly conceived, postmodernism is an attitude toward the social world at the current stage of its historical development—more of a diagnosis than a theory. It is radically interdisciplinary in character and rejects conventional styles of academic discourse. Many scholars claim that it is characterized by its opposition to four central doctrines that form the core of the Enlightenment tradition: (a) the notion of a rational, autonomous subject—a self that has an essential human nature; (b) the notion of *foundationalist epistemology* (and foundationalist philosophy in general); (c) the notion of reason as a universal, a priori capacity of individuals; and (d) the belief in social and moral progress through the rational application of social scientific theories to the arts and social institutions (law, family, education, etc.). Postmodernism is also characterized by its distrust of and incredulity toward all 'totalizing' discourses or metanarratives—those large-scale or abstract theoretical frameworks that purportedly explain culture, society, and human agency. In place of these metaframeworks, postmodern theory endorses heterogeneity, difference, fragmentation, and indeterminacy.

Not all scholars associated with postmodern thought describe their work as postmodern or themselves as postmodernists. In fact, few scholars agree on what exactly the term means, except perhaps that it represents a reaction to, critique of, or departure from modernism to which the Enlightenment gave birth. This definition, however, is also problematic for the following reasons: If modernity is a historical stage in the development of society, then modernism is a reaction to modernity. The historical period of modernity is characterized by faith in reason, representation, certainty, continuity of meaning, essentialism, foundationalism, and a commitment to abstraction, grand theorizing, rationalization, and instrumentality in thought and society. Modernism is characterized as significant and varied critique of all these notions in architecture, literature, art, philosophy, and so on. None of the scholars and artists engaged in this critique, however, would be labeled postmodernists. Hence, postmodernism cannot simply be a reaction to or antithesis of modernism. It must be characterized by something other than the kind of opposition that has been mounted from within modernity. One way in which this difference has been drawn is to argue that modernist critiques of modernity generally exhibited faith that the problems of modernity could be solved. In other words, critics of modernity believed that they could at once be both subversive and redemptive, critical and utopian. Although postmodernism shares many of the same criticisms as modernism, what distinguishes it is that postmodern critics completely relinquish all faith in the redemptive power of modernist thought. **See also CRISIS OF LEGITIMATION, CRISIS OF REPRESENTATION, GRAND NARRATIVE, GRAND THEORY.**

Key References

Best, S., & Kellner, D., *Postmodern Theory*. New York: Guilford, 1991.

Crotty, M., *The Foundations of Social Research*. London: Sage, 1998.

Harvey, D., *The Condition of Postmodernity*. Oxford, UK: Blackwell, 1989.

Posnock, R., *The Trial of the Century: Henry James, William James, and the Challenge of Modernity*. Oxford, UK: Oxford University Press, 1991.

Rosenau, P., *Post-Modernism and the Social Sciences*. Princeton, NJ: Princeton University Press, 1992.

POSTPOSITIVISM   This term is used in several ways in the literature. It can mean 'nonpositivism'—that is, any epistemology other than that of *positivism* or *logical positivism*. It can more narrowly refer to a less strict form of positivism, namely, *logical empiricism*. Also, it is sometimes used as a synonym for *postempiricism*.

Key References

Crotty, M., *The Foundations of Social Research*. London: Sage, 1998.

Phillips, D. C., & Burbules, N. C., *Postpositivism and Educational Research*. Lanham, MD: Rowman & Littlefield, 2000.

POSTSTRUCTURALISM   This is the general name for a critique of *structuralism* that arose largely in France in the early 1970s through the work of Georges Bataille (1897-1962), Jacques Derrida, Michel Foucault (1926-1984), Julia Kristeva, Jean-François Lyotard (1924-1998), Roland Barthes (1915-1980), and Jean Baudrillard. Poststructuralism shares many of the same concerns of structuralism (e.g., it is resolutely anti-metaphysical and antihumanist, and it accepts the fact that language plays a central role in the constitution of subjectivity and social reality). Whereas structuralism was informed by the constructive scientific vision of identifying both social and linguistic order, post-structuralism is resolutely *de*constructive in intent. Although there is considerable variation among the views of the cluster of scholars identified as poststructuralist, several central themes are identifiable. First is the decentering of the notion of an individual, self-aware condition of being a subject. Poststructuralists question the value and existence of the metaphysical notion of a human being or conscious subject as a datum. The 'I' is not immediately available to itself because it derives its identity only from its position in language or its involvement in various systems of signification. Hence, subjects, authors, and speakers are irrelevant to the interpretation of texts. Second is pantextualism—everything is a *text*—and all texts are interrelated, which makes for 'intertextuality.' Third, meaning is unstable, never fixed, never determined or determinable, and never representational. Finally, *deconstructionism* is a poststructuralist strategy for reading texts that unmasks the supposed 'truth' or meaning of text by undoing, reversing, and displacing taken-for-granted binary oppositions that structure texts (e.g., right over wrong, subject over object, reason over nature, men over women, speech over writing, and reality over appearance). **See also** SEMIOTICS.

Key References

Culler, J., *On Deconstruction*. Ithaca, NY: Cornell University Press, 1982.

Giddens, A., "Structuralism, Poststructuralism and the Production of Culture," in A. Giddens & J. H. Turner, eds., *Social Theory Today*. Stanford, CA: Stanford University Press, 1987.

Seidman, S., *Contested Knowledge: Social Theory in the Postmodern Era*, 2nd ed. Oxford, UK: Blackwell, 1998.

PRACTICE   See PRAXIS.

PRAGMATISM   Perhaps the only uniquely American philosophy, pragmatism is best known through the work of William James (1842-1910), John Dewey (1859-1952), and Charles Sanders Peirce (1839-1914), and its revival as neopragmatism in the works of Richard Rorty. There are many versions of pragmatism, and some are radically different (e.g., the pragmatism of Peirce and that of Rorty). Generally speaking, however, this philosophy views knowledge as an instrument or tool for organizing experience, and it is deeply concerned with the union of theory and practice. For qualitative inquiry, pragmatism or the pragmatic outlook is important for at least two reasons: (a) Pragmatism is a philosophical source of *symbolic interactionism* and the *Chicago school of sociology*, and (b) the contemporary pragmatic outlook comprises a set of ideas that are often appealed to in defending qualitative inquiry as a viable option in the social sciences. Richard J. Bernstein (1991, p. 326ff) identifies these substantive themes as (a) antifoundationalism; (b) a "thoroughgoing fallibilism where we realize that although we must begin any inquiry with prejudgments and can never call everything into question at once, nevertheless there is no belief or thesis—no matter how fundamental—that is not open to further interpretation and criticism"; (c) "the social character of the self and the need to cultivate a critical community of inquirers"; (d) an "awareness and sensitivity to radical contingency and chance that mark the universe, our inquiries, our lives"; and (e) the view that there can be no escape from the plurality of traditions, perspectives, and philosophic orientations. **See also INSTRUMENTALISM.**

Key References

Bernstein, R. J., *The New Constellation: The Ethical-Political Horizons of Modernity/Postmodernity.* Cambridge: MIT Press, 1991.

Diggins, J., *The Promise of Pragmatism: Modernism and the Crisis of Knowledge and Authority.* Chicago: University of Chicago Press, 1994.

Joas, H., *Pragmatism and Social Theory.* Chicago: University of Chicago Press, 1993.

Mounce, H. O., *The Two Pragmatisms: From Peirce to Rorty.* New York: Routledge, 1997.

West, C., *The American Evasion of Philosophy: A Genealogy of Pragmatism.* Madison: University of Wisconsin Press, 1989.

PRAXIS   There is a long history of this notion in Marxism, existentialism, and pragmatism, but perhaps it is currently best known to qualitative inquirers as occupying a central place in the hermeneutic philosophies of Hans-Georg Gadamer and Jürgen Habermas. It is a term for a particular form of human activity that means something different than our common usage of the word *practice.* Practice typically means the domain of everyday activity (i.e., the world of the practitioner) in which theory is applied or used; practice is about action and doing (whereas theory is about knowledge and thinking). In the literature on action research, considerable criticism is directed at theory for being too 'academic' and abstract and hence distant from or irrelevant to practice in this sense. Consequently, considerable attention is paid to improving practice by designing ways of getting knowledge (theory) somehow better aligned with or connected to practice (e.g., by beginning an inquiry with practitioners' own knowledge and doing coresearch). This distinctly modernist notion of practice as the everyday work of practitioners that should be informed and hence improved or perfected by theory (i.e., knowledge generated through the application of method) is not what Gadamer and

Habermas have in mind. In fact, it is precisely this connection between theory and practice that they find problematic. The source of this difference lies in efforts of Gadamer and Habermas to revitalize Aristotle's (*Nicomachean Ethics,* Book VI) scheme of knowledge and action that is based on a threefold distinction between theory (*episteme*) and two forms of practical knowledge (*techné* and *phronesis*). This distinction is summarized as follows:

1. *Theory* as an activity arises in the life of contemplation; it is separate from the practical and productive life of the polis (the life of individuals in society; the realm of morality, ethics, political life, education, etc.). Theory yields knowledge of necessary and eternal truths (*episteme*); such knowledge is not possible in the polis because of its inherently changeable and uncertain nature.

2. Two other forms or modes of activity are the *productive (poiesis)* and the *practical (praxis)*:

   2.1. *Productive activity (poiesis)*: Requisite knowledge is *techné*. This is a form of activity under the firm control of an objective, impersonal method. It is an activity that has to do with making or fabrication. It is craftsmanship—an activity designed to bring about and terminate in a product or result. The product or result is separable from the one who produces it, and the knowledge required for (or that governs) this activity is also separable from the user of that knowledge. It is a kind of activity in which one can decide to willfully participate or not participate.

      2.1.1. This particular kind of activity is associated with a type of practical knowledge called *techné*. This is the kind of knowledge possessed by an expert in a specialized craft—a person who understands the principles underlying the production of an object or state of affairs (e.g., a house, a table, a safe journey, and a state of being healthy). Moreover, this kind of knowledge fits smoothly into a means-end framework: The materials and tools (including method) of this kind of practical knowledge are means used by the maker to bring about the end product or result. Practical knowledge (*techné*) is a means to the achievement of the final product as the end of the activity.

2.2. *Practical activity (praxis)*: Requisite knowledge is *phronesis*. This is a form of activity that has to do with the conduct of one's life and affairs as a member of society. It is about doing the right thing and doing it well in interactions with fellow humans. It is an activity that leaves no separably identifiable outcome as its product, hence the end (aim) of the activity (i.e., being a 'good' human being, teacher, doctor, lawyer, etc.) is realized in the very doing of the activity. This is the kind of activity from which one cannot 'rest'—unlike the practical activity of *poiesis*, it is not an activity that one can set aside at will. Joseph Dunne (1993) explains that praxis is a "type of human engagement that is embedded within a tradition of communally shared understandings and values, that remains vitally connected to peoples' life experience, that finds expression in their ordinary linguistic usage, and that, rather than being a means through which they achieve outcomes separate from themselves, is a kind of enactment through which they constitute themselves as persons in a historical community" (p. 176).

2.2.1. The distinct mode of practical knowledge associated with praxis is *phronesis*. This is neither a technical nor a cognitive capacity that one has at one's disposal but, rather, is bound up with the kind of person that one is and is becoming. This kind of practical-moral knowledge characterizes a person who knows how to live well; it is acquired and deployed in one's actions with one's fellow human beings. It demands an intellectual and moral disposition toward right living and the pursuit of human good and hence a different form of reasoning and knowledge. This kind of knowledge is variously referred to as deliberative excellence, practical wisdom, or practical reason. Associated cognitive virtues are understanding, judgment, and interpretation.

> Phronesis is intimately concerned with the timely, the local, the particular, and the contingent (e.g., "What should I do *now*, in *this* situation, given *these* circumstances, facing *this* particular person, at *this* time?").

Both Gadamer and Habermas argue that modernity is characterized by an assimilation of theory and *episteme* to *poiesis* and *techné*. Modern science invented a new form of theoretical knowledge based on methods, completely displacing the notion of theory as a contemplative ideal with a new form of *techné*. Scientific theory is pursued with the attitude of the technician (i.e., within the form of activity that Aristotle would have called poiesis). In other words, technical control through the use of an impersonal method is the defining perspective, framework, and interest within which scientific theory is assembled. In modern science, the only kind of knowledge that counts as both theory and a source of production is that given by science—that is, knowledge based on method (this is a definition of *scientism*).

For both Gadamer and Habermas, an even more troubling and dangerous feature of modernity is the assimilation of praxis (the practical domain of personal and social affairs) into *techné*. Roughly, this is equivalent to treating every human situation in which practical-moral judgment is required (e.g., in teaching, managing, and providing health care or social services) as presenting a technical problem to be solved by the application of knowledge generated via method. They both seek to recover the centrality of praxis to our self-understanding.

Both Gadamer and Habermas draw on the Aristotelian conception of knowledge and action to restore a sense of praxis to our life in society, and both agree that *hermeneutics* (understanding) plays an intrinsic role in this recovery. In other words, practical life/practical reason (in the sense of No. 2.2 listed previously) is the medium in which understanding takes place. This is so because in praxis we must continually understand and interpret each other's language in gestures and speech, and without the reliable background of such understanding praxis would be impossible. Moreover, praxis is not external to understanding—that is, one does not first understand (by generating knowledge based on method) and then 'apply' that understanding to praxis. Rather, in the 'event' of understanding, there is already an element of praxis (action-oriented self-understanding). Thus, for Gadamer, as we come to a clearer view of the nature of understanding, we possess a more adequate conception of praxis.

For Gadamer, recovering Aristotle's notions of *phronesis* as a form of knowledge is a key to understanding what it means to 'do' hermeneutics. *Phronesis* is a model of the problems of hermeneutics—the model helps to destroy the notion that knowledge (understood as *techné*) has authority or sovereignty over being (praxis). In Gadamer's view, the kind of knowledge and understanding that characterizes praxis is not technical knowledge anchored in method but, rather, *phronesis.* Understanding is an event that happens within a relationship of vulnerability to that which one seeks to understand. The interpreter surrenders to an interaction in which he or she is always at risk and always in a situation demanding situated reflection (see also **PLAY**).

Habermas develops a conception of praxis that is deeply informed by critique. Gadamer believes that the possibilities for restoring our sense of the centrality of critical moral-political judgment in daily life lie within the tradition of praxis. Habermas disagrees, arguing that praxis is distorted by ideology; thus, we must have a vantage point outside of tradition, outside of praxis, from which to develop a critique of praxis. **See also CRITICAL HERMENEUTICS, PHILOSOPHICAL HERMENEUTICS, THEORY.**

Key References

Bernstein, R. J., *Beyond Objectivism and Relativism.* Philadelphia: University of Pennsylvania Press, 1983.

Bernstein, R. J., *Praxis & Action.* Philadelphia: University of Pennsylvania Press, 1999.

Dunne, J., *Back to the Rough Ground: 'Phronesis' and 'Techne' in Modern Philosophy and in Aristotle.* Notre Dame, IN: University of Notre Dame Press, 1993.

Gadamer, H.-G. *Reason in the Age of Science.* F. G. Lawrence, trans. Cambridge: MIT Press, 1981.

Habermas, J., *Knowledge and Human Interests.* J. J. Shapiro, trans. Boston: Beacon, 1971.

Habermas, J., *The Theory of Communicative Action*, Vol. 1. T. McCarthy, trans. Boston: Beacon, 1981.

Lobkowicz, N., *Theory and Practice: History of a Concept from Aristotle to Marx*. Notre Dame, IN: University of Notre Dame Press, 1967.

P

PREJUDICE   See **BIAS, PHILOSOPHICAL HERMENEUTICS.**

(THE) PROBLEM OF THE CRITERION   The following is the problem of the criterion: How can we specify *what* we know without specifying *how* we know it, and vice versa? Although there is no generally accepted resolution to this skeptical argument, the central project of *epistemology* remains the justification of knowledge claims: How are we to decide that any particular account or interpretation of the world is valid, genuine, legitimate, and true? Philosophers and methodologists have devoted much effort to specifying the appropriate *criteria* for making such an assessment.

The legitimization of social scientific inquiry has hinged on the fact that it is particularly preoccupied with means for developing and testing accounts of social phenomena for their accuracy or truth. The advent of *postmodernism* and *poststructuralism* in social thought has cast the project of epistemological justification, and hence the traditional grounds of authority for social science, into question. For some scholars, issues of epistemological criteria no longer matter; what does matter is political justification. For other scholars, the epistemological and the political are collapsed into an interlocking larger issue. Of course, social science has always had scholars who focused on the political nature of the enterprise. In recent decades, however, concerns about the politics of method, hostility toward allegedly authoritative claims of *representation,* denials of the possibility of truth, and so forth have called into question the importance of the search for *epistemic criteria* in social science. For many social theorists, the central problem of social science is no longer one of developing the best criteria for establishing genuine knowledge but rather one of unmasking the values and politics of the enterprise of social inquiry that were hidden within the epistemological project. **See**

also CRISIS OF REPRESENTATION, POLITICS OF RESEARCH, VALID-
ITY.

Key Reference

Smith, J. K., *After the Demise of Empiricism: The Problem of Judging Social and Educational Inquiry.* Norwood, NJ: Ablex, 1993.

P

PROPOSITIONAL KNOWLEDGE   On a relatively commonsense interpretation, propositions are sentences or statements that express in written or spoken language what we believe, doubt, affirm, or deny. (Of course, we express these dispositions in other ways as well.) Assertions, interpretations, evaluations, conclusions, findings, hypotheses, and the like are familiar kinds of propositions or statements. Propositional knowledge is knowing-that—an assertion *that* something is so. It is a kind of knowledge distinguishable from knowing-how—knowledge of how to do something.

The phrase *propositional knowledge* is often used in the literature on qualitative inquiry in a way that connotes something more like abstract formal language. Logic is such a language—its grammar and interpretation are determined solely by rules defining its symbols. Propositional knowledge thus often means something like the expression of scientific knowledge claims in a formal mathematical calculus. (A propositional calculus employs symbols for variables in combination with logical operators also expressed in symbolic form—for example, $p \supset q$ is read "if p then q" or "p implies q," and $p \equiv q$ is read "p is equivalent to q" or p if and only if q.") The logical positivists argued that all genuine scientific knowledge should be capable of expression in this kind of formal language. They believed that by stating (and analyzing) claims about the world using the tools of formal logic, one could arrive at a way of expressing knowledge claims in propositions that were unambiguous, timeless, and expressive of unchanging relations. Qualitative inquiry in general opposes this view. Hence, when the phrase *propositional knowledge* is used in contrast to notions such as tacit knowledge, experiential knowledge, and practical knowledge, it may be a way of expressing opposition to the idea that there is only one way to speak of what constitutes genuine, legitimate knowledge of the world. **See also NARRATIVE PSYCHOLOGY, TACIT (PERSONAL) KNOWLEDGE.**

Key Reference

Bunge, M., *Finding Philosophy in Social Science.* New Haven, CT: Yale University Press, 1996.

PURPOSIVE SAMPLING   See **SAMPLING LOGIC.**

QUALITATIVE   This is a not-so-descriptive adjective attached to the varieties of social inquiry that have their intellectual roots in *hermeneutics, phenomenological sociology,* and the *Verstehen* tradition. Many scholars use the phrase *qualitative inquiry* as a blanket designation for all forms of social inquiry that rely primarily on qualitative data (i.e., data in the form of words), including *ethnography, case study research, naturalistic inquiry, ethnomethodology, life-history methodology,* and *narrative inquiry.* To call a research activity qualitative inquiry may broadly mean that it aims at understanding the *meaning* of human *action.* Perhaps the clearest use of the adjective is to distinguish between qualitative data—nonnumeric data in the form of words—and quantitative data—numeric data. The term is also used, however, as a modifier for *method, methodology, research,* and *paradigm* and as a synonym for *nonexperimental* and *ethnographic.* Because the adjective is used in so many different ways, it does not clearly signal a particular meaning or denote a specific set of characteristics for qualitative research.

Often, the use of the term *qualitative* involves both implicit and explicit comparisons to some equally ambiguously used adjective, "quantitative"—as, for example, in the phrase "qualitative methods versus quantitative methods." Broadly speaking, qualitative methods are procedures including unstructured, open-ended interviews and participant observation that generate qualitative data, whereas so-called quantitative methods (e.g., structured questionnaires, psychometric measures, and tests) are means of generating quantitative data. One, however, could easily generate qualitative data via an open-ended interview, transform those data into numbers, and analyze them by means of nonparametric statistics. Hence, what precisely comprises a so-called qualitative method is not all clear.

Qualitative denotes of or relating to quality. A *quality* is an inherent or phenomenal property or essential characteristic of some thing (object or experience). Ironically, there appears to be only one variety of qualitative inquiry that takes the definition of quality as its starting point. Elliot Eisner's (*The Enlightened Eye*, Macmillan, 1991) explication of qualitative inquiry begins from the point of view that inquiry is a matter of the perception of qualities of some object or event and an appraisal of their value. The work of Eisner and his students aims to define and illustrate an aesthetics that explains how qualitative aspects of the experiences and settings of teaching and learning are to be perceived, appreciated, interpreted, understood, and criticized. The metaphors he employs for capturing the dual features of his methodology are connoisseurship and criticism. **See also FIELD STUDIES.**

Key References

Denzin, N. K., & Lincoln, Y. S., eds., *Handbook of Qualitative Research*, 2nd ed. Thousand Oaks, CA: Sage, 2000.

Richardson, J. T. E., ed., *Handbook of Qualitative Research Methods for Psychology and the Social Sciences*. Leicester, UK: British Psychological Society, 1996.

QUALITATIVE EVALUATION   This is a broad designation for a variety of approaches to evaluating (i.e., determining the merit, worth, or significance of) social and educational programs, policies, projects, and technologies that make use of typically 'qualitative' methods for generating data (e.g., unstructured *interviewing, observation,* and *document analysis*) and nonstatistical means of analyzing and interpreting those data. These approaches arose in the mid-1970s as a reaction to the dominance of randomized and quasi-experimental designs and the use of standardized measures of achievement as the primary means of evaluation. Included here are approaches known as case study evaluations, responsive evaluation, illuminative evaluation, and *naturalistic inquiry* or fourth-generation evaluation. The so-called qualitative versus quantitative debate continues to be an issue in the field of evaluation. **See also MIXED METHODS.**

Key References

Guba, E., & Lincoln, Y. S., *Fourth Generation Evaluation.* Newbury Park, CA: Sage, 1989.

Patton, M. Q., *Qualitative Evaluation and Research Methods,* 2nd ed. Newbury Park, CA: Sage, 1990.

Reichardt, C. S., & Rallis, S. F., eds., *The Qualitative-Quantitative Debate: New Perspectives,* New Directions for Program Evaluation No. 61. San Francisco: Jossey-Bass, 1994.

QUANTIFICATION   See **QUANTITATIVE.**

QUANTITATIVE   This is an adjective indicating that something is expressible in terms of quantity (i.e., a definite amount or number). Thus, it is accurate to talk of quantitative measures and quantitative data. The term, however, is often used as a synonym for any design (e.g., experimental and survey) or procedure (e.g., statistical) that relies principally on the use of quantitative data and is then contrasted with 'qualitative' accordingly, but so-called qualitative studies can and often do make use of quantitative data. Quantification is the activity or operation of expressing something as a quantity or amount—for example, in numbers, graphs, or formulas. Quantification or the reliance on quantitative data is a near ubiquitous phenomenon not simply in the sciences but also in all aspects of the administration of social life. **See also QUALITATIVE.**

Key Reference

Porter, T., *Trust in Numbers: The Pursuit of Objectivity in Science and Public Life.* Princeton, NJ: Princeton University Press, 1995.

RADICAL HERMENEUTICS See DECONSTRUCTIONISM.

RATIONALISM   This philosophical position is composed of many variations that generally hold that reason is the primary way we acquire knowledge. Moderate rationalism is equivalent to faith in reason—a belief in the value of critical discussion and valid argumentation. Thus conceived, moderate rationalism is an essential aspect of modernity because it is opposed to superstition, dogma, and authoritarianism. It is the opposite of irrationalism—the view that it is pointless to engage in rational discussion; rather, one must trust in feeling and intuition. Modern cultural, social, scientific, technological, governmental, and administrative practices all reflect trust in reason and, hence, a moderate rationalism. More extreme or radical rationalism (often associated with Descartes [1596-1650], Kant [1724-1804], and Leibniz [1646-1716]) is equated with faith in the ability of reason unaided by perception, experiment, or action. The radical rationalist argues that minds have a priori structures or categories of understanding that organize and give meaning to our sense experiences. Hence, data are neither the primary source of knowledge nor the final arbiter of what constitutes a legitimate knowledge claim.

   In the social sciences, rationalism is most often opposed to *empiricism* that privileges sense experience as the basis for all knowledge. In the philosophy of social science, Karl Popper's (1902-

1994) critical rationalism is a strong critique of the strict empiricism of *logical positivism.* In practice, contemporary natural and social science reflects a blend of rationalism and empiricism, reason and observation.

Key References

Bunge, M., *Finding Philosophy in Social Science.* New Haven, CT: Yale University Press, 1996.

Hollis, M., *The Philosophy of Social Science: An Introduction.* Cambridge, UK: Cambridge University Press, 1994.

RATIONALITY   This is a state or characteristic of being reasonable. The question of what it means to behave rationally when faced with competing (different and contradictory) interpretations is a central issue in debates between *objectivism* and *relativism.* Objectivists typically argue that to resolve a dispute between competing interpretations one must have a set of *criteria.* As Bernstein (1986) explains, they believe that

> if we cannot come up with universal fixed criteria to measure the plausibility of competing interpretations, then this means that we have no *rational* basis for distinguishing better and worse, more plausible or less plausible interpretations, whether these be interpretations of texts, actions, or historical epochs. (p. 358)

Their fear is that without such criteria, reasonable choice between competing interpretations is impossible, and the only alternative is relativism—all evaluation of competing interpretations becomes relative to some particular culture, society, theoretical framework, or conceptual scheme. What it means to behave rationally or reasonably in the face of competing claims thus appears to be framed in terms of an either-or choice: either objectivism (rational behavior) or relativism (irrational behavior).

There are at least two major alternative views, however. One is a strong skeptical view that holds that the objectivists' search for *foundational* criteria is not simply misguided but dangerous. Strong skeptics argue that if being reasonable or rational means having foundational criteria, then the very idea of being rational requires deconstruction. They hold that searching for criteria that can decisively resolve interpretive disputes encourages an intolerance of 'otherness,' ambiguity, and diversity of views. Thus, new strategies are required for circumventing or subverting that demand for answerability to reason through which, it is believed, power and control are exercised. The radical relativist seeks to make space in thought for that which is allegedly nonassimilable to reason—namely, diversity, heterogeneity, pluralism, and difference. A second view is a more moderate skepticism that does not necessarily seek to deconstruct the idea of rationality but aims to recover a different kind of rationality. Moderate skeptics agree that we can never find a set of foundational criteria that can settle disputes regarding competing interpretations in an objective, impartial manner because criteria are always socially formulated, negotiated, interpreted, and applied. They claim, however, that we need not, as a result, be suspicious of the very idea of rationality. Rather, we must recover the idea of practical rationality—that is, how in our practices we exercise a kind of contextually embedded and situationally sensitive practical judgment of the particular (see PRAXIS) and support our comparative judgments with arguments and the appeal to good reasons. Bernstein (1983) holds that

> central to this new understanding is a dialogical model of rationality that stresses the practical, communal character of rationality in which there is choice, deliberation, interpretation, judicious weighing and application of criteria, and even rational disagreement about which criteria are relevant and most important. (p. 172)

Key References

Bernstein, R. J., *Beyond Objectivism and Relativism*. Philadelphia: University of Pennsylvania Press, 1983.

Bernstein, R. J., "What Is the Difference That Makes a Difference? Gadamer, Habermas, and Rorty," in B. R. Wachterhauser, ed., *Hermeneutics and Modern Philosophy*. Albany: State University of New York Press, 1986.

Burbules, N. C., "Moving Beyond the Impasse," in D. C. Phillips, ed., *Constructivism in Education: Opinions and Second Opinions on Controver-*

sial Issues, 99th Yearbook of the National Society for the Study of Education. Chicago: University of Chicago Press, 2000.

Smith, N. H., *Strong Hermeneutics: Contingency and Moral Identity.* London: Routledge, 1997.

Taylor, C., *Philosophical Arguments.* Cambridge, MA: Harvard University Press, 1995.

REACTIVITY   This is a state of affairs that results from the use of any means to generate data that influences the respondents, participants, or subjects who provide the data. Reactivity is typically regarded as a threat to *validity* and something that can be prevented through the use of completely unobtrusive observation or measurement. The notion of reactivity, however, is actually part of a more encompassing condition of all research that can never be eliminated—namely, that there are *always* effects of the audience and the context on what people say and do. Thus, rather than wrestle with the elimination of reactivity through finding the right, allegedly nonreactive procedure, a wiser choice is to recognize that all accounts produced by researchers must be interpreted within the context in which they were generated. Interpretations must examine, as carefully as possible, how the presence of the researcher, the context in which data were obtained, and so on shaped the data. **See also REFLEXIVITY.**

Key Reference

Hammersley, M., & Atkinson, P., *Ethnography: Principles in Practice.* London: Tavistock, 1983.

REALISM   Broadly conceived, this is the doctrine that there are real objects that exist independently of our knowledge of their existence. On a daily basis, most of us probably behave as garden-variety empirical realists—that is, we act as if the objects in the world (things, events, structures, people, meanings, etc.) exist as independent in some way from our experience with them. Also, we regard society, institutions, feelings, intelligence, poverty, disability, and so on as being just as real as the toes on our feet and the sun in the sky. More than this commonsense realism is often at stake in the literature on qualitative inquiry, however. Hence, it is important to distinguish several varieties of realism.

In terms of a theory of perception, *naïve (or direct) realism* denies the importance of a mental entity (an awareness *of* some object) that is interposed between the perceiver and the object. Direct realism claims that the external, independently existing physical object is directly perceived—the things in the world just are as they appear. This theory contrasts with representative realism, which argues that we do not directly perceive external objects but rather we perceive the effects (images, ideas, impressions, etc.) that these objects have on us. These two theories are of considerable significance in the current debate about *representation* in contemporary qualitative inquiry, although one seldom sees an examination of the philosophical issues involved here in that literature.

Metaphysical realism is the doctrine that the world exists independently of consciousness. A related epistemological doctrine called meaning realism holds that meaning exists in objects (including human actions and events) independent of whether we as agents are aware of same. The distinction in these two forms of realism is important for understanding the philosophy of constructivism. The constructivist believes that meaning does not have an independent existence; meaning is not 'objective' in this sense or simply 'out there' awaiting discovery. Rather, meaning comes into existence only through the engagement of knowers with the world. One could, without contradiction, quite readily accept metaphysical realism (there is a world of things, events, and objects 'out there' whether I can conceive of them or not) and still be a constructivist with regard to epistemology—that is, what those things, events, and so on mean. This is the kind of constructivism characteristic of the *philosophical hermeneutics* of Hans-Georg Gadamer and Charles Taylor. More radical versions of constructivism deny both metaphysical realism and meaning realism and hold that it is not simply what one makes of the world that is constructed but also that the world is constructed.

Scientific realism is the view that scientific theories refer to real features of the world or the view that real things just exactly are as science takes them to be. *Real* here refers to whatever it is in the universe (i.e., forces and structures) that causes the phenomena that we perceive with our senses. Scientific realism argues that what is 'real' is not necessarily only that which we can directly observe. To understand this idea, it may help to contrast it with the view of the logical positivists. Logical positivists did not deny that there was a real world; they insisted that the world consists of observable particulars. They rejected, however, any elements of realism in their *epistemology* (i.e., in their theory of what constituted a legitimate scientific explanation). The logical positivists believed that what is real is a world of discrete or particular events that are observable. These events actually exist whether we observe them or not. The interest of logical positivists regarding questions of reality stopped there, however. They argued that the only sure path to knowing this world is the experience of the senses. Thus, logical positivists were thoroughgoing empiricists. They believed that reality is that which can be observed, and what we can observe is only the constant conjunction of events—some set of events is followed by the appearance of events of another kind. Explanations are thus simply a question of locating an event to be explained in (i.e., 'covering it' with) an observed regularity. For the logical positivist, there is nothing deeper, so to speak, to the notion of explanation than the proper logical arrangement of well-verified observations. The test of whether a theory is true or false is nothing more than a test of its success or failure at predicting events. Hence, there is no need to talk of whether theories actually refer to causes, forces, necessities, mechanisms, or any other such unobservable 'real' underlying entities. All such talk is metaphysical speculation and has no place in what constitutes genuine, legitimate scientific knowledge.

Scientific realism agrees with logical positivism that there is a world of events 'out there' and that there are patterns or regularities of events that can be observed. Scientific realists, however, distinguish the empirical (that which we observe with our senses) from the real (the processes that generate the events we observe). Realism rejects logical positivist epistemology. It holds that to claim one has genuine, scientific knowledge, it is important to decide whether theories are 'really' true or false (and not just valid by virtue of their ability to predict); whether a cause really exists; and whether there really are things out there such as electrons, gravity, force fields, society, and social structures. Realists believe that a genuine scientific explanation must go beyond statements of observed regularities to get at the mechanisms, processes, structures, or whatever unobservable, real, underlying forces actually account for the regularities (constant conjunctions) that we observe.

Doctrines of this kind of scientific (or ontological) realism are met by strong opposition from varieties of ontological relativism, such as expressed by Richard Rorty. The latter views claim that the world is just what we take it to be according to our current interpretive practices. In other words, the truth of scientific theories is not a matter of determining whether they in fact mirror the real world. Rather, the meaning and truth of theories are matters decided within a particular conceptual scheme or language game—a particular habit of construing evidence according to some logic of inquiry that we have adopted that answers to our own ideas of what is good in the way of belief. This antirealist stance is characteristic not only of Rorty's neo-pragmatism but also of much social *constructivism.* See also EMPIRICISM, ETHNOGRAPHIC REALISM, OBJECTIVISM, REPRESENTATION.

Key References

Bhaskar, R., *Reclaiming Reality: A Critical Introduction to Contemporary Philosophy.* London: Verso, 1989.

Crotty, M., *Foundations of Social Research.* London: Sage, 1998.

Outhwaite, W., *New Philosophies of Social Science: Realism, Hermeneutics and Critical Theory.* New York: St. Martin's, 1987.

Rorty, R., *Philosophy and the Mirror of Nature.* Princeton, NJ: Princeton University Press, 1979.

REALIST TALE   See ETHNOGRAPHIC REALISM.

RECIPROCITY   This is a kind of social behavior—a mutual give and take and an exchange of gifts or services—in which we routinely engage in social life but that is especially important in *field* studies in which the researcher is accorded the privilege of access to the lives of those he or she studies. Paying respondents, informants, and participants and doing small favors, such as giving them a ride to work, picking up their dry cleaning, baby-sitting their children, and buying them a meal, are reciprocal social acts that might be performed by a field researcher. Reciprocity is part of the larger ethical-political process of building trust, cultivating relationships, and demonstrating genuine interest in those whom one studies. Which of these kinds of activities to engage in or how far to take the act of reciprocity are matters of ethical judgment regarding what is appropriate in the circumstances in question and hence requires practical wisdom. See also FIELD RELATIONS.

Key References

Johnson, J. M., *Doing Field Research*. New York: Free Press, 1975.

Wolcott, H. F., *The Art of Fieldwork*. Walnut Creek, CA: AltaMira, 1995.

R

REDUCTIONISM   This is the idea that we can (and should) replace one vocabulary (set of concepts and theory) by a second vocabulary (set of concepts and theory) that is more primary. Examples of attempts at reductionism include the logical positivists' bid to reduce the vocabulary of theory to the vocabulary of observation statements; logicism—the bid to reduce mathematics to logic; the reduction of psychology to neurology; the reduction of social science explanations to natural science explanations, especially those of physics; and methodological individualism—reducing explanations about social reality to statements about individual human actions. See also HOLISM.

Key Reference

Collin, F., *Social Reality*. London: Routledge, 1997.

REFLEXIVITY   Discussion of the meaning and consequences of reflexivity in the conduct and writing of qualitative inquiry is extensive. In *ethnomethodology*, reflexivity refers to the fact that all accounts (in speech and writing) are essentially not just *about* something but are also *doing* something. Written and spoken accounts do not simply represent some aspect of the world but are in some way involved in that world. This kind of (ontological) reflexivity is simply unavoidable.

The term reflexivity is also used in a methodological sense to refer to the process of critical self-reflection on one's biases, theoretical predispositions, preferences, and so forth. This kind of self-inspection can be salutary for any kind of inquiry, and field-workers are often encouraged to record and explore these evolving dispositions in personal notes in their *field journals*. Reflexivity in a methodological sense can also signal more than inspection of potential sources of bias and their control. It can point to the fact the inquirer is part of the setting, context, and social phenomenon he or she seeks to understand. Hence, reflexivity can be a means for critically inspecting the entire research process, including reflecting on the ways in which a field-worker establishes a social network of informants and participants in a study and examining one's personal and theoretical commitments to determine how they serve as resources for generating particular data, for behaving in particular ways vis-à-vis respondents and participants, and for developing particular interpretations. Reflexivity understood in this way is held to be a very important procedure for establishing the *validity* of accounts of social phenomena. This is particularly true for many critical researchers concerned with the charge that their research can become nothing more than a self-serving ideology and for feminist researchers wary of duplicating androcentric perspectives and race and class bias in their investigations.

Reflexivity is also used in an ideological sense to signal various strategies for composition and writing that reflect specific theoretical, political, and intellectual agendas. This kind of reflexivity is characteristic of "messy texts"—forms of experimental writing that reject the 'finished' appearance of a *realist tale* written by a detached observer. They reflect an open-endedness, incompleteness, the full presence of the writer in the text, and the continual movement back and forth between description, interpretation, and multiple voices. Ethnopoetics and *autoethnography* are examples. **See also BIAS, REPRESENTATION.**

Key References

Denzin, N. K., *Interpretive Ethnography: Ethnographic Practices for the 21st Century*. Thousand Oaks, CA: Sage, 1997.

Marcus, G. E., "What Comes (Just) After 'Post?' " in N. K. Denzin & Y. S. Lincoln, eds., *Handbook of Qualitative Research.* Thousand Oaks, CA: Sage, 1994.

Potter, J., *Representing Reality: Discourse, Rhetoric and Social Construction.* London: Sage, 1996.

Sanjek, R., "On Ethnographic Validity," in R. Sanjek, ed., *Fieldnotes: The Makings of Anthropology.* Ithaca, NY: Cornell University Press, 1990.

RELATIVISM   In general, this is the doctrine that denies that there are universal truths. There are several interrelated senses of the term, however:

1. *Epistemological relativism* is a doctrine about our experience of or knowledge of the world. It is the belief that notions of rationality, truth, goodness, rightness, and reality can be understood *only* as relative to some specific theoretical framework, language game, conceptual scheme, set of social practices, or culture.

2. *Ontological relativism* is a doctrine about the nature of reality. It is the belief that reality is determined by our language or conceptual scheme.

3. *Descriptive cultural relativism* is a long-standing perspective in anthropology. This is the view that acceptable social practices (or the morality of such practices) differ from society to society or culture to culture. Cultural relativists (those who simply describe differing social practices), however, are not necessarily ethical relativists.

4. An *ethical relativist* holds that there are no universally valid moral principles.

5. *Cognitive relativism* is the belief that there are no universal truths about the world. In poststructuralist thought, this kind of relativism is often associated with universal perspectivalism and thus leads to radical *skepticism.* Universal perspectivalism is attributable to Friedrich Nietzsche (1844-1900), who argued for the interpretive and radically perspectival character of all knowing. He argued that there can be no such thing as absolute

knowledge that transcends all perspectives; we must face the fact that there are only interpretations of interpretations. Hence, we can never know whether there is any such thing as valid knowledge. Contemporary versions of cognitive relativism that are not simultaneously given to radical Nietzschean skepticism are offered by Rorty, Goodman, and Putnam.

Key References

Bernstein, R. J., *Beyond Objectivism and Relativism*. Philadelphia: University of Pennsylvania Press, 1983.

Fay, B., *Contemporary Philosophy of Social Science*. Oxford, UK: Blackwell, 1996.

Goodman, N., *Ways of World Making*. Indianapolis, IN: Hackett, 1978.

Krausz, M., & Meiland, J., eds., *Relativism: Cognitive and Moral*. Notre Dame, IN: University of Notre Dame Press, 1982.

Putnam, H., *The Many Faces of Realism*. LaSalle, IL: Open Court, 1987.

Rorty, R., *Objectivity, Relativism and Truth: Philosophical Papers*, Vol. 1. Cambridge, UK: Cambridge University Press, 1991.

RELIABILITY   This is an *epistemic criterion* thought to be necessary but not sufficient for establishing the truth of an account or interpretation of a social phenomenon. An account is judged to be reliable if it is capable of being replicated by another inquirer. Traditionally, social scientists assume that although not all repeatable or replicable observations or accounts are necessarily valid, all valid accounts are (at least in principle) replicable. Opinion is divided among qualitative researchers regarding whether this criterion has any meaning whatsoever in judging the accuracy of fieldwork accounts. Some scholars emphasize the importance of repeatability of observations within a given study both diachronically (the stability of a field-worker's observations across data drawn from different time periods) and synchronically (similar observations within the same time period across different methods, e.g., observation and interview). Others argue that reliability can and must be addressed in fieldwork by using conventionalized methods for recording fieldnotes and analyzing transcripts as well as making interrater checks on coding and categorization procedures and results. Still others have called for establishing *dependability*—an analog to reliability—through careful documentation of procedures for generating and interpreting data. Here, reliability is a matter of assembling dependable evidence, and the methods used to assemble this evidence matter. (Making a claim about the meaning of this evidence is a *validity* issue.) Finally, some argue that reliability in qualitative study is a fiction because no investigator can ever literally replicate another's fieldwork.

Key References

Kirk, J., & Miller, M., *Reliability and Validity in Qualitative Research.* Beverly Hills, CA: Sage, 1986.

Lincoln, Y. S., & Guba, E. G., *Naturalistic Inquiry.* Beverly Hills, CA: Sage, 1985.

Sanjek, R., "On Ethnographic Validity," in R. Sanjek, ed., *Fieldnotes: The Makings of Anthropology.* Ithaca, NY: Cornell University Press, 1990.

Silverman, D., *Interpreting Qualitative Data.* London: Sage, 1993.

REPRESENTATION   Depicting, portraying, or describing social phenomena is a goal not simply of qualitative inquiry but of all forms of social science. Representation in its many forms—as resemblance, replication, repetition, description, and duplication—is central to the modernist project of understanding the world. Whether inquirers should claim that they 'represent' the social world in their studies and precisely what they are doing when they try to represent, however, is a matter of great dispute.

Naturalistic inquiry assumes the importance of faithful representation of the life-worlds of those one studies. Few such inquirers cling to naïve *realism* and argue that their accounts are a literal mirror or representation of an external reality; few, however, would also abandon the idea that their portrayals, depictions, or descriptions, although fictions (in the sense of invented or crafted), should not also be accurate. Many struggle with the idea of fallible representation—seeking to find ways to give evidence or good reasons for their accounts that represent social phenomena without claiming that those accounts are certain or beyond revision.

Many postmodernists find the idea of representation reprehensible. They claim that the practice of taking one thing for another assumes (a) the ability to reproduce and duplicate reality and (b) the ability to make the transfer without loss of content. For these postmodernists, there is no such thing as the 'original' of anything that stands in some relation of equivalence to its representation; there is only the endless play of different representations. Hence, they believe that representation assumes *objectivism,* and that the goal of *deconstructionism* is to reveal the foolishness of all representational claims. Postmodern-inspired qualitative studies claim that they 'evoke' rather than 'represent.' Pauline Rosenau (1992) summarizes the radical postmodernist view:

> Representation is politically, socially, culturally, linguistically, and epistemologically arbitrary. It signifies mastery. ... It signals distortion; it assumes unconscious rules governing relationships. It concretizes, finalizes, and excludes complexity.... [It] is fraudulent, perverse, artificial, mechanical, deceptive, incomplete, misleading, insufficient, wholly inadequate for the postmodern age. (pp. 94-95)

See also AUTHORITY, CRISIS OF REPRESENTATION, DESCRIPTION, ETHNOGRAPHIC REALISM, EXPERIENCE, OBSERVATION.

Key References

Danto, A. C., *The Body/Body Problem*. Berkeley: University of California Press, 1999.

Denzin, N. K., *Images of Postmodern Society*. London: Sage, 1991.

Gubrium, J. F., & Holstein, J. A., *The New Language of Qualitative Method*. Oxford, UK: Oxford University Press, 1997.

Rosenau, P., *Post-Modernism and the Social Sciences*. Princeton, NJ: Princeton University Press, 1992.

Van Maanen, J., ed., *Representation in Ethnography*. Thousand Oaks, CA: Sage, 1995.

RESEARCH DESIGN   Designs or plans for conducting qualitative studies vary considerably; there are no prescribed designs as, for example, one might find in survey research, experimental, and quasi-experimental studies in the social sciences. That does not mean, however, that qualitative researchers conduct studies without careful forethought and planning. Every qualitative study requires some combination of theoretical claims and empirical evidence to produce an argument that answers the research question or problem that the study examines. Jennifer Mason explains that, generally speaking, all plans for qualitative studies require fashioning answers to three broad questions: (a) What is my research about? (i.e., What is the phenomenon to be investigated? What might constitute evidence of that phenomenon? and Why is this phenomenon worth investigating?) (b) What is the strategy for linking research questions, methods, evidence? and (c) How will the proposed research take account of relevant ethical, political, and moral concerns? **See also** EMERGENT DESIGN, SENSITIZING CONCEPTS.

Key References

Alford, R. R., *The Craft of Inquiry*. Oxford, UK: Oxford University Press, 1998.

Mason, J., *Qualitative Researching*. London: Sage, 1996.

RESPONDENT   See ETHICS OF QUALITATIVE INQUIRY, **INFORMANT.**

RESPONDENT VALIDATION   See MEMBER CHECK.

REVIEW OF LITERATURE   All reviews involve combining multiple studies for the purpose of demonstrating their collective relevance for solving some problem, for understanding some issue, for explaining some relationship, and so on. Reviewing is an interpretive undertaking insofar as it is an effort to make sense of these studies and to establish their meaning. A widely held view is that reviews are a means of collecting and organizing the results of previous studies so as to produce a composite of what we have already learned about a particular topic. This approach assumes that knowledge accumulates within a field, and hence understanding of some phenomenon can be built up piece by piece, brick by brick, eventually yielding a more complete, thorough, and, hence, trustworthy understanding, which in turn can be more confidently applied to solving a problem of a particular kind.

This traditional notion of the literature review is based on a biomedical model of combining multiple single studies that address related or identical causal hypotheses to arrive at a valid generalization of a causal relationship. For example, we want to know the efficacy of a treatment A (e.g., some particular pharmaceutical therapy) for condition X (some particular form of cancer), so we examine all single studies of this relationship seeking, by means of induction, to synthesize the individual findings into a general conclusion.

This way of reasoning is extended to social phenomena when we ask about the general conclusion that can be drawn from various single studies about, for example, the effects of homework on academic achievement, the effects of busing on school desegregation, and the effects of site-based management on parent and student satisfaction with public schools. Procedures for these kinds of integrative research reviews and meta-analyses are well established. Moreover, although we often think of such reviews as employing mathematical techniques for comparing, synthesizing, and analyzing results of multiple studies, statistical techniques are not a necessary feature of such reviews. For example, we might imagine a review that examines multiple case studies of school disciplinary practices with the goal to understand what social structures serve as prominent causes of this social action or to understand what social rules, institutional practices and norms, and so on comprise the underlying 'grammar' that gives such practices their meaning. Judging the quality of all such reviews is a matter of determining whether the review in question clarifies and resolves inconsistencies in the various studies under consideration and whether the synthesis is consistent, parsimonious, fruitful, useful, and so on. These, of course, are 'interpretive' criteria, subject to changing definition.

Margaret Eisenhart (1998) argues for an alternative to this traditional conception of literature reviews. She holds that an interpretive review should be consistent with the spirit of interpretive scholarship. That scholarship, she notes, is marked by (a) its power to disrupt conventional wisdom by revealing something surprising, startling, or new; (b) its commitment to demonstrating how the meaning of human action varies by sociocultural context; and (c) its goal of enlarging the universe of discourse, expanding our ways of understanding how we interpret ourselves to ourselves. Hence, she suggests that an interpretivist-oriented review should "offer surprising and enriching perspectives on meanings and circumstances"; it should "shake things up, break down boundaries, and cause thinking to expand" (p. 396). A review should be less like a synthesis or consolidation of existing studies that aims to settle an issue or understanding and more like a reexamination or reconsideration that unsettles or disturbs what we might take for granted as "already learned." **See also** METAETH-NOGRAPHY.

Key References

Eisenhart, M., "On the Subject on Interpretive Reviews." *Review of Educational Research*, 1998, 68(4), 391-399.

Strike, K., & Posner, G., "Epistemological Problems in Organizing Social Science Knowledge for Application," in S. Ward & L. Reed, eds., *Knowledge Structure and Use*. Philadelphia: Temple University Press, 1983.

Strike, K., & Posner, G., "Types of Syntheses and Their Criteria," in S. Ward & L. Reed, eds., *Knowledge Structure and Use*. Philadelphia: Temple University Press, 1983.

SAMPLING LOGIC   There are two general strategies or logics for selecting units (organizations, events, people, documents, locations, etc.) to study in qualitative work: an empirical or statistical strategy and a theoretical or purposive strategy. Both can be employed in the same study, although many qualitative studies rely only on the latter. In the logic of sampling based on an *empirical* or *statistical strategy*, sample units are chosen based on their representativeness of some wider population of units. A population of units is defined and enumerated, and sample is chosen from within that population using a procedure that ensures that all samples have an equal or known probability of being selected. Statistical means are used to judge the probability that characteristics and patterns observed in the sample are reflected in the population.

   In the logic of sampling based on a *theoretical* or *purposive strategy*, units are chosen not for their representativeness but for their relevance to the research question, analytical framework, and explanation or account being developed in the research. Relevance may be a matter of choosing a unit(s) because there may be good reason to believe that "what goes on there" is critical to understanding some process or concept or to testing or elaborating some established theory. Relevance may also be a matter of choosing a unit because on the basis of prior knowledge, it is known to be an extreme, typical, deviant, unique, or particularly revelatory unit for shedding light on the issues that the researcher is seeking to elaborate. Finally, relevance may be a matter of choosing multiple places, cases, or sites to facilitate comparisons either because these different units are likely to yield predictable contrasts in understanding the definition of social action or because they are likely to show the same or similar definition of social action. There are two critical issues in the logic of theoretical or purposive sampling. First is the explicit establishment (and explanation) of a relevant criterion (or criteria) on the basis of which the selection of units will be made. Failing to specify and explain this criterion results in sampling in an ad hoc, unspecifiable, and convenient manner, making it impossible to explain why particular units were chosen for study (i.e., Why *these* people, *this* event, and *this* organization?). Second is the use of a strategy for checking that the units one is using are not simply chosen because they support the developing account. The most common strategy employed here is *negative case* analysis.

When a researcher is studying complex social action within a particular locale (an organization, classroom, social service agency, etc.), additional considerations arise regarding sampling *within* that locale or site. Here, the researcher seeks assurances that what is being observed is usual or customary, something that typically goes on there (rather than something being staged for the benefit of the researcher). Thus, a researcher may develop a representational map of the site that creates a working picture of the temporal, ritual, and routine features of the persons, organizations, or social actions under study (N. Denzin, *The Research Act,* 3rd ed., Prentice Hall, 1989). Representational maps also guide the selection of those specific events, activities, interactions, and so on that will be studied within the site. Imagine, for example, that a field-worker has selected a court room as a profitable place in which to study the way in which lawyers and judges frame the behavior of juveniles charged with a crime. Before forming conclusions about the kinds of frames employed in that site, the field-worker would want to be sure that he or she observed on several different occasions in court (mornings, afternoons, weekends, Mondays, Fridays, etc.), over several different events (complicated and uncomplicated cases), and across several different types of plaintiffs (males and females, Caucasians, Hispanics, African Americans, etc.) and (if appropriate) several different kinds of lawyers and judges (experienced and inexperienced, male and female, etc.). **See also CROSS-CASE ANALYSIS, GENERALIZATION.**

Key References

Flick, U., *Introduction to Qualitative Research*. London: Sage, 1998.

Hammersley, M., & Atkinson, P., *Ethnography: Principles in Practice*. London: Tavistock, 1983.

Mason, J., *Qualitative Researching*. London: Sage, 1996.

Patton, M. Q., *Qualitative Evaluation and Research Methods*, 2nd ed. Newbury Park, CA: Sage, 1990.

SCIENCE   One aspect of the contemporary (political) debate about the academic status of qualitative inquiry is whether it can properly be called a science. In this regard, it is worth noting that the German term for science (*Wissenschaft*) has a much broader sense than that associated with the English use of the term *science*, which is typically restricted to physics, chemistry, biology, and so forth. *Wissenschaft*, however, is not narrowly limited to those forms of science that employ the empirical methods of observation and experimentation but refers to any systematic, rational form of inquiry with rigorous and intersubjectively agreed on procedures for validation. *Wissenschaft* includes both the sciences of mathematics and logic and the hermeneutic and phenomeno- logical disciplines concerned with the interpretation of meaning and the description of experience, respectively. The intellectual tradition encompassing all the methodological and epistemological concerns of the natural sciences is referred to as *Naturwissenschaften*, and that tradition sets them apart from the tradition of the human or social sciences or *Geisteswissenschaften*. **Naturalism** is a defense of the former tradition, whereas **antina- turalism** defends the latter. Many poststructuralists would likely disavow any and all attempts to form something called a science of any kind, viewing such attempts as nothing more than linguistic inventions of totalizing, all-encompassing worldviews or metanarratives. **See also EXPLANATION.**

Key References

Outhwaite, W., *Understanding Social Life*, 2nd ed. London: Allen & Unwin, 1986.

Polkinghorne, D., *Methodology for the Human Sciences*. Albany: State University of New York Press, 1983.

SCIENTIFIC METHOD   See METHOD.

SCIENTISM   The term may have originated with F. A. Hayek (*The Counter-Revolution of Science: Studies in the Abuse of Reason*, 1955), who traced the idea to the French positivists Auguste Comte (1798-1857) and Henri Saint-Simon (1760-1825). In general terms, twentieth-century Continental philosophy (e.g., phenomenology, existentialism, philosophical hermeneutics, critical theory, and poststructuralism) is characterized by its reaction to scientism. Jürgen Habermas (1971) provides the following succinct definition: "Scientism means science's belief in itself: that is, the conviction that we can no longer understand science as *one* form of possible knowledge, but rather must identify knowledge with science" (p. 4). In various ways, Continental philosophers have argued that the extension of scientific method and rationality (and the cognitive authority bestowed on same) beyond the subject matter of science to all aspects of social life has led to a narrowing of the pubic sphere, the transformation of moral-political issues into technical problems to be solved, a loss of personal identity, and the erosion of personal responsibility for decision making.

Key References

Cooper, D. E., "Modern European Philosophy," in N. Bunnin & E. P. Tsui-James, eds., *The Blackwell Companion to Philosophy*. Oxford, UK: Blackwell, 1996.

Habermas, J., *Knowledge and Human Interests*. J. J. Shapiro, trans. Boston: Beacon, 1971.

Ross, D., *The Origins of American Social Science*. Cambridge, UK: Cambridge University Press, 1991.

SEMIOTICS   Also called semiology, this is the theory of signs or the theory investigating the relationship between knowledge and signs. A *signifier* is an acoustic image of a spoken word as heard or read by a recipient of a vocal, written, or otherwise displayed message. The *signified* is the meaning called forth in the mind of the recipient resulting from the stimulation of the signifier. A *sign* is a unity of signifier and signified. A sign is understood to be an entity or object that carries information—for example, a word, gesture, map, road sign, model, picture, and diagram. *Semiosis* is the symbolic activity (speaking, drawing, dancing, writing, etc.) or process of interpreting or producing meaningful signs—the activity of taking one thing as a sign of another thing.

   The major original contributors to this theory were the Swiss linguist Ferdinand de Saussure (1857-1913) and the American philosopher Charles Sanders Peirce (1839-1914). Saussure's semiotic theory demonstrated that words do not derive their meaning from standing for things in the world; rather, they derive their meaning from sets of relationships and contrasts with other signs. Saussure argued that the proper object for linguistic investigation was *langue* (the shared set of structural properties or rules underlying language use). This focus on structure marks his theory as one of structural linguistics. Criticism and extensions of Saussure's work foreground French poststructuralist semiotic theory (e.g., Roland Barthes [1915-1980], Jacques Derrida, Michel Foucault [1926-1984], and Julia Kristeva). **See also POSTSTRUCTURALISM, STRUCTURALISM.**

Key References

Barthes, R., *Mythologies*. London: Palladin, 1972.

Hawkes, T., *Structuralism and Semiotics*. London: Methuen, 1977.

Saussure, F., *Course in General Linguistics*. London: Peter Owen, 1960. (Original work published 1919)

SENSITIZING CONCEPTS   This term was coined by Herbert Blumer to refer to the way in which symbolic interactionists (and now qualitative inquirers more generally) make use of concepts in their research. Sociopsychological concepts, such as family, victim, stress, and stigma, are held loosely at the outset of a study;

they are not given full operational definitions so that the inquirer might explore how the concept is manifest and given a particular meaning in the set of circumstances under investigation. Sensitizing concepts are not *emic* or indigenous concepts but generated by the inquirer from existing studies and theory. They are used to provide a general sense of direction and reference for a study.

Key References

Blumer, H., *Symbolic Interactionism.* Englewood Cliffs, NJ: Prentice Hall, 1969.

Van den Hoonaard, W. C., *Working With Sensitizing Concepts.* Thousand Oaks, CA: Sage, 1997.

SKEPTICISM   Radical skepticism is the belief that we can never know whether there is any knowledge (cognitive skepticism) or universally valid moral principles (ethical skepticism). More moderate versions of skepticism doubt that there is knowledge of certain kinds. A radical skeptical attitude characterizes the work of many postmodernist scholars who hold that there is no such thing as knowledge understood as justified belief. **See also EPISTEMOLOGY, RELATIVISM.**

Key Reference

Bohman, J. F. "Holism Without Skepticism: Contextualism and the Limits of Interpretation," in D. R. Hiley, J. F. Bohman, & R. Shusterman, eds., *The Interpretive Turn.* Ithaca, NY: Cornell University Press, 1991.

SOCIAL CONSTRUCTIONISM   See CONSTRUCTIVISM.

SOCIOLOGY OF SCIENTIFIC KNOWLEDGE (SSK)   Also spoken of as social studies of science, this is a broad label for a loose collection of scholars, including those in the Strong Programme of the Edinburgh school (e.g., Barry Barnes and David Bloor), the Bath school (e.g., Harry Collins), and others such as Steven Shapin, Simon Schaffer, Steve Woolgar, Bruno Latour, and Karin Knorr-Cetina, who conduct ethnographic studies of scientific practice (in, for example, the laboratories in which scientists work). The work is broadly social constructivist in its orientation —it regards cognition as socially determined—although not all those affiliated with this kind of work use the term *constructivism.*

Traditional sociology of science is principally concerned with the social conditions and norms that enable epistemic justification of scientific claims (or the generation of genuine [i.e., true] knowledge) and with the study of social and psychological factors that lead to discoveries and to errors. SSK studies are more concerned with understanding how it is that scientific activity generates or constructs the facts about the physical world. Controversy surrounds these studies when they claim that it is not simply the facts about the world that are constructed but that physical reality is constructed through the activity of scientists.

Key References

Bloor, D., *Knowledge and Social Imagery,* 2nd ed. Chicago: University of Chicago Press, 1991.

Collins, H. M., *Changing Order: Replication and Induction in Scientific Practice.* London: Sage, 1985.

Knorr-Cetina, K. D., & Mulkay, M., eds., *Science Observed: Perspectives on the Social Study of Science.* London: Sage, 1983.

Pickering, A., ed., *Science as Practice and Culture.* Chicago: University of Chicago Press, 1992.

SPECTATOR THEORY OF KNOWLEDGE   See OBSERVATION.

STANDPOINT EPISTEMOLOGIES   These are ways of thinking about the nature of knowledge that begin with the assumption that there is no universal, Archimedean vantage point (no 'view from nowhere') from which we can know the world. All efforts to know, and all knowledge, are socially situated. Various kinds of standpoint epistemologies (e.g., from the standpoint of women, gays, lesbians, people of color, and people experiencing colonial oppression) share the assumption that 'knowing' must begin in the experiences, interests, and values of some traditionally excluded group because in this way dominant knowledge claims can be effectively criticized and revised. Standpoint epistemologies are a means of deconstructing what has passed for knowledge so as to expose its exclusions and dominant perspectives (e.g., masculinist, eurocentric, racist, and straight). Standpoints are almost always linked to some liberatory, emancipatory, or critical aim. A key issue for standpoint epistemologies is the consequence for knowledge of substituting 'views from everywhere' for the idea of a 'view from nowhere.' The position that is emerging here, influenced by postmodern thought, is that all views (standpoints) are partial and incomplete—it is impossible to imagine uniting them into a single complete or collective view of what knowledge is; knowing is always an act of living within limits and contradictions.

Key References

Asante, M. K., *The Afrocentric Idea*. Philadelphia: Temple University Press, 1987.

Collins, P. H., *Black Feminist Thought*. New York: Routledge, 1991.

Denzin, N. K., *Interpretive Ethnography: Ethnographic Practices for the 21st Century*. Thousand Oaks, CA: Sage, 1997.

Harding, S., *Whose Science? Whose Knowledge?* Ithaca, NY: Cornell University Press, 1991.

Smith, D. E., *Everyday World as Problematic*. Boston: Northeastern University Press, 1987.

STATISTICAL EXPLANATION   This is a form of causal explanation in which evidence of statistical correlation is combined with knowledge of causal factors or mechanisms through which observed correlations evolve. These explanations differ from *deductive-nomological explanations* only to the extent that they imply probabilistic as opposed to deterministic claims. These kinds of explanations are rare but not completely unknown in qualitative studies. A weak analog to this idea is found in M. Miles and A. M. Huberman's *Qualitative Data Analysis* (2nd ed., Sage, 1994). They describe various means for developing empirically supportable causal networks, causal models, and causal chains linking variables. Although the associations between variables

are not measured mathematically, the scheme reflects the underlying idea of establishing correlations among variables and developing a causal story explaining the mechanisms linking the variables into a network or chain. **See also** CAUSAL ANALYSIS,
EXPLANATION.

Key Reference

Little, D., *Varieties of Social Explanation: An Introduction to the Philosophy of
Social Science*. Boulder, CO: Westview, 1991.

STATISTICAL GENERALIZATION   See GENERALIZATION,
SAMPLING LOGIC.

STRUCTURALISM   This is both a way of thinking about the world
and a methodology for investigating the world that is concerned
with identifying and describing its underlying structures that
cannot be observed but must be inferred. What exactly a structure
is varies depending on the discipline in which structures are discussed. For example, the underlying determinate structure may
be economic, as in the case of Marxism; a particular 'grammar' of
language in the case of linguistics; a 'system' in system analysis; or
gender relations in the case of some feminist structural analyses.
Jean Piaget (1896-1980) (*Structuralism*, C. Maschler, ed. & trans.,
Routledge Kegan Paul, 1971) provides a general definition of a
structure as an arrangement of entities that are characterized by
wholeness or internal coherence, dynamism and the capability of
transforming or processing new material, and self-regulation.
Structuralist theories descended from the work of the Swiss linguist Ferdinand Saussure (1857-1913) and the adaptation of
Saussure's ideas for the analysis of language to the analysis of culture by the anthropologist Claude Lévi-Strauss in the 1960s.
Roughly, Lévi-Strauss viewed aspects of cultural behavior—ceremonies, kinship relations, rites, totemic systems, marriage laws,
myths, and so on—not as entities in their own right but as structures in the larger whole or system called culture. Taken together,
these aspects form a kind of language of culture, and each aspect is
a partial expression of the total language. The organization of cul-

ture becomes intelligible through an analysis of its relational structures in much the same way that the organization of a language is made clear by analyzing its grammar.

Structuralist thinking spread beyond the boundaries of linguistics and anthropology to influence other disciplines, including philosophy, literary theory, biology, physical anthropology, and political theory. Its central idea of widespread structural regularities across time and space and its commitment to forming a scientific basis for the study of the innate properties of human nature, human cognition, language, and sociocultural phenomena have found an appeal in these disciplines. **See also** FUNCTIONALISM, POSTSTRUCTURALISM.

Key References

Boyne, R., "Structuralism," in B. S. Turner, ed., *The Blackwell Companion to Social Theory*. Oxford, UK: Blackwell, 1996.

Giddens, A., "Structuralism, Post-Structuralism and the Production of Culture," in A. Giddens & J. H. Turner, eds., *Social Theory Today*. Stanford, CA: Stanford University Press, 1987.

S

SUBJECTIVISM   There are two different senses of this term. First, it is a doctrine that holds that all judgments (claims, interpretations, assertions, etc.) are *nothing but* reports of an individual speaker's feelings, attitudes, and beliefs, or that whatever one claims to be the case is nothing but a matter of personal opinion or taste. This understanding of subjectivism is compatible with *relativism*—that is, the view that 'anything goes' or that any interpretation is as good as any other. Second, it is a doctrine that holds that subjectivity is the ultimate reality, so to speak. Edmund Husserl's (1859-1938) phenomenology of transcendental subjectivism is a well-known example. Husserl offered two kinds of arguments against the doctrine of *realism:* He attempted to show that there is no real world that is wholly independent of the 'subject' that knows or experiences that world, and that the knowing subject does not belong to the world that it knows or experiences—that is, this subject is the "transcendental Ego." This understanding of subjectivism is clearly not equivalent to relativism because Husserl sought to show that transcendental subjectivity was a *universal* truth. **See also** OBJECTIVISM.

Key References

Bunge, M., *Finding Philosophy in Social Science*. New Haven, CT: Yale University Press, 1996.

Hammond, M., Howarth, J., & Keat, R., *Understanding Phenomenology*. Oxford, UK: Blackwell, 1991.

SUBJECTIVITY   From an epistemological point of view, this notion has been discussed in terms of (a) the personal view of an individual, (b) an unwarranted or unsupported (or unwarrantable and insupportable) claim, or (c) a biased or prejudiced account. These three senses of the term are not necessarily equivalent. For example, just because a statement or claim is someone's personal view, it does not necessarily follow that it is unwarranted or biased. Thomas Kuhn in *The Essential Tension* (University of Chicago Press, 1977) sought to distinguish the *judgmental* character of a choice, decision, or statement from its *subjective* character. He argued that there are some kinds of subjective choices that are simply matters of taste—for example, when one expresses "I like ice cream." When one is called on to make a personal judgment, however, then one must give reasons that support that judgment. To be rational and reasonable in this case is to give reasons for one's judgment.

The term has also been used more broadly to refer to the notion of *lived experience* in its historical, political, and physical contexts. Here, the primary issues are the (subjective) experience of sense and self as evident, for example, in discussions of *reflexivity* and *emotion* in qualitative work.

Many postmodernists reject the language of subject and subjectivity altogether as being the trappings of modernity. They are postsubjective or champion the decline of subjectivity, which means they aim to deemphasize the subject as focus for analysis. They also seek to do away with the idea of a rational, unified subject as knower, arguing that there are multiple and contradictory subjectivities that are produced by discursive practices. **See also**

INTERSUBJECTIVITY, JUDGMENT, OBJECTIVITY, SUBJECTIVISM, SUBJECT-OBJECT RELATIONSHIP.

Key References

Ellis, C., & Flaherty, M. G., eds., *Investigating Subjectivity*. Newbury Park, CA: Sage, 1992.

Rosenau, P., *Post-Modernism and the Social Sciences*. Princeton, NJ: Princeton University Press, 1992.

SUBJECT-OBJECT RELATIONSHIP   The conceptual distinction, dualism, or dichotomy of subjects (knowers and thinkers) and objects (what they know or think about) is central to most Western philosophy. (Of course, subjects can be objects of thought and knowledge as is assumed in the notion of *reflexivity*.) The subject-object (S-O) relationship receives a great deal and wide variety of criticism in the literature in qualitative inquiry, most of which is directed at the idea that this dualism is central to the doctrine of *objectivism*, in which it is mistakenly regarded as a substantive (i.e., real) distinction. To regard the S-O relationship as a real distinction, the argument goes, is to believe that the subject stands independently of, apart from, or over against objects of knowledge. Subjects stand alone as fully separate, self-defined entities; the state of being a subject ('subjectivity') is characterized by its ability to have a purely theoretical, contemplative, rational, or intellectual grasp of objects (including both self and world). Furthermore, meaning resides in objects and is discoverable. To fully grasp and to correctly represent that meaning, subjects must exercise their faculty or capacity to reason in a way free from the effects of standpoint—that is, independent of historical context, prejudices, tradition, and so on. Reason thus requires the correct use of *method* (whether Descartes's method of rational doubt or empirical method) because method or procedure is a device that helps prevent reason from being corrupted by prejudice, tradition, and so forth. Following the rules of method helps ensure the distancing of the object of study from the observer (subject and knower), thereby making objective knowledge possible.

Critics call this portrayal of the *epistemology* and *ontology* of the S-O relationship a stance of disengagement. Disengagement is equivalent to objectification, best captured in the German word *Gegenstand*. It means that an object is that which stands over against the subject (knower) who experiences or encounters it. To objectify that which one seeks to understand is thus to treat things that do not stand over against the knower as if they did. Drawing on the intellectual traditions of phenomenology and philosophical hermeneutics, critics argue that the fundamental relationship of self to world (human agency) is actually one of engagement. As Gallagher (1992) explains, "The living human being understands the world as he [sic] finds himself already in it, not as an anemic egological entity eruditely confronting an opposing objective entity" (p. 45). Subjectivity is always, already in the world, situated in relation to objects; subjects are always in dialogue, participating in making sense of self and world. Views of human agency as embodied, of self as dialogical, of meaning as constructed in interaction, and of knowledge as something we participate in (vs. something we acquire as individuals through cognitive mechanisms of input and processing) all follow from these criticisms of the disengaged S-O relationship. **See also BODY, INTENTIONALITY.**

Key References

Adorno, T. W., & Horkheimer, M., *Dialectic of Enlightenment*. J. Cumming, trans. New York: Herder & Herder, 1972.

Crotty, M., *The Foundations of Social Research*. London: Sage, 1998.

Gallagher, S., *Hermeneutics and Education*. Albany: State University of New York Press, 1992.

Smith, M. J., *Social Science in Question*. London: Sage (in association with the Open University Press), 1998.

Taylor, C., *Philosophical Arguments*. Cambridge, MA: Harvard University Press, 1995.

SYMBOLIC INTERACTIONISM   This social psychological and sociological theory has it roots in American *pragmatism*. Like all frameworks informing qualitative studies, this theory comes in a variety of forms and thus is difficult to summarize briefly. Many of the shared assumptions of this school of thought derive from the work of Herbert Blumer (*Symbolic Interactionism: Perspective and Method*, Prentice Hall, 1969), who in turn was influenced by the philosopher and social theorist George Herbert Mead (1863-1931). The Blumer-Mead version of symbolic interactionism rests on three premises. First, humans act toward the objects and people in their environment on the basis of the meanings these objects and people have for them. Second, these meanings derive from the social interaction (communication, broadly understood) between and among individuals. Communication is symbolic because we communicate through language and other symbols and in communicating create significant symbols. Finally, meanings are established and modified through an interpretive process undertaken by the individual actor. The influence of pragmatism on symbolic interactionism is evident in the latter's claim that humans are purposive agents who confront a world that must be interpreted rather than a world composed of a set of stimuli to which the individual must react. The meanings an actor forms in interpreting the world are instruments for guiding and forming action. Symbolic interactionism is thus characterized by its rejection of associationist or behaviorist psychologies. It also evinces a profound respect for the empirical world; to understand the process of meaning making, the inquirer must attend carefully to the overt behaviors, speech, and particular circumstances of behavior settings in which interaction takes place. The inquirer can understand human action only by first actively entering the setting or situation of the people being studied to see their particular definition of the situation, what they take into account, and how they interpret this information.

Key References

Denzin, N. K., *Symbolic Interactionism and Cultural Studies*. Oxford, UK: Blackwell, 1992.

Joas, H., "Symbolic Interactionism," in A. Giddens & J. H. Turner, eds., *Social Theory Today*. Stanford, CA: Stanford University Press, 1987.

Plummer, K., "Symbolic Interactionism in the Twentieth Century: The Rise of Empirical Social Theory," in B. S. Turner, ed., *The Blackwell Companion to Social Theory*. Oxford, UK: Blackwell, 1996.

TACIT (PERSONAL) KNOWLEDGE   Tacit knowledge is having an awareness of certain things in a way that is quite different from focusing attention on them. In contrast to explicit knowledge, in which a knower is self-aware of the state of having knowledge, tacit knowledge is implicit. It is genuine knowledge one can have without being self-consciously aware of having it. Yvonna Lincoln and Egon Guba argued that the tacit knowledge of the field researcher as "human instrument" plays a significant role in distinguishing the methods of *naturalistic inquiry* from the methods of conventional social inquiry. Tacit knowledge enables field researchers to be situationally responsive and to key into potentially important information. Lincoln and Guba claim that this kind of adaptability and flexibility of the "human instrument" marks naturalistic inquiry as uniquely different from experimental and quasi-experimental inquiry that relied on paper-and-pencil instruments (i.e., questionnaires) and mechanical recording devices for data gathering.

Viewed more broadly, a defense of the importance (even necessity) of tacit or personal knowing in scientific inquiry plays a significant role in criticisms of *logical positivism* and *logical empiricism.* These philosophies sought to eliminate from science (or at least greatly minimize) tacit knowledge or, more broadly, any kind of knowing that would be regarded as personal *judgment* and appraisal. The chemist and philosopher Michael Polanyi is generally credited with explaining why the ideal of scientific detachment is suspect and pointing out that the personal participation of the knower in all acts of knowing (including scientific knowing in the context of justification) is essential. Polanyi argued that the inevitable inclusion of personal, tacit assessments and judgments in all aspects of knowledge acquisition did not necessarily undermine the objectivity of science but rather called for an alternative analysis of scientific objectivity. Polanyi (Polanyi & Prosch, 1975) summarized his argument as follows:

> [T]he processes of knowing (and so also of science) in no way resemble an impersonal achievement of detached objectivity. They are rooted throughout (from our selection of a problem to the verification of a discovery) in personal acts of tacit integration. They are not grounded on explicit operations of logic. Scientific inquiry is accordingly a dynamic exercise of the imagination and is rooted in commitments and beliefs about the nature of things. It is a fiduciary act. It is far from skepticism itself. It depends upon firm beliefs. . . . Science is not thus the simon-pure crystal-clear fount of all reliable knowledge and coherence, as it has for so long been presumed to be. Its method is not that of *detachment* but rather of *involvement.* It rests, no less than our other ways of achieving meaning, upon various commitments which we personally share. (p. 63)

Other postempiricist philosophers of science incorporate this insight into their arguments about the rationality of science. Thus, it seems reasonable to say that tacit or personal knowing plays an important role in *all* forms of scientific investigation. **See also PROPOSITIONAL KNOWLEDGE, *WELTANSCHAUUNG.***

Key References

Brown, H., *Perception, Theory and Commitment: The New Philosophy of Science.* Chicago: University of Chicago Press, 1977.

Lincoln, Y. S., & Guba, E. G., *Naturalistic Inquiry.* Beverly Hills, CA: Sage, 1985.

Polanyi, M., *Personal Knowledge: Towards a Post-Critical Philosophy.* Chicago: University of Chicago Press, 1958.

Polanyi, M., & Prosch, H., *Meaning.* Chicago: University of Chicago Press, 1975.

TELEOLOGY   The Greek word *telos* means purpose or end, and teleology is the doctrine that human beings (and/or nature) have a
basic purpose (what that purpose is and where that purpose comes from are debated among teleologists). If human beings have a
telos, that means that they pursue that end or purpose as part of
their nature or essence. A nonteleological view holds that purposes or ends are something that human beings impose on the
world and themselves. Teleological explanation of human behavior is often contrasted with mechanistic explanation characteristic
of *behaviorism;* the latter does not include references to final
causes, ends-in-view, and the like but aims to explain behavior in
terms of physiochemical processes or stimulus response. In the
philosophy of science, functional explanations found in biology
and anthropology are often referred to as teleological because
they explain the occurrence of an event or trait in terms of the purpose it serves (e.g., a biological trait is explained because it is useful to the organism's survival).

Key Reference

Taylor, C., *The Explanation of Behaviour.* London: Routledge Kegan Paul,
1964.

TEXT   There are at least three related ways in which to think of the
importance of the notion of text in qualitative work. The broadest
conception is explained by Clifford Geertz: We can ask, "What
analogies do social scientists use to imagine what social life (the
object of social inquiry) is like, and how it can be best explained?"
Traditionally, social science has looked to analogies drawn from
the natural sciences to explain social life in terms of laws, forces,
structures, and mechanisms. In approximately the past three decades, however, it has become increasingly popular for social theorists to borrow analogies from the humanities and, hence, to
view and explain social *action* as if it were like moves by players
in a game, performances by actors in a drama, and sentences in a
text. Of these three kinds of analogies, the textual analogy, as
Geertz suggests, is perhaps the most venturesome and least obvious. Geertz (1983) notes, however, that it is a potentially very
powerful analogy, not least because it refigures social explanation:

To see social institutions, social customs, social changes as in
some sense "readable" is to alter our whole sense of what [so-
ciological and anthropological] interpretation is and shift it
toward modes of thought more familiar to the translator, the
exegete, or the iconographer than to the test giver, the factor
analyst, or the pollster. (p. 31)

The second, more narrow or technical understanding of text is
specifically related to the textual paradigm of *hermeneutics*. The
phenomenon of the text—biblical, classical, legal, and so on—and
the interrelated issues of interpretation, language, and meaning in
understanding a text lies at the heart of what it means to do hermeneutics. Although the work of Martin Heidegger (1889-1976) and
Hans-Georg Gadamer established the notion of ontological hermeneutics—not simply a textual hermeneutics but a universal,
philosophical hermeneutics that reveals that interpretation is an
inescapable feature of human experience—the 'text' still serves as
the paradigm for philosophical hermeneutics.

To be considered a viable framework for the social sciences,
philosophical hermeneutics had to be extended to address the
subject matter of the social sciences. This required an argument by
analogy: Social action can be read like a written text. This argument is most clearly explained by Paul Ricoeur. Ricoeur accepted
the premise that the object of social science was meaningful social
action construed as a whole (see CONTEXTUALISM), and he pro-
ceeded to explain why (a) this object displayed some of the same
features constitutive of a written text and (b) the methodology of
hermeneutics employs similar procedures in understanding this
object as in interpreting written texts. Charles Taylor also develops this analogy in his defense of hermeneutical social science.
Ricoeur's and Taylor's arguments lend support to the broad textual analogy for social theorizing explained by Geertz.

A third understanding of text is offered by poststructuralists,
who, following Jacques Derrida, hold that *everything* (life experiences, events, relationships, activities, practices, cultural artifacts, etc.) is a text. This radical extension of the textual paradigm
is often referred to as pantextualism, textualism, or the primacy of
language. In this view, texts have several characteristics: (a) Texts
(textual accounts) do not refer transparently to the social world;

(b) they are 'writerly' texts capable of, indeed requiring, rewriting in every encounter by a reader (vs. a traditional notion of 'readerly' texts destined for a passive reader and read for a specific message); (c) every text is related to every other text—this is known as intertextuality (which can also refer to the broad poststructuralist theme that issues and concerns once thought distinct to a discipline are now blended and intertwined across multiple disciplines and fields of thought); and (d) every text is open-ended and indeterminate and thus the site of an infinite number of interpretations. **See also ACTION, CRISIS OF REPRESENTATION, POSTSTRUCTURALISM.**

Key References

Barthes, R., "From Work to Text," in J. Harari, ed., *Textual Strategies: Perspectives on Post-Structuralist Criticism.* Ithaca, NY: Cornell University Press, 1979.

Geertz, C., "Blurred Genres: The Refiguration of Social Thought," in C. Geertz, ed., *Local Knowledge.* New York: Basic Books, 1983.

Ricoeur, P., "The Model of the Text: Meaningful Action Considered as a Text," in J. B. Thompson, ed. & trans., *Hermeneutics and the Human Sciences.* Cambridge, UK: Cambridge University Press, 1981.

Taylor, C., "Interpretation and the Sciences of Man," in C. Taylor, ed., *Philosophy and the Human Sciences: Philosophical Papers.* Cambridge, UK: Cambridge University Press, 1985. (Original work appeared in the *Review of Metaphysics,* 1971, 25, 3-51)

TEXTUAL ANALYSIS, METHODS OF   Researchers can regard a text as an object suitable for analysis. A text can consist of words or phrases (such as responses to structured interviews or questionnaires) or more lengthy segments (as found, for example, in narrative research, analysis of written documents, or responses to open-ended and unstructured interviews). Methods for analyzing data in the form of texts vary along a continuum anchored on one end by methods that emphasize content or *what* was said and on the other end by methods that emphasize form or *how* something was said. Analysis of texts undertaken in *content analysis* and *objectivist hermeneutics* is primarily concerned with content. Analysis undertaken by ethnomethodological means aimed at making sense of talk-in-interaction (*conversation analysis* and *discourse analysis*) is more concerned with form. *Narrative analysis* and the kind of analyses undertaken in *semiotics* generally are concerned with both form and content.

Key References

Bernard, H. R., & Ryan, G. W., "Qualitative and Quantitative Methods of Text Analysis," in H. R. Bernard, ed., *Handbook of Methods in Cultural Anthropology*. Walnut Creek, CA: AltaMira, 1998.

Coffey, A., & Atkinson, P., *Making Sense of Qualitative Data*. London: Sage, 1996.

Manning, P., *Semiotics and Fieldwork*. Newbury Park, CA: Sage, 1987.

Silverman, D., *Interpreting Qualitative Data: Strategies for Analyzing Talk, Text and Interaction*. London: Sage, 1993.

TEXTUALISM   See **TEXT**.

TEXTUALIZATION   See **TRANSCRIPTION**.

THEORETICAL CANDOR   This is a procedure for establishing the *validity* of analysis and interpretation in ethnography. The disciplinary perspectives and formal theories held by the *field-worker* determine the site, problems, and objectives brought to the *field*, thereby giving ethnography a particular purpose and meaning. In other words, theory has an a priori function in shaping research questions, problems, and initial hypotheses. In addition, once fieldwork is under way, the field-worker develops something like a local theory about people, places, interactions, and events that determine much of what is heard and seen. Theoretical candor means making both kinds of theoretical decisions explicit in writing an interpretive account.

Key Reference

Sanjek, R., "On Ethnographic Validity," in R. Sanjek, ed., *Fieldnotes: The Makings of Anthropology*. Ithaca, NY: Cornell University Press, 1990.

THEORETICAL SAMPLING   See **SAMPLING LOGIC**.

THEORETICAL SATURATION   See **GROUNDED THEORY METHODOLOGY.**

THEORY   There are four different ways in which the term theory is used in qualitative inquiry and, more broadly, in all social science. Theory$_1$—theory as a set of tested empirical generalizations; Theory$_2$—theory as a unified, systematic causal *explanation* of a diverse range of social phenomena. Theory of this kind is evaluated in terms of the familiar criteria of parsimony, completeness, predictive power, scope, and so on. Examples from different social science disciplines include exchange theory, kinship theory, cognitive dissonance theory, and Keynesian economic theory. Although what constitutes an adequate causal explanatory account is a matter of debate, there is general agreement among naturalists, some critical social scientists, and pluralists that developing Theory$_2$ is the proper goal of the social sciences; Theory$_3$—theoretical orientations or perspectives (e.g., functionalism, symbolic interactionism, behaviorism, phenomenology, hermeneutics, feminism, and poststructuralism) that are approaches to framing problems, solving problems, and understanding and explaining social reality; and Theory$_4$—critical theory, which refers both to a way of theorizing and to the product of that theorizing. It is distinguishable from the traditional empiricist way of thinking about theorizing and theory (Theory$_1$ and Theory$_2$) in the following ways:

1. It is a way of submitting the very 'givenness' or taken-for-granted character of the social world (its concepts, understandings, cultural categories, etc.) to critical reconsideration and is thus part of the self-reflective public discourse of a democratic society. Traditional theory fails to recognize that theory constitutes the way we access the world—that theory provides the categories through which we think about and experience the world.

2. It regards theory as intimately related to *praxis.* In the empiricist tradition, the theorist does not regard his or her activity of theorizing as part of social practice. Rather, the theorist is disinterested and views theorizing as an activity that takes place

alongside all the other activities that comprise social life but has no immediately clear connection to those activities. In a separate step that is not part of the theorist's work, theory must be applied to practice. In sharp contrast, critical theorizing is 'interested' and simultaneously empirical and normative.

3. It is a kind of theory that employs the method of immanent critique, working from within categories of existing thought to radicalize those categories, reveal their internal contradictions and shortcomings, and demonstrate their unrecognized possibilities.

See also CRITICAL SOCIAL SCIENCE, DISINTERESTED SOCIAL SCIENCE, EMPIRICISM.

Key References

Bernstein, R. J., *The Restructuring of Social and Political Theory*. Philadelphia: University of Pennsylvania Press, 1976.

Calhoun, C., "Social Theory and the Public Sphere," in B. S. Turner, ed., *The Blackwell Companion to Social Theory*. Oxford, UK: Blackwell, 1996.

Horkheimer, M., *Critical Theory*. M. J. O'Connell, trans. New York: Continuum, 1972. (Original German text published 1937)

THEORY-LADEN OBSERVATION   See **THEORY-OBSERVATION DISTINCTION.**

THEORY-OBSERVATION DISTINCTION   The philosophy of *logical positivism* drew a sharp distinction between theory (concepts) and observation and assigned epistemological priority to observation statements. In other words, knowledge was said to rest on a foundation of unambiguous observations. Concepts and theories were entirely dependent for their meaning on the particular observation statements into which they could be unpacked. Thus, the logical empiricist Herbert Feigl argued in classic inductivist fashion that theoretical concepts grow out of the "soil" of observation: Theory is meaningful only and precisely because of an "upward seepage" of meaning from observation statements to theoretical concepts.

This sharp theory-observation separation was strongly criticized by postempiricist philosophers of science, who argued that considerations such as *tacit knowledge,* prior theory, and metaphysical commitments influenced both the making of observations and decisions about what constituted fact. They challenged the relative priority of observation statements over theoretical statements characteristic of the strict inductivist approach of logical positivism and attempted to restore theoretical considerations to an equal footing with observation statements in our picture of the development of scientific knowledge. They demonstrated that although theory does not necessarily determine fact, all observations are in an important sense theory laden. They also demonstrated that all theories are underdetermined by observation or evidence. In other words, there is no body of evidence (data) that can conclusively demonstrate the superiority of one theory over another. Theories can, in various ways, be made to fit the evidence (or, in some cases, to disregard the evidence as anomalous). There is now general agreement in the philosophy of science that the formation, testing, and success of scientific theories is not solely an empirical matter—that is, it does not depend on an unshakable foundation of observations. Rather, there is some sort of dynamic interplay between theory (concept) and observations (evidence) in what constitutes genuine scientific knowledge.

The abandonment of a strict theory-observation distinction and the recognition that theoretical presuppositions (concepts, conceptual schemes, theoretical orientations, etc.) play an important role in observation and testing do not necessarily lead to a relativist epistemology. For naturalists and many antinaturalists, it simply means that there is no absolutely reliable foundation for knowledge that the logical positivists hoped for. Some scholars, however, couple the dissolution of the hard-and-fast theory-observation distinction with a doctrine of radical conceptual difference to draw a relativist conclusion as follows: (a) All empirical evidence is theory laden—i.e., observation is dependent on a conceptual scheme; (b) every conceptual scheme is relative to some language and norms of a particular group, community, or culture of inquirers; (c) these conceptual schemes are incommensurable; and, hence, (d) all knowledge is relative to a conceptual scheme, and comparisons across conceptual schemes are not possible. **See also DESCRIPTION, EMPIRICISM.**

Key References

Feigl, H., "The 'Orthodox' View of Theories," in M. Radner & S. Winokur, eds., *Minnesota Studies in the Philosophy of Science IV*. Minneapolis: University of Minnesota Press, 1970.

Hesse, M., *Revolutions and Reconstructions in the Philosophy of Science*. Bloomington: Indiana University Press, 1980.

THEORY OF SIGNS   See SEMIOTICS.

THEORY-PRACTICE RELATIONSHIP   See PRAXIS, THEORY, USE OF QUALITATIVE INQUIRY.

THICK DESCRIPTION   Following advice given by Clifford Geertz in his widely cited 1973 essay "Thick Description: Toward an Interpretive Theory of Culture," many qualitative inquirers emphasize the importance of "thick" as opposed to "thin" description. It is not entirely clear just what thick description is, however. Most efforts to define it emphasize that thick description is not simply a matter of amassing relevant detail. Rather, to thickly describe social action is actually to begin to interpret it by recording the circumstances, meanings, intentions, strategies, motivations, and so on that characterize a particular episode. It is this interpretive characteristic of description rather than detail per se that makes it thick. **See also** CONTEXTUALISM, INSCRIPTION, REPRESENTATION, TRANSCRIPTION.

Key Reference

Geertz, C., "Thick Description: Toward an Interpretive Theory of Culture," in C. Geertz, ed., *The Interpretation of Cultures*. New York: Basic Books, 1973.

TRANSCRIPTION   This is a written account—a *text*—of what a respondent or informant said in response to a field-worker's query or what respondents said to one another in conversation. Transcription is the act of recording and preparing a record of the respondents' own words. The transcription may result from retyped handwritten notes or audio recordings. When a field-worker records a speech made by a respondent, a respondent's description of an event, a conversation between respondents, a series of answers to a set of interview questions, and so on, the field-worker is preparing a transcription. James Clifford argued that when reports of *fieldwork* are based largely on texts produced through transcription, they may have the effect of breaking up the monological authority of the field-worker-as-privileged-author or interpreter of human action. He and other ethnographers, however, caution that transcription is not some kind of innocent recording of the way things really are. For example, John Van Maanen (1988) explains that transcriptions (and all other forms of *fieldnotes*) are mediated

> many times over—by the field-worker's own standards of relevance for what is of interest; by the historically situated queries put to informants; by the norms current in the field-worker's professional community for what is proper work; by the self-reflection demanded of both the field-worker and the informant; by the intentional and unintentional ways a field-worker or informant is misled; and by the field-worker's mere presence on the scene as an observer and participant. (p. 95)

Van Maanen borrows from Paul Ricoeur the term *textualization* —the process whereby 'unwritten' behavior, beliefs, traditions, and so on become fixed, discrete, particular kinds of data—to claim that it is only in textualized form that data yield to analysis. Hence, he concludes, "the process of analysis is not dependent on the events themselves [as recorded in allegedly innocent transcriptions], but on a second-order, textualized, field-worker-dependent version of events" (p. 95). **See also INSCRIPTION, INTERVIEWING.**

Key References

Clifford, J., "On Ethnographic Authority." *Representations*, 1983, 1(2), 188-146.

Van Maanen, J., *Tales of the Field*. Chicago: University of Chicago Press, 1988.

TRANSFERABILITY   See GENERALIZATION, TRUSTWORTHINESS
CRITERIA.

TRIANGULATION   This is a procedure used to establish the fact
that the criterion of *validity* has been met. The field-worker makes
inferences from data, claiming that a particular set of data supports a particular definition, theme, assertion, hypothesis, or
claim. Triangulation is a means of checking the integrity of the inferences one draws. It can involve the use of multiple data sources,
multiple investigators, multiple theoretical perspectives, multiple methods, or all these. The central point of the procedure is to
examine a conclusion (assertion, claim, etc.) from more than one
vantage point. For example, to understand the nature of communication between geriatric patients and internists in an outpatient
clinic, the field-worker might compare data from early and late
phases of fieldwork, from different patient-physician pairs, from
different times in the temporal cycle of the encounter (taking the
medical history—testing—diagnosis—prescribing a treatment
plan—follow-up), and so forth. Also, data from observations of
patient-physician interactions may be compared with data from
interviews with each party, and so on.
   The strategy of triangulation is often wedded to the assumption
that data from different sources or methods must *necessarily* converge on or be aggregated to reveal the truth. In other words, so
the argument goes, triangulation is both possible and necessary
because research is a process of discovery in which the genuine
meaning residing within an action or event can be best uncovered
by viewing it from different vantage points. Many researchers argue that because triangulation is typically wedded to this assumption of *meaning realism,* it is inappropriate for qualitative research. Others disagree. For example, Martyn Hammersley and
Paul Atkinson (1983) believe that the notion can be salvaged and
made serviceable provided the advice that

> one not adopt a naively "optimistic" view that the aggrega-
> tion of data from different sources will unproblematically
> add up to produce a more complete picture . . . *differences* be-

tween sets or types of data may be just as important and illuminating. . . . [W]hat is involved in triangulation is not just a
matter of checking whether inferences are valid, but of discovering which inferences are valid. (pp. 199-200)

Key References

Denzin, N. K., *The Research Act*, 3rd ed. Englewood Cliffs, NJ: Prentice
Hall, 1989.

Hammersley, M., & Atkinson, P., *Ethnography: Principles in Practice*. London: Tavistock, 1983.

Mason, J., *Qualitative Researching*. London: Sage, 1996.

Seale, C., "Quality in Qualitative Research." *Qualitative Inquiry*, 1999,
5(1), 465-178.

TRUSTWORTHINESS CRITERIA   This is the name given by
Yvonna Lincoln and Egon Guba to one set of *criteria* that have
been offered for judging the quality or goodness of qualitative inquiry. In *Naturalistic Inquiry* (1985), they described criteria (and
associated procedures) that were more appropriate than traditional epistemic criteria (e.g., internal and external validity) and
procedures for judging the trustworthiness of naturalistic investigations. Trustworthiness was defined as that quality of an investigation (and its findings) that made it noteworthy to audiences.
They developed four criteria that served as the naturalist's equiv-
alents to conventional criteria. First, *credibility* (parallel to internal
validity) addressed the issue of the inquirer providing assurances
of the fit between respondents' views of their life ways and the inquirer's reconstruction and representation of same. Second, *transferability* (parallel to external validity) dealt with the issue of *generalization* in terms of case-to-case transfer. It concerned the
inquirer's responsibility for providing readers with sufficient information on the case studied such that readers could establish the
degree of similarity between the case studied and the case to
which findings might be transferred. Third, *dependability* (parallel
to reliability) focused on the process of the inquiry and the inquirer's responsibility for ensuring that the process was logical,
traceable, and documented. Finally, *confirmability* (parallel to objectivity) was concerned with establishing the fact that the data

and interpretations of an inquiry were not merely figments of the inquirer's imagination. It called for linking assertions, findings, interpretations, and so on to the data in readily discernible ways. For each of these criteria, Lincoln and Guba also specified a set of procedures that could be used to meet the criteria. For example, *auditing* was described as a procedure useful for establishing both dependability and confirmability, and *member check* and *peer debriefing*, among other procedures, were defined as most appropriate for credibility.

Several years later, in *Fourth Generation Evaluation* (1989), Guba and Lincoln reevaluated this initial set of criteria. They explained that trustworthiness criteria were parallel, quasi-foundational, and clearly intended to be analogs to conventional criteria. Furthermore, they held that trustworthiness criteria were principally methodological criteria and thereby largely ignored aspects of the inquiry concerned with the quality of outcome, product, and negotiation. Hence, they advanced a second set of criteria called *authenticity criteria*, arguing that this second set was better aligned with the constructivist epistemology that informed their definition of qualitative inquiry. **See also VALIDITY.**

T

Key References

Guba, E. G., & Lincoln, Y. S., *Fourth Generation Evaluation.* Newbury Park, CA: Sage, 1989.

Lincoln, Y. S., & Guba, E. G., *Naturalistic Inquiry.* Beverly Hills, CA: Sage, 1985.

TRUTH   This is one of the most difficult of all philosophical topics, and controversies surrounding the nature of truth lie at the heart of both apologies for and criticisms of varieties of qualitative work. Moreover, truth is intimately related to questions of *meaning,* and establishing the nature of that relationship is also complicated and contested. There is general agreement that *what* is true or what carries truth are statements, propositions, beliefs, and assertions, but *how* the truth of same is established is widely debated. Major theories of truth include the familiar *correspondence theory,* which holds that a statement is true or false depending on whether the content of a statement or belief accurately matches or represents some state of affairs in the world. (A companion theory called the picture theory of meaning holds that a statement is true or false depending on whether reality matches the picture represented by the belief.) A *consensus theory* of truth, as found, for example, in the work of Jürgen Habermas, holds that the truth of a statement is a matter of consensus on beliefs and values that responsible people would reach in an ideal speech situation (i.e., a situation free from the distortions of everyday communication). A *coherence theory* of truth judges the truth of falsity of a statement in terms of the degree to which it is coherent with a background of settled (agreed on and warranted) beliefs. A *contextualist theory* of truth, as held by Richard Rorty, claims that truth is not something about which there can ever be an important philosophical theory because truth is a just a term of agreement; a statement is justified or regarded as true relative to some particular community or culture of inquirers. Many social constructionists are agnostic with respect to the idea of whether truth is a property of the content of statements and focus instead on how telling the truth is socially accomplished or how in interactions people construct a description or statement as 'being true.' A *pragmatic theory* of truth as held, for example, by John Dewey, claims that truth of assertions is determined by whether they function well in helping us understand the world. Dewey argued that the term truth should be replaced by the notion of warranted assertability. For Hans-Georg Gadamer, Charles Taylor, and others in the tradition of philosophical hermeneutics, truth (and meaning) is something that is disclosed in the relationship of interpreter to the object of interpretation. Generally speaking, truth is a property or content over which interpretations "compete," and the better (more perspicuous and perspicacious) account offers an epistemic gain over the account that is less so. For Michel Foucault and followers, truth is not at all a term of appraisal, as is the case in the previous definitions. Foucault argues that an inescapable relationship of power and knowledge characterizes self and society in which truth is something produced and reproduced in particular systems of domination. Some postmodernists, such as Lyotard, hold an even more radical notion of truth (that at times seems close to a contextualist theory)—namely, that a true statement is simply one that is 'good' to make given the relevant criteria accepted within one's social circle of interlocutors.

A good deal of the current criticism (and confusion) about the nature and meaning of truth derives from the fact that truth is often assumed to be a construct that principally acquires its meaning in the doctrine of *realism*. In other words, it is held that to call a statement true is to claim that it accurately accounts for and explains events that actually occur in the real world. Hence, criticisms of the notion of truth are often directed at an epistemology of *representation* and associated epistemic values such as accuracy. Some critics argue that the term truth has no meaning other than as a socially constructed term because there is no 'actual' meaning 'out there' in events, objects, and interactions. Others accept that meaning is constructed in interaction but do not find that idea incompatible with the notion of truth as a real content. Truth is also traditionally related to the notion of *objectivity*, when the latter is understood in a substantive way—that is, when "objective" refers to the semantic content of a statement. In other words, to claim that a statement is objective may be to claim that it is true (or aims at being true) because the content of the statement reflects accurately the way things really are. Hence, criticisms of the notion of truth may be directed more broadly at criticism of the notions of objectivity and *objectivism*. **See also VALIDITY.**

Key References

Abbinnett, R., *Truth and Social Science*. London: Sage, 1998.

Bunnin, N., & Tsui-James, E. P., eds., *The Blackwell Companion to Philosophy*. Oxford, UK: Blackwell, 1996.

Smith, N. H., *Strong Hermeneutics*. London: Routledge, 1997.

UNDERDETERMINATION OF THEORY BY DATA   See **THEORY-OBSERVATION DISTINCTION.**

UNDERSTANDING   To say that we understand what others are doing or saying or that we have an understanding of them is to claim something quite different than that we 'know.' To understand is literally to stand under, to grasp, to hear, get, catch, or comprehend the meaning of something. To know is to signal that one has engaged in conscious deliberation and can demonstrate, show, or clearly prove or support a claim. In Anglo-American thought, at least, knowing and knowledge are more often than not associated with intellectual achievement, cognitive performance, or a special kind of mastery of subject matter—we say, "She really knows her stuff." That understanding is an activity different than knowing is perhaps more evident in the German words for "understanding" *Verständis*, which means comprehension, insight, and appreciation, and *Verstehen,* which we translate as "understanding," also means to have an appreciation for something, to comprehend it *(für etwas Verständis haben).* In German, a difference between knowing and understanding is expressed in the questions *"Woher weißt du das?"* ("How do you know that?") and *"Wie verstehen Sie das?"* ("What do you make of that?").

To claim that we can achieve an understanding means that we also acknowledge the risk that we might misunderstand—that is, fail to grasp, catch, hear, or comprehend the meaning of something; fail to actually 'make something' out of our observation and listening; or construct an understanding that is not in concert with the circumstances of the event or interlocutor we aim to understand. (At times, it appears that some approaches to qualitative inquiry that claim they are given to understanding as an aim of their work fail to take seriously the possibility and risks of misunderstanding.)

Achieving an understanding of others or of the meaning of social *action* is often spoken of as the goal of the human sciences (vs. *explanation* as the goal of the natural sciences). How understanding is accomplished, however, is a matter of some dispute. Some view understanding as an act of discovery or exegesis in which one extracts the meaning inherent in text or speech (see INTENTIONALISM). Others regard understanding as an act of cocreation in which understanding the meaning of text or speech (how a text or a person 'speaks' to the interpreter) is accomplished only through dialogue and a posture in which the interpreter genuinely risks her or his own prejudices (prior understandings).

For example, Gadamer claims that when we seek to understand what others are doing and saying, we are always standing in a liminal space between familiarity and strangeness. He adds that we are "pulled up short" when we encounter situations and people that challenge our expectations and assumptions—those situations in which answers to the question "What should I make of this?" are not easy to come by. Gadamer explains that we can make sense of these challenging encounters with others in three ways. The first is to try to discover the typical behavior of the other and to make predictions about others on the basis of experience. We thereby form what we call knowledge of human nature. Here, subjects (knowers) regard *the other* as an object in a free and uninvolved way in much the same way as they would any other object in their experiential field. This is the methodological attitude of the social sciences—the idea of disinterested theoretical contemplation of an object of understanding.

In a second way of understanding the other, the interpreter acknowledges the other as a person, but this understanding is a form of self-relatedness. Here, the interpreter claims to know the other from the other's point of view and even to understand the other better than he or she understands himself or herself. To be sure, the interpreter understands the immediacy of the other's claim, but it is co-opted from the standpoint of the interpreter. This can be understood as a form of sympathetic listening in which we interpret others in our own terms and refuse to risk our own prejudgments in the process. Gadamer notes that by claiming to know the other in this way, one robs him or her claims of their legitimacy, and Gadamer argues that charitable or welfare work often operates in this way.

A third way of understanding begins from the full acknowledgment that as interpreters we are situated within a tradition. It is only from such a posture that an interpreter can experience the other truly as an other and not overlook his or her claim but let him or her really say something to us. Gadamer (1989) states that "without such openness to one another there is no genuine human bond. Belonging together always means being able to listen to one another" (p. 361). Thus, it seems that it is only the interpreter who is awake to this living in between that can have new experiences and learn from them. Understanding requires an openness to experience, a willingness to engage in a dialogue with that which challenges one's self-understanding. To be in a dialogue requires that one listen to the other and simultaneously risk confusion and uncertainty both about oneself and about the other person one seeks to understand.

It is only in a dialogical engagement of this kind, in a genuine conversation, that understanding is possible. As Gadamer (1989) states, "The miracle of understanding is not a mysterious communion of souls, but sharing in a common meaning" (p. 292). That common meaning can arise only in a dialogue wherein one does not simply defend one's own beliefs or criticize what the other believes but rather seeks to become clear about oneself—about one's own knowledge and ignorance. It is only if an engagement is a genuine conversation that one can engage in checking, amending, and perhaps abandoning one's own prejudices by exposing them to the contribution of the other. See also INTENTIONALISM, MEANING.

Key References

Gadamer, H.-G., *Truth and Method*, 2nd rev. ed. J. Weinsheimer & D. G. Marshall, trans. New York: Crossroad, 1989.

Kerdeman, D., "Hermeneutics and Education: Understanding, Control, and Agency." *Educational Theory*, 1998, 48(2), 241-266.

Risser, J., *Hermeneutics and the Voice of the Other: Re-Reading Gadamer's Philosophical Hermeneutics*. Albany: State University of New York Press, 1997.

UNITY OF METHOD   See LOGICAL EMPIRICISM, NATURALISM.

USE OF QUALITATIVE INQUIRY   How one conceives of the use of qualitative inquiry is related to conceptions of the purpose or aim of such research. As traditionally conceived, the aim of social science is the development of empirical, explanatory *theory*. Particular cases are studied for the purpose of forming general theoretical knowledge; they are not interesting in their own right. Once we are in possession of theory, we can, over time, achieve intellectual and practical mastery of the social world (in much the same manner that possessing a body of empirical explanatory theory in the natural sciences facilitates mastery of the physical world). A particular relationship between theory and practice or action is assumed here: The way to change the social circumstances of education, health care, work life, and so forth is through the technical application of social scientific knowledge (especially knowledge of the probable consequences of different courses of action) to social problems. Hence, here the notion of the use of social inquiry is largely instrumental. Also, instrumental use can take at least two forms: It can be a direct application of a research finding to a problem, or it can be more indirect or 'enlightening,' helping practitioners of various kinds better understand or appreciate the scope and complexity of a problem and its various solutions.

Other notions of use are less technical or instrumental and more educative. For example, research approaches informed directly or indirectly by *critical theory* assume that research should be a kind of cultural criticism—both a way of better understanding ourselves and our society and a way of changing or transforming same. In the tradition of *philosophical hermeneutics*, the kind of understanding one acquires from interpreting a text, culture, speech, and so on is not distinguished from 'use.' In other words, there are not two separate activities of (a) acquiring an understanding and then (b) applying or using it. Rather, the understanding or knowledge that one acquires in interpretation is already a kind of action-oriented self-understanding (this is a view of use shared by Habermas as well). Another educative sense of use follows from the view that we study the particular case to train perception and increase the capacity for practical reasoning and deliberation in those many situations in life that are full of too many details, idiosyncrasies, and exceptional aspects to permit the application of general knowledge. In this conception of use, previous case studies are regarded as useful not to the extent that they make possible general theoretical knowledge but rather because they help develop the capacity to attend to the morally and politically relevant features of the case at hand and thereby enhance practical wisdom. **See also GENERALIZATION.**

Key References

Denzin, N. K., "Interpretive Ethnography for the Next Century." *Journal of Contemporary Ethnography*, 1999, 28, 510-519.

Fay, B., *Critical Social Science.* Ithaca, NY: Cornell University Press, 1987.

Misgeld, D., & Nicholson, G., eds., *Hans-Georg Gadamer on Education, Poetry, and History: Applied Hermeneutics.* Albany: State University of New York Press, 1992.

VALIDATION HERMENEUTICS See CONSERVATIVE
HERMENEUTICS.

VALIDITY   In ordinary usage, validity is a property of a statement, argument, or procedure. To call one of those things valid is
to indicate that it is sound, cogent, well grounded, justifiable, or
logically correct. Psychologically, validity means having confidence in one's statements or knowledge claims. In social science,
validity is one of the *criteria* that traditionally serve as a bench-
mark for inquiry. Validity is an epistemic criterion: To say that the
findings of social scientific investigations are (or must be) valid is
to argue that the findings are in fact (or must be) true and certain.
Here, "true" means that the findings accurately represent the phenomena to which they refer and "certain" means that the findings
are backed by evidence—or warranted—and there are no good
grounds for doubting the findings, or the evidence for the findings
in question is stronger than the evidence for alternative findings.
    There is much discomfort with and some outright rejection of
this criterion among some social inquirers committed to
constructivist, postmodernist, feminist, and pragmatic perspectives. Their objections are many and interrelated. A few of the
more salient ones are singled out here. First, some criticisms are
based on a rejection of naïve or direct *realism*—the idea that we
can have direct, unmediated knowledge of the world. Critics of
this kind argue that if truth means that our ideas about the world
must correspond to the way the world really is, and if validity is a
test of this correspondence, then there can be no validity because

there is no unmediated, observer-independent account of experience to which an account can mirror or correspond. Second, and in a related way, other critics reject the notion that we discover the truth about the world—that is, that truth is somehow 'out there.' They hold that all accounts of the world are language bound. Thus, if there is such a thing as truth, it is arbitrary, and validity would be relative to some particular language system or worldview. Third, still other critics reject the association of validity with *objectivism*—the doctrine that there must be permanent, ahistorical benchmarks or foundations for judging the truth of claims. Any attempt to associate validity with objectivism is greeted at least with *skepticism*. One additional even stronger objection to truth and validity comes from radical postmodernists, who hold that the very idea of truth as essential to knowledge or as a goal of science is a modernist, Enlightenment value associated with order, rules, logic, rationality, and reason, all of which are considered suspect at best and oppressive at worst.

What this all means is that there are at least four different perspectives from which to understand the notion of validity:

1. Fallibilism: The fallibilist might argue that assessing the validity of a claim is indeed a test of whether the claim accurately represents the social phenomena to which it refers. The fallibilist, however, would explain that no claim ever actually reproduces an independently existing meaning, and no claims (no matter how warranted) are ever absolutely certain. Defenders of this view hold that one can have good reasons for accepting an account as more or less valid (true or false), but an account is always subject to error and revision. Martyn Hammersley, for example, argues that we judge the validity of an account by checking whether it is plausible; whether it is credible given the nature of the phenomenon being investigated, the circumstances of the research, and the characteristics of the researcher; and, if we doubt either plausibility or credibility, by inspecting the credibility of evidence offered in support of the claim. In this view, all procedures typically cited as means of establishing validity (e.g., *analytic induction* for testing hypotheses, *triangulation, member check,* providing fieldwork evidence, and *theoretical candor*) are nothing more or less than

fallible means of making a case for a plausible and credible account.

2. Contextualism: Here, the validity of an account is regarded as relative to the standards of a particular community at a particular place and time. What is considered 'valid' is judged in terms of the current consensus about words, concepts, standards, and so on in a given community of interpreters.

3. Radical relativism: The most radical of postmodernists would argue that it is meaningless to talk of a valid (i.e., true) account of the world; there are only different linguistically mediated social constructions. In this radical perspectivalist view, validity is an empty issue (not simply because the term is a social construction) because no single interpretation or account can be judged superior to any other. There is only an endless interplay of different interpretations.

4. Replacement or displacement of validity: The central argument here is that the traditional epistemological concern with validity cannot be decoupled from aesthetic or rhetorical criteria, on the one hand, and political agendas, on the other hand. Hence, the focus shifts from determining whether an account is true to how the account was developed in conversation between inquirer and participants, how it was crafted in writing by the writer of the account, and whether the account advances a social agenda or offers cultural criticism. **See also (THE) PROBLEM OF THE CRITERION.**

Key References

Denzin, N. K., "Aesthetics and the Practices of Qualitative Inquiry." *Qualitative Inquiry*, 2000, 6(2), 256-265.

Hammersley, M., *Reading Ethnographic Research.* New York: Longman, 1990.

Kvale, S., "The Social Construction of Validity." *Qualitative Inquiry*, 1995, 1(1), 19-40.

Lather, P., "Fertile Obsession: Validity After Poststructuralism." *Sociological Quarterly*, 1993, 34(4), 673-693.

Maxwell, J., "Understanding and Validity in Qualitative Research." *Harvard Educational Review*, 1992, 62, 279-300.

VALUE-FREE SOCIAL SCIENCE   See DISINTERESTED SOCIAL SCIENCE, FACT-VALUE DISTINCTION.

VALUE-NEUTRALITY   See DISINTERESTED SOCIAL SCIENCE, FACT-VALUE DISTINCTION, POLITICS OF RESEARCH.

VERIFICATION   This is the activity of determining whether a statement is true or accurate. To verify is to confirm, substantiate, or validate a claim. Thus, financial auditors verify and then attest to the fact that a client's claims about the value of inventory, cash balances, amounts of short- and long-term debt, and so forth are in fact what the client says they are.

In the philosophy of science, verification (also called the principle of verifiability or the verifiability criterion of meaning) has a more specific and technical meaning associated with *logical positivism*. In that philosophy, verification is a criterion for determining whether a statement is a suitable candidate for genuine scientific knowledge. Only those statements capable of verification —capable of being shown to be either true or false by means of either observation or logical reasoning—are considered cognitively meaningful. The logical positivists used this criterion to exclude all other statements (such as those in metaphysics, ethics, or theology) as meaningless with regard to establishing genuine knowledge. Their goal was to establish a foundation for all knowledge claims in the bedrock of observation statements. A variety of critics of logical positivism demonstrated that the verifiability principle was an impossible criterion to maintain. Currently, in the philosophy of science, it is widely acknowledged that verification is not a viable strategy for substantiating a hypothesis or theory; more appropriate criteria are testability and falsifiability. In all social science, it is also generally understood that talk of verifiability (in a strict sense of conclusive confirmation or disconfirmation) as a process of validating or warranting a statement or claim is mistaken. At best, a researcher assembles an argument to substantiate the inference (conclusion) drawn from the data he or she has generated. Substantiation is a matter of demonstrating the likelihood (never the certainty) that the conclusion is correct, genuine, or true or, at least for the time being, not incorrect or false. Thus, it is disturbing so see the term verification discussed in the literature as a process suitable for establishing the validity of claims made in qualitative inquiry. **See also EVIDENCE.**

Key References

Ayer, A. J., *Language, Truth and Logic.* London: Gollancz, 1936.

Creswell, J. W., *Qualitative Inquiry and Research Design.* Thousand Oaks, CA: Sage, 1998.

VERISIMILITUDE   This term originates in Karl Popper's (1902-1994) philosophy of science. Popper held that the goal of science is increasing verisimilitude, where verisimilitude meant an approximation toward or closeness to the truth about the way the world really is. He argued that we could compare scientific theories by examining the relative amounts of truth or falsity contained within each theory. This proved to be an indefensible position, although the notion of verisimilitude has been salvaged in modified form by the philosopher of science W. H. Newton-Smith.

The term verisimilitude, as it appears in discussions about the methodologies of qualitative inquiry, is used in ways quite different from that intended by Popper. There are three overlapping definitions of the term, all dealing with a quality of the text:

1. Verisimilitude as a criterion (others include plausibility, internal coherence, and correspondence to readers' own experience) sometimes cited as important for judging narrative inquiry: A narrative account (referring either to the narratives generated from or by respondents or to the narrative report produced by the inquirer) is said to exhibit the quality of verisimilitude when it has the *appearance* of truth or reality. (Note that what Popper meant by approximation to the truth is quite different from appearance of truth.)

2. Verisimilitude as a criterion for judging the evocative power or sense of authenticity of a textual portrayal: This is a style of writing that draws readers into the experiences of respondents in such a way that those experiences can be felt.

3. Verisimilitude as the relationship of a particular text to some agreed on opinions or standards of a particular interpretive community: A particular text (e.g., book review, scholarly essay, speech to a scholarly society, and research report) has verisimilitude to the extent that it conforms to the conventions of its genre.

A related word in poetics is *vraisemblance,* which refers broadly to the plausibility of any text and encompasses the three senses of verisimilitude noted previously.

As a criterion for **narrative inquiry,** verisimilitude and related nonepistemic criteria have met with strong opposition by scholars who claim that just because a story or narrative is compelling, plausible, lifelike, seemingly authentic, and so on, it does not follow that it is necessarily true. These scholars argue that although not all stories or narrative accounts need be true—for example, provocative, entertaining fiction has its place—in cases in which it is claimed that the narrative is explanatory or knowledge bearing, a judgment about whether the account is true or false does matter.

Key References

Culler, J., *Structuralist Poetics: Structuralism, Linguistics, and the Study of Literature.* Ithaca, NY: Cornell University Press, 1975.

Newton-Smith, W. H., *The Rationality of Science.* London: Routledge Kegan Paul, 1968.

Phillips, D. C., *The Expanded Social Scientist's Bestiary.* Lanham, MD: Rowman & Littlefield, 2000.

VERSTEHEN   This is a German term for "understanding" used to refer both to the aim of human sciences and to their method. Reacting to the growing prominence of empiricist and positivist epistemologies in the late nineteenth and early twentieth century, the German philosopher and historian Wilhelm Dilthey (1833-1911) set out to establish the unique nature of historical and cultural knowledge. He argued that what fundamentally distinguished the natural sciences (*Naturwissenschaften*) from the human (mental) sciences (*Geisteswissenschaften*) was that the former aimed at developing causal explanations (*Erklärung*) from the outside, so to speak, through the use of general laws, whereas the latter aimed at understanding meaning (*Verstehen*) from the agent or actor's point of view by grasping the subjective consciousness of action from the inside: "Nature we explain; psychic life we understand." Dilthey relied heavily on the analysis of inner, psychic experience as distinct from (but related to) outer experience of external nature. He emphasized that the social inquirer must engage in a psychological reenactment (*Nacherleben*) or imaginative reconstruction of the experience of human actors to understand human social life and history. Hence, his view of *Verstehen* had strong overtones of psychologism (the doctrine that reduces the objects of consciousness to mental states).

This distinction between the natural and human sciences and the role and meaning of *Verstehen* was further elaborated by neo-Kantian philosophers Wilhelm Windelband (1848-1915) and Heinrich Rickert (1863-1936), who objected to the psychologism inherent in Dilthey's view. Windelband argued that the natural sciences seek nomothetic knowledge (general laws), whereas the historical sciences seek to describe unique events (idiographic knowledge). Unlike Dilthey, he held that there was no essential difference in the *objects* that the two sciences studied, only a difference in *method*. Any kind of object (e.g., mental events and physical objects) could be studied by means of both methods. Windelband claimed that positivism's error was in believing that every event must be viewed nomothetically. Rickert developed a connection between ideal or transcendent cultural values and historical events, arguing that it was only through grasping this connection that the meaning of historical events could be made clear. He used the term *Kulturwissenschaften*—cultural sciences—to signal a revision of Dilthey's focus on inner, psychic experience.

Max Weber's (1864-1920) efforts to establish an interpretive sociology (**Verstehende sociology**) predicated on an understanding of actors' perspectives of their social action were, in turn, indebted to the work of these predecessors. Weber distinguished two kinds of *Verstehen*: "direct observational understanding," in which the purpose or meaning of human **action** is immediately apparent, and "explanatory understanding" that required grasping the motivation for human behavior by placing the action in some intelligible, inclusive context of meaning. Weber argued that human action is both open to and requires interpretation in terms of the subjective meaning that actors attach to that action. Social scientific (causal) explanation of human action had to be predicated on this kind of understanding.

The phenomenological sociologist Alfred Schutz (1899-1956) sought to clear up the meaning of *Verstehen* by distinguishing three senses of the term:

1. As "the experiential form of commonsense knowledge of human affairs": *Verstehen*, in this definition, has nothing to do with introspection or the subjective states of human agents. Rather, it refers to the intersubjective character of the *life-world* and the complex processes by which human beings come to recognize their own actions and those of their fellow actors as meaningful.

2. As an epistemological problem: The central issue here is how *Verstehen* (as a kind of knowledge) is possible. Here, Schutz drew on Edmund Husserl's (1859-1938) considerable work on the concept of the life-world (*Lebenswelt*). Husserl had argued that the life-world was ontologically prior; all scientific, logical, and mathematical concepts originate in this life-world. The life-world is the grounds of all understanding.

3. As a method unique to the human sciences: Schutz argued that social reality has a specific meaning and relevance structure for human beings living, acting, and thinking within it. *Verstehen* thus refers to a first-order process by which we all interpret the world. The interpretation of the world sought by the social scientist must begin by grasping this first-order understanding. The social scientist then fashions a second-order interpretation of that world by employing the constructs of the social sciences. *Verstehen* thus also means a second-order process, a special means of entry into the life-world, by which the social inquirer seeks to understand the first-order process.

Despite the efforts of Schutz and others to clarify what is meant by *Verstehen* or interpretive understanding, *logical empiricists* (e.g., Theodore Abel and Otto Neurath) seized on the tendency to equate the act of understanding with grasping subjective, mental states. They argued that *Verstehen* defined as psychological empathy or getting inside other people's heads was interesting only as a heuristic device for generating objectively testable hypotheses. This logical empiricist formulation of *Verstehen* has persisted to the present day and continues to be refuted. For example, echoing Schutz, Charles Taylor, in his often-cited essay "Interpretation and the Sciences of Man" (*Review of Metaphysics*, 1971, 25, 3-51), argued that *Verstehen* has to do not with inner organic or psychological states but with understanding intersubjective meanings constitutive of social life. These meanings, in turn, are not grasped via empathy but by means of a hermeneutic process. In addition, in defending interpretive anthropology, Clifford Geertz (1983) found it necessary to explain that ethnographers cannot claim "some unique form of psychological closeness" with their subjects. He argued that interpretive understanding of the meaning of human action is forthcoming more from the act of looking over the shoulders of others:

> The trick is not to get yourself into some inner correspondence of spirit with your informants. Preferring, like the rest of us to call their souls their own, they are not going to be altogether keen about such an effort anyhow. The trick is to figure out what the devil they think they are up to. (p. 58)

Hans-Georg Gadamer accepted Dilthey's idea that the operation of *Verstehen* is profoundly different than explaining the events of nature, but he too rejected the view that understanding depends on a psychological reenactment of the experiences of human actors. In *Truth and Method* (2nd rev. ed., Continuum, 1989), he argued, "*Verstehen ist sprachgebunden*" ("Understanding is tied to language"). Language is the medium of intersubjectivity and the concrete expression of traditions that give human actions particular meaning. *Verstehen* is achieved by entering into a conversation or dialogue with those traditions.

Jürgen Habermas's (1971) theory of critical social science accepts the view that the historical-hermeneutic sciences aim at interpretive understanding or *Verstehen* serving the *interest* of clarifying the conditions for communication and intersubjectivity. These social sciences stand in contrast to the empirical-analytic sciences that aim at explanation in the interest of controlling and manipulating the social world. Habermas, however, argues that each kind of science, although not reducible to each other, makes the mistake of claiming that it provides the fundamental knowledge of human action. He defends a third, more basic, emancipatory cognitive interest that permits the dialectical synthesis of the other two interests and forms the basis of his understanding of a critical social science. **See also EXPLANATION, UNDERSTANDING.**

Key References

Geertz, C., " 'From the Native's Point of View': On the Nature of Anthropological Understanding," in *Local Knowledge*. New York: Basic Books, 1983.

Habermas, J., *Knowledge and Human Interests*. J. J. Shapiro, trans. Boston: Beacon, 1971.

Outhwaite, W., *Understanding Social Life: The Method Called Verstehen*. London: Allen & Unwin, 1975.

Schutz, A., *Collected Papers*, Vol. 1. M. Natanson, ed. & trans. The Hague, The Netherlands: Martinus Nijhoff, 1967.

Weber, M., "Basic Sociological Terms," in G. Roth & C. Wittich, eds., *Economy and Society*. New York: Bedminster, 1968.

VERSTEHENDE SOCIOLOGY   Also referred to as *interpretivism,* this is a shorthand way of referring to several social theories (e.g., *symbolic interactionism, phenomenological sociology,* and *ethnomethodology*) that assign a central place to the method of **Verstehen**. These approaches are also often called *hermeneutic* because they accept the premise that interpretation or understanding is the fundamental way that human beings participate in the world. The hermeneutic tradition that traces its roots to Hans-Georg Gadamer and is developed by Charles Taylor, Jürgen Habermas, Anthony Giddens, Paul Ricoeur, and others, however, is actually critical of *Verstehende* sociology. Criticisms center on two ideas: First, *Verstehende* sociology confines itself largely to the study of subjective meanings—the meanings that reside within individual actors. The hermeneutic tradition argues that this approach ignores the more general underlying structures of intersubjective meanings. Second, the defenders of hermeneutical approaches argue that *Verstehende* sociology retains a subject-object dichotomy and an objectivist conception of *method.*

Key References

Giddens, A., *New Rules of Sociological Method,* 2nd ed. Stanford, CA: Stanford University Press, 1993.

Habermas, J., *On the Logic of the Social Sciences,* trans. S. W. Nicholsen & J. A. Stark. Cambridge: MIT Press, 1988.

VOICE   Two overlapping senses of this term are important in contemporary qualitative inquiry: One stems from the *literary turn* in the social sciences and the other from feminist philosophy. The increasing interest in the literary analysis of social science texts involved importing conceptual tools from literary criticism and narratology (the study of the nature, form, and structure of narrative) into social science discourse. *Voice* is one of those concepts that has become a particularly useful tool. It is the set of textual signs that characterize the narrator in a text. Identifying signs of first-person narratives or third-person narratives is part of this notion. Voice includes analysis of all aspects of a text that provide information about who the narrator is—who "speaks." The associations between voice, authority, and the representation of social (and natural) phenomena are a central concern in the literary turn in the social sciences. Experiments with multivoiced, dialogic, and polyphonic texts are, in part, efforts to break up or decenter the monological voice of authority of the lone field-worker who writes as if he or she is transparently and unproblematically reproducing social reality in an ethnographic account.

The concern with the connection between who speaks, who is heard, and what is voiced or given a voice is central to much feminist scholarship (although whether there is a necessary connection between voice and feminist scholarship is debated). Although this scholarship shares the concern with voice as defined in the literary turn (and, in many ways, feminist work actually leads the criticism of authorial voice here), it also addresses issues in the politics of voice—for example, how women's voices have been silenced by means of various social practices (including methodologies of social inquiry), how critiques of these practices can be used to nurture women's voices and bring them to the fore, and how women's voices have been absent from social science (and natural science) investigations. **See also CRISIS OF REPRE-SENTATION, STANDPOINT EPISTEMOLOGIES.**

Key References

Bakhtin, M. M., *Speech Genres and Other Late Essays.* C. Emerson & M. Hol-quest, eds., V. W. McGee, trans. Austin: University of Texas Press, 1986.

Fine, M., *Disruptive Voices.* Ann Arbor: University of Michigan Press, 1992.

Genette, G., *Narrative Discourse: An Essay in Method.* Ithaca, NY: Cornell University Press, 1980.

Tierney, W. G., & Lincoln, Y. S., eds., *Representation and the Text: Re-Framing the Narrative Voice.* Albany: State University of New York Press, 1997.

WELTANSCHAUUNG   This is a German term for "worldview" or "philosophy of life." The *Weltanschauung* analysts was a name given to several philosophers of science (including Stephen Toulmin, Thomas Kuhn, Norwood Hanson, and Paul Feyerabend) who were highly critical of how logical positivist epistemology construed the rationality of science as completely free of issues of human judgment. In contrast, they claimed that scientific theorizing was dependent not only on empirical observations but also on the scientist's worldview or conceptual perspective that determine which questions are worth investigating and which answers are acceptable.

Key Reference

Suppe, F., ed., *The Structure of Scientific Theories,* 2nd ed. Champaign: University of Illinois Press, 1977.

WRITING STRATEGIES   With the advent of the *literary turn* in the social sciences, the purpose(s) of and strategies for writing or composing an account of qualitative inquiry (or, more broadly, any social scientific account) have become contested. In addition to familiar, traditional advice on techniques for composing a research report, a new tradition is emerging for conceiving of the purpose, style, and ethics of writing. Perhaps the greatest difference in the two ways of thinking about writing centers on the way in which each conceives of the relationship between language and science. The former regards language as necessary to science: After all, scientists must clearly express themselves in writing, but language is really not much more than a medium that the scientist employs, in more or less effective ways, to display the conclusions or findings resulting from a research practice. In contrast, the concerns about poetics and rhetoric characteristic of the new ways of writing are marked by a belief that science, like literature, is an activity *situated in* language. This means that scientists-authors now look to practices other than research (e.g., literature, creative arts, and introspection) for ideas on how both to model and to represent their activity of making sense of the world of others (to understand what others are doing and saying), and that scientists-authors more self-consciously and publicly display the fact that they are artisans displaying the craft of composition. These ways of thinking about writing are discussed in various new genres, including *autoethnography,* ethnographic fiction, ethnographic poetry, ethnographic drama, and narratives about the writing process.

Key References

Becker, H. S., *Writing for Social Scientists: How to Start and Finish Your Thesis, Book, or Article.* Chicago: University of Chicago Press, 1986.

Ellis, C., & Bochner, A., eds., *Contemporary Ethnography: Alternative Forms of Qualitative Writing.* Walnut Creek, CA: AltaMira, 1996.

Richardson, L., *Writing Strategies: Reaching Diverse Audiences.* Newbury Park, CA: Sage, 1990.

Wolcott, H., *Writing Up Qualitative Research.* Newbury Park, CA: Sage, 1990.

About the Author

Thomas A. Schwandt is Professor of Education at the University of Illinois Urbana-Champaign, where he also holds appointments in the Unit for Criticism and Interpretive Theory and the Interdisciplinary Concentration in Cultural Studies and Interpretive Research. Previously, he was a faculty member at Indiana University (IU) and a fellow of the IU Poynter Center for Ethics and American Institutions, a member of the faculty in medical education at the University of Illinois at Chicago, and was employed as a evaluator and organizational consultant in the private sector. He has lectured on interpretive methodologies and theory of evaluation in Norway, Sweden, and Denmark and held visiting appointments at both research institutions and universities in those countries. His papers on qualitative methodology, issues in the philosophy of social science, and evaluation have appeared in a variety of books and journals. His latest book is *Evaluation Practice Reconsidered*, which is scheduled for publication in 2002.